for the amateur parent ...

Child Rearing for Fun

Trust Your Instincts and Enjoy Your Children

Anne Atkins

ZONDERVAN™

GRAND RAPIDS, MICHIGAN 49530 USA

We want to hear from you. Please send your comments about this
book to us in care of zreview@zondervan.com. Thank you.

ZONDERVAN™

Child Rearing for Fun
Copyright © 2004 by Anne Atkins

Requests for information should be addressed to:
Zondervan, *Grand Rapids, Michigan 49530*

Library of Congress Cataloging-in-Publication Data

Atkins, Anne (Anne D.)
    Child rearing for fun : trust your instincts and enjoy your children / Anne
    Atkins.—1st ed.
        p. cm.
    ISBN 0-310-25417-5 (softcover)
    1. Parenting. 2. Child rearing. 3. Parent and child. I. Title.
    HQ755.8.A773   2004
    649'.1—dc22
                                                                2004015764

Anne Atkins asserts the moral right to be identified as the author of this work.

The website addresses recommended throughout this book are offered as a resource to
you. These websites are not intended in any way to be or imply an endorsement on
the part of Zondervan, nor do we vouch for their content for the life of this book.

This book is for informational purposes only and medical issues should be handled by
a health care professional.

Please note that some names of people in the stories contained within have been changed
to protect their privacy.

Interior design by Beth Shagene

Printed in the United States of America

04 05 06 07 08 09 10 /❖ DC/ 10 9 8 7 6 5 4 3 2 1

'I think it should be "Dedicated to my dear, sweet children."
(Hem, hem, enuff said.)'

Bink

Contents

Acknowledgements

I would like to thank the following: Ruth Brinkman of Zebedee Nursery School. Mr Richard and Miss Clare – indeed, absolutely everyone: Miss Henrietta, Caroline, Terri and Hedi – from Finton House School. John Young for his music and humour, and Colin Foran for his science and humility. Dean Close School, particularly the Rev. Timothy Tasty Spliff – I mean Hastie-Smith – Rod Pellereau and Lee Edmond. Dr Peter Cramer of Winchester College. The Rev. Lindsay Collins. Steven Boyes at Mander Portman Woodward. Dr Isobel Heyman of the Maudsley Hospital. And Professor Simon Baron-Cohen of the Autism Research Centre. All professionals, but with the hearts of amateurs.

While we're on the subject, Bink has insisted that I mention David and Mary Briggs, her grandparents and two of the best teachers in the world: professional amateurs, as it were.

And I suppose I ought to thank the five people who have reorganized my life, my priorities and my bedtime. And some of the mess in the house. Thanks.

anyone can do it

What *is* all the fuss about?

Anyone would think bringing up children an impossible task, doomed to failure, understood only by psychiatrists, social workers and authors of books on the subject. Even with expert advice we will get it horribly wrong, our children will rebel against us, and future therapists' couches will reverberate with the history of all our ghastly mistakes.

Something doesn't add up. Correct me if I'm wrong, but surely the human race has been rearing children for millennia? By and large we seem to have done it successfully, without any of the help now considered essential. Generations have come and gone, laughed and wept, loved and lived, raising offspring without professional intervention. And – surprise, surprise – until recently children were thought to be a joy and a blessing, happy the man his quiver full of them.

Is it possible (whisper who dares) that child rearing isn't so difficult after all? That, contrary to the current creed, it is not an obstacle course surmountable only by specialists? Maybe, if left alone, we will do the right thing anyway. Could bringing up children even be an instinctive process, as natural as making love? In which case we should presumably welcome tips from those who have done it before, but basically follow our noses. Raising children might even be *fun*.

So, you ask reasonably, why do we need another book on the subject? Because we are *not* left alone: everyone is interfering. Because we have lost our confidence. Because even as I put pen to paper, one of the main political parties is on its annual conference, devising new ways of coming between us and our children.[1] We live in a culture that is not only anti-family but peculiarly anti-parent. The work of child rearing is almost certainly the most vital any of us will ever do. We ought to revere and respect parents far more than we do politicians or pop singers, film stars or footballers – merely the icing on the cake of society. And yet parliamentarians presume to intrude; shrinks suggest they know better; counsellors dare to criticize. So we no longer believe in ourselves, and feel we must keep referring to so-called professionals for guidance and approval. As Frank Furedi says in his wonderfully liberating book, *Paranoid Parenting*, 'The role of bumbling amateurs has been assigned [parents] by the self-appointed experts. Consequently a lack of self-belief tinged with an intense level of anxiety informs the parenting style of our times.'[2]

I don't think this makes us better parents. Bringing up children is like many other amateur activities: riding a bicycle, making bread. Of course we need to know what the basic principles are. But after that, sometimes the more we analyze, criticize and worry about the way we're doing it, the more of a mess we make. Certainly the less we enjoy it. Let's face it, in the rather dreary, politically correct climate of modern society an awful lot of the joy seems to have gone out of raising children. And the trouble is that if parents are not self-confident and happy, the children will not be either. Ironically, one consequence of the so-called 'Children's Rights' movement is that it has stripped parents of the assurance we need to bring up our children properly. To give a trivial example, if you do not have the authority to teach your child table manners – if you can't make him listen and obey you when you tell him not to snatch or eat with his mouth open – he is the one who will suffer: after a while, no one will invite him to tea.

Perhaps we need Parents' Lib. A Mothers' and Fathers' Empowerment Movement. Consciousness-raising for Parental Carers. However, as most of us are rather too busy wiping noses to descend on Westminster with placards, I suggest more subversive tactics. It is possible to rebel quietly and unobtrusively at home. Resist the trend. Refuse to be cowed. Decide that we are in charge of our children's upbringing, and we will rear them in the way we believe to be best. We might even dare to admit that we like our children and take pleasure in having them around.

So here goes. Take courage. Believe in yourself. God has given us the essential qualities we need: the love, commitment and dedication. Success is not impossible, or even improbable. It is within our grasp.

The necessary qualifications

When I first started as agony aunt for the *Daily Telegraph* a few people asked, rather belligerently, what my qualifications for the job were. In one sense the answer was absolutely none. (Happily, this didn't seem to matter to those who wrote to me for advice.) In another sense, however, this was not true at all. I had the supreme qualification that the editor had asked me to do it.

Similarly, when I first discussed this book with my publisher, we considered my expertise. Had I a doctorate, medical training or recognition from any professional body? No, I said. On the contrary, I live with five genuine experts who can say with absolute authority that I am merely an amateur. So in lieu of letters after my name my editor suggested using as much personal detail as possible, including all the problems my family and I might have encountered.

I strongly resisted this. I am wary of subjective data: the fact that I have found something to be so is not good enough reason to believe that it is. In addition, dwelling on trials and tribulations is not usually constructive: it is dispiriting, sometimes self-indulgent, and not something I like to do. Recently, however, a colleague asked me what I was working on. When he went on to enquire what my take on bringing up children would be, I replied that I wanted to reassure parents that the job is not so difficult after all. He made no comment for some time. When he did return to it an hour or so later, he said tentatively, 'Perhaps you could say something for the parents of handicapped children.' He was far too polite to say he thought my thesis almost criminally loopy, but he went on to tell me about his four-year-old, brain-damaged at birth and now partially sighted and mentally and physically handicapped, and how much work it is just to get him through the day.

Much humbled, I thanked him for his implied and gentle rebuke. But then I asked him whom he considered the ultimate experts on caring for his son. His wife and himself? Or the 'specialists'? After due consideration he said that (except on matters of technical medical information) the two of them knew best; they understood their son and his needs far more profoundly than anyone else.

That is the nub of it. Parenting is done by parents, not professionals. And we know what we are doing. Sadly, though, we are often led to believe that we do not.

Critics may disagree with this book. Anyone who considers himself an expert on family life will probably feel like burning it. Go ahead. But I would be sorry to alienate fellow combatants, other parents, because they might have found the going tough and erroneously assume we have led a charmed life. We have not.

Every parent has discouragements and disappointments, and Shaun and I are no exception. It's not because we have found parenting plain sailing that I have come to my conclusions. We have experienced what people sometimes refer to as our 'share' of downs as well as ups – not that such matters are ever shared out with any concession to fairness.

Such difficulties give me no more or less authority to write this book. But we live in an age that judges competence by experience, and experience by adversity. So I am obliged to pre-empt the objection that I only say parenting is easy because we've never had it hard. In no particular order, therefore, here are some of the challenges we have had to overcome.

One of our children was the victim of inappropriate conduct by a hospital consultant. To help with recovery, I requested the services of a psychologist. After one meeting she concluded that our child had been abused and, against the advice of all her superiors, referred our family to the police and social services for the inclusion of our child on the At Risk register. We had to fight ruthlessly, and sleeplessly, to get the case dropped. The irony was that the actual abuse that took place, in hospital, was never addressed: we were far too relieved to get the care of our child back to mention it again.

Another of our children was diagnosed with Asperger's syndrome, a form of autism. The school most sympathetic to his needs thought he had a fifty-fifty chance of surviving the educational process, while the consultant who diagnosed him told me he would never form a lasting relationship and was unlikely to hold down a job. At five he went to a school that had no understanding of his condition and tried to discipline it out of him. At ten he was offered a scholarship by a boarding school where the head assured us he would be understood and cared for, so we handed over various medical and psychological reports for him to share with his staff. Not only did he not do this, but he never told any of his colleagues there was anything different about our son. Consequently, the teachers repeatedly punished him until he climbed onto the school roof to kill himself.

Shortly after this, our twelve-year-old went missing for forty-eight hours. The police mounted a round-the-clock forty-man search, scouring the Thames for the body. They were particularly concerned that one sibling can pick up the idea of suicide from another. Happily, she was found safe and well.

A few years later one of our children was found to have severe Obsessive Compulsive Disorder, resulting in several months' psychiatric hospitalisation and, to date, two years' loss of schooling. OCD is generally thought to be genetic in origin (my nephew spent much of last year in hospital with it too). If diagnosed early, it is susceptible to a straightforward and often successful cure. Our child was given the wrong treatment for the first eighteen months. This made the condition many times worse and compromised further help.

This in turn caused depression in two of our other children, in one case severe enough to prompt repeated suicidal inclinations.

Most recently, when I was seven months pregnant with our youngest, I was told that several scans showed an unambiguous case of talipes, or club foot. This is frequently caused by chromosomal abnormality, making it likely that our child had Down's syndrome. We prepared for both handicaps as best we could. Happily, the scans had been misinterpreted.

I have also experienced two six-month bouts of caring for the children alone, when Shaun was bedridden with Chronic Fatigue Syndrome. And we have had five miscarriages.

There is never a point at which one can say, 'I can't cope' – just as no pain, not even labour pain, is ever, strictly speaking, unbearable. If you have no choice, you bear it. And if you are a parent, you cope. But I have been there, and have some idea what it is like.

I don't believe any of these experiences give me more qualifications to comment on parenting than any other parent. But they do give me an opportunity to reassert that child rearing is simple, straightforward and spontaneous, and that the parent is the expert. Every mother and father reading this will have endured problems, some more manageable, others infinitely harder than ours. But, on the basis of twenty-one years' experience, I now know for certain that, whatever challenges arise in any family, the principles of parenting are not complicated; and also that we, the parents, are the ones who know best, are best equipped to cope, and are the ultimate authority on our children.

But are we treated as such? Some years ago I was on a radio programme with Peter Tatchell, who was putting forward the case for the modification of a particular law governing teenagers. He argued that the experts were all in favour of change, and quoted organizations such as the NSPCC, Barnardo's, The Children's Society, ChildLine and so on. I'm sorry? These are *not* the people who know and understand children best. Yet parents are considered amateur when the welfare of young people is considered. No wonder we often feel crippled by uncertainty and low self-esteem.

Those with 'qualifications' are considered proficient. And sometimes they are. But they don't spend nearly as much of their time working with children as we who bring them up. Nor, indeed, can they offer help comparable to that from the friend on the end of the telephone or the neighbour around the corner. After all, the most important goals in the world are achieved, not by professionals, but by those very amateurs we disparage: by those who do it for love.

Introduction

Who knows most about the act of love itself? Is it the professional, the prostitute engaged for mercenary reward? Certainly she has more, and wider, experience. No doubt, too, she is technically superior. Perhaps she even has higher standards of performance, since her living depends on it. She could marshal plenty of reasons to prove that she knows more than anyone else about love-making. Fair enough. I am only an amateur in the bedroom. I imagine you are too. Sometimes we are unimaginative. Sometimes we are clumsy. Sometimes, I'm sorry to say, we just fall asleep. The professional never does this. So should we concede that we are incompetent, and allow that this is yet another activity best left to the specialist? No. The professional is not the same as the expert. The professional may know more *about* love, but only the amateur knows true love.

And the professional may know more about children, but only you know your child. When it comes to rearing children it is we, the parents, who are the real experts, the amateurs, trained by experience, motivated by devotion, labouring for love. This is true even if we start out knowing next to nothing. I was hopelessly ill-prepared, being the youngest child in my family. I think our eldest was the first baby I had ever touched. I didn't know what a nappy was until after she was born. My mother had given me a pile of fluffy terries a few months earlier, and I put them in the airing cupboard thinking they were hand towels for the guest room. The midwife had to tell me what they were and what to do with them.

But there you go: even I could put a nappy on by child number three or four. We pick it up somehow. Soon we become more competent than anyone else (apart from grannies). Your GP may know more about your child's measles, your teacher about his GCSE syllabus, a psychiatrist about her anorexia – though it is amazing how quickly parents become competently versed in all these matters. *But you know your child.* Take the specialist knowledge by all means, but take it with a pinch of salt.

Just as I had no qualifications to be an agony aunt other than the only one that mattered – that the editor had appointed me – so I have no qualifications to be a parent other than having children. I don't suppose you have either. But this is the only qualification there is.

Anyone can do it

When I was twenty-one I had quite a shock. I fell in love. It was about eleven-thirty on a bright Monday morning a week after St Valentine's Day, somewhere between St Peter's College and the Radcliffe Camera, and it changed my life. We both knew that, whether we married or not, neither of us would ever be the same again.

Paradoxically, however, a few years later it happened again. I woke up early one Thursday and there, in the April sunlight under the billowing curtains, on a fresh new sheepskin in a borrowed wicker cot, was a new human being, not a day old. It was as if someone had dropped her there like dew in the night. We both felt absolutely astonished. (I agree, it's odd that it took us so much by surprise. There had been indications, after all; particularly during the preceding forty-eight hours.)

Loving our children may have changed us even more than falling in love with each other. I am English, and don't go in for mawkish displays of sentimentality, but I don't know how else to describe what started that sunny spring morning. When our fourth was born, Shaun admitted he thought he had become blasé about birth and parenthood … but he was bowled over yet again. And early last summer, twenty years after that bright April morning, it happened to us again: a new person is even now sitting outside in an ancient carriage pram under the cherry blossom, waving at the spring sunshine, laughing at the sky, watching a white feather drift by on the breeze; working her unconscious magic on all of us again, filling our days with a laughter and joy and hope and purpose, revolutionizing us forever. Bink's reaction, when she met her new sister the morning she was born, summed it up. 'This is the most extraordinary thing in the world', she said. 'And anyone can do it.'

When I was her age I longed to achieve greatness, and thought in terms of *Hamlet* or Beethoven's Fifth. But Bink is right: being a parent is more of a privilege, more important and influential, and – I now believe – more satisfying and fulfilling than almost anything else in the world. True, it is also more painful and heartbreaking, more exhausting and exasperating, and sometimes just more darned expensive. But it has brought enough bliss to compensate us a hundredfold. And *anyone can do it.*

So perhaps we should start by acknowledging this, that anyone can indeed do it, and that all the other parents out there are probably doing it rather well. Initially we may find this difficult. When confidence is low it is comforting to take solace from other people's apparent mistakes. Parenting is so much under attack nowadays that we all tend to feel incompetent, and the idea that others may be even more so is an attractive one. I must confess to having done this myself. So-and-so's child has dropped out of school, or has bulimia, or is unbelievably rude. Surely this is because the so-and-sos undermine their children, or spend too much money on them, or do something or other. If only they were more strict, or more approachable, or weren't going through a divorce, or didn't neglect them or spoil them or drink or smoke … Give the child to me for a few weeks and I'd sort him out.

Actually, this is extremely unlikely. So-and-so has probably tried all the obvious solutions. The issue could be an inevitable part of growing up, have nothing to do with the external circumstances, and be a phase the child would have gone through however the mother and father had handled it. More to the point, this attitude is insidious. If our neighbour, or sister, or best friend can be criticized for bringing her children up badly, why then, so can we.

Look around you at the other parents you know. Enumerate all the things they are doing well. Support them, believe in them, and tell yourself how well they are doing. Soon you may find you even believe in yourself too.

I want to confess at the outset that I am not a good parent. It is the sort of thing one ought to say when writing a book about parenting. (And it is certainly what I feel, much of the time.) But I don't think it would be true. You see, it may be what I *feel*, but it is not what I *believe*. I believe that all parents are good. I know the media are full of dreadful people who don't care if their offspring go around knifing old ladies and boiling policemen's heads, but the truth is that every father I see loves his children, and every mother I know is doing a great job.

So let me be honest and say, instead, that I am under no illusion that I am a better parent than any other. If I had ever been tempted to think so (I wasn't), living with my children would have put me straight pretty fast. And I have, over the years, gleaned great confidence and assurance from simple, effective, tried and tested guidelines from those who have done it before. I am happy to say there is nothing new about most of it. Child rearing is like theology: if it is genuinely original, it is almost certainly wrong.

The analogy I use is that of building a house. First the foundations must be laid. They are often put down even before anyone is aware of the work being done, and they may never be visible to outsiders, but without them the whole edifice might one day crumble and fall. The most important aspect of parenting is the character and relationship of the parents themselves, not so much what we do as who we are. Our children initially depend on us for everything: we must be secure and strong. The first section of the book outlines qualities that are important for all parents, of whatever type. And once these are in place (even if this is before the children are born), a good deal of the essential work has been done already.

Next, the shape and structure of the house begin to appear. Much of this is a question of personal taste and resources: some like small, modern, practical bungalows; others prefer rambling, romantic mansions. Whatever your preference in fashioning this visible aspect of your home, provided the unseen foundations are secure, the structure will stand. Some adore noisy, boisterous, individualistic children; others believe in formality, early bedtimes, smart clothes. As long as you know roughly what you want and are happy with the outcome, it is rather up to you. If I suggest a certain style it is not because it is necessarily the right or only way, but rather to give an example of how you can put your own principles into practice.

Finally, and most important of all, the home should be filled with spirit and life. What is the point of your family, your children, the love you have for them? What is your ultimate ambition on their behalf? Where will they end up eventually? Many intelligent, responsible, wonderful parents bring up bright, kind, gorgeous children without ever asking these questions. It is perfectly possible to do this. However, my belief is that there are some things that are even more important to our children than their health and happiness.

So, is parenting easy? Well no, perhaps it is not easy, exactly. Indeed, it is sometimes very hard work. But it is hard in the way that climbing a mountain is, rather than in the way that complicated brain surgery is. We may get jolly tired sometimes, but we all basically know how to do it: we put one foot in front of the other. It does not require years of technical training or a degree in psychology. Of course we will make mistakes. Of course parenting is quite dauntingly demanding. But, contrary to expectations, it is not unduly complicated. The principles are almost insultingly plain: not necessarily easy to *implement*, but remarkably easy to *understand*. Or, to put it another way, it is not so much that child rearing is *easy*, but it is *straightforward*.

Once we have grasped the principles, we can get on with the process of loving our children and living with them and earning a living to support them. After all, bringing up children is natural, instinctive, in some ways almost automatic. It is rather refreshingly down to earth. One might almost say it is child's play.

······· Action Page ···········

1. Appreciate your own parents

Make a list of some of the good things your own parents did for you. This might include:

a. Feeding you.

b. Buying you shoes.

c. Making sure you went to school.

d. Not wearing a hat or kissing you on Sports Day.

e. Teaching you 'This little piggy went to market'.

f. Lending you the car.

g. Giving you puce sugar icing on your birthday cake. (All the other eighteen-year-old boys had a night at the pub, but no, you wanted puce sugar icing.)

Highlight in yellow the things you appreciated most at the time, and in pink those items that you are most grateful for now. The main purpose of this is to see the yucky colour you get when you put fluorescent pink over lurid yellow. Horrid, isn't it?

Put the list somewhere where you can't lose it, like in your head.

2. Appreciate your in-laws

Do the same for your spouse's parents. You may need some help here. Consider it one of those toe-curlingly embarrassing touchy-feely exercises you have to do together, if your relationship is ever going to go into these dark corners where you don't want it to go.

Fair enough: why should you indeed. All right, go for a brisk and bracing walk instead, and ask her what aspects of her childhood she most enjoyed. That's not too bad, is it?

3. Appreciate your spouse

Make a list of all the ways in which your spouse is (or is going to be) a great parent; particularly those ways in which he is (or will be) different from you.

If you have recovered from the embarrassment of the previous exercise, you might mention these qualities occasionally.

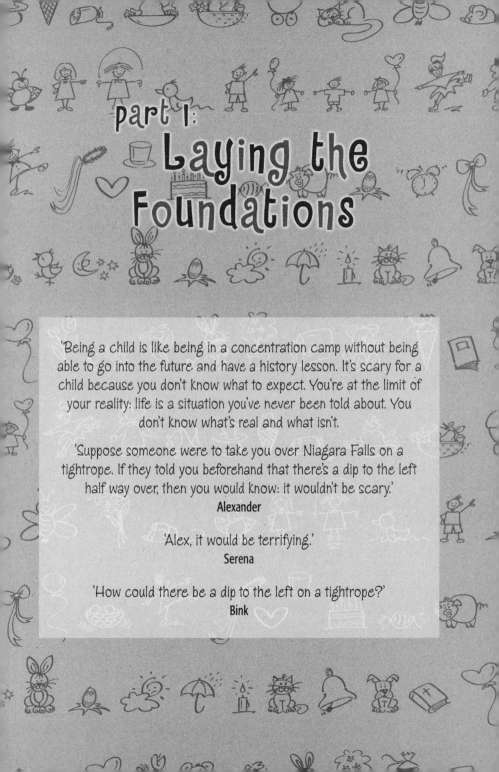

part I:
Laying the Foundations

'Being a child is like being in a concentration camp without being able to go into the future and have a history lesson. It's scary for a child because you don't know what to expect. You're at the limit of your reality: life is a situation you've never been told about. You don't know what's real and what isn't.

'Suppose someone were to take you over Niagara Falls on a tightrope. If they told you beforehand that there's a dip to the left half way over, then you would know: it wouldn't be scary.'
Alexander

'Alex, it would be terrifying.'
Serena

'How could there be a dip to the left on a tightrope?'
Bink

All human beings have the same basic needs. We each want security, self-worth and significance. Different theories abound as to who wants which most: I have heard it said that men crave significance and like to be important, whereas women value self-worth, preferring to be cherished. This may be true in a general sort of way, but it is misleading if it suggests that boys don't long to be cared for, or girls to be respected. Every child has a deep-seated desire for each of these three things.

Our yearning for *security* is satisfied by the world around us. At its most basic level, it relates to our physical wellbeing: will we be fed when we are hungry, clothed when we are cold? This is the most elemental aspect of child rearing.

So how encouraging is that? We are not yet into the first chapter, and already we are fulfilling our most important obligation towards our children, to feed, clothe and house them. Add to this the fact that they are probably being bathed at night and educated by day (if they are old enough), and they have much to thank us for, like Desdemona:

> My noble Father,
> To you I am bound for life, and education:
> My life and education both do learne me
> How to respect you.[1]

We are also meeting their need for emotional security. In eighteenth-century France a cruel experiment was allegedly conducted, in which a hundred orphan babies were kept warm and fed but never spoken to, picked up or cuddled. Every one of the babies died. Such an exercise could only be done with orphans: it would be impossible to stop parents hugging and talking to our children, the instinct to dose is so strong. So we are supplying this need too, giving them early emotional stability which will enable them to approach life with confidence, grace and fortitude – and cope with hardship – later on. And they, like us, will barely have perceived it. Children who have their basic requirements met are usually blissfully unaware how fortunate they are (until they meet, or hear of, others who are less so). Security, then, is a matter of finding the world about us to be nurturing and welcoming; and the safer it is, the less we tend to notice it.

Self-worth, by contrast, is to do with our relationship with ourselves. When we turn our gaze inside, is what we find acceptable? After all, it would be possible to be in a secure environment, and yet feel worthless. We all need to know that we are valuable and lovable. We don't have to have stratospheric IQs, or beatific bodies, or an unusual talent. We simply need to be satisfied with the way God has made us. I knew a boy who positively exuded this happy self-confidence. He came from a family of exceptionally gifted people: his father was world famous in his field and his siblings were unusually clever. By contrast he himself was quite ordinary, except in one respect: he was completely content with who he was. Consequently, he was one of the easiest people I've known, spreading sunshine wherever he went. He was as much a tribute to his parents as his high-achieving brothers and sisters.

Why do we think our own children brighter and better and more beautiful than anyone else's? Because they need us to affirm and value them. We have an innate instinct to fulfil this requirement too. Every time we feel proud of them or tell them we love them we are feeding their self-worth. Are you ever tempted to believe you have given birth to, or begotten, God's gift to mankind? Spoil yourself: it is a temptation to be thoroughly indulged.

If security is concerned with our environment, and self-worth with ourselves, then *significance* is a question of how the one relates to the other. What can I contribute to those around me? Do I matter? Does the way I behave have any meaning for others, or make any impact? Children may feel wonderfully safe, and extraordinarily good about themselves, but they still need to be taught consideration for others, and the importance of kindness and honesty and self-discipline. Again the process is intuitive. Your baby smiles: you smile back. Without even thinking about it you are teaching her how to behave, rewarding her sociable conduct and encouraging her to do it again. When we reinforce pleasant attributes and discourage unpleasant ones we are shaping our children's characters to be the people we want them to be. This third aspect of child rearing is the one which is most consciously taught – through what we say, as well as what we do: this, and not that, is what we expect of you. It is perhaps slightly less instinctive, but also rather less important than the other two. And it depends on them. A child who is not safe and loved will not respond well to being told how to be good. Nonetheless, it too is innate.

We have hardly started, and already we are giving our children the most important aspects of their upbringing, unconsciously, intuitively, almost involuntarily. We probably deserve a coffee break and a KitKat for getting so far so soon . . .

Security
'I am safe'

'There's usually enough food on the table. But there are never enough fajitas. Certainly not after you get there, Mother.'
Benjamin

I was sitting at the top of the stairs, after school. The afternoon sun slanted through the balcony window, catching the dancing motes of dust and casting tiny shadows on the woollen stair carpet. My mother sat next to me, in her maroon and blue tweed skirt, honey-coloured stockings and navy leather shoes.

I had a best friend called Imelda. She had a large, rambling house and a garden with little unexpected statues lurking by hidden ponds. She also had a handsome older brother and lots of sisters, and I liked going there for Sunday lunch. Her mother was slightly awe-inspiring (she used to offer both Chinese and Indian tea at four o'clock) but kind and polite to me, and her father was wonderful. He was a university don, inventive and funny, with a beautiful working golden retriever called Lucky (after whom I later named my own dog), and he used to put me on his knee and make up stories about a miniature family called the Parkers – possibly inspired by his fountain pen.

My mother had sat down beside me, on the top stair, to tell me about Imelda's father. He was dead. He had shot himself. Presumably with the gun he used when he went out with Lucky. I remember trying to take in the sorrow of it all, and the tragedy it meant for my friend. But then my mother said an odd thing. I think she was crying when she tried to explain that the news was sad, not just for Imelda herself, but also for her mother. I couldn't understand this. To lose a father was a terrible, unimaginable loss – almost as bad as losing a mother. But a husband? Surely you could get another any time? The only relationship that meant anything to me was that between a parent and a child.

For a young child the bond between parent and child is paramount. I was made aware of this again some years ago, when I was praying with one of our children at bedtime and mentioned a friend who had cancer. Suddenly I realized there were tears in his eyes, and moments later he was racked with sobs, so distraught he had to sleep that night in our bed. I was surprised by the strength of his reaction because he didn't know this person well. How could he be so upset? It wasn't until he said some-thing just before he fell asleep that I understood. The friend in question had a son his own age, and he asked me how he would cope. Of course, what had distressed him was not so much for the grown-up who was dying, but for the child who would be orphaned.

I used to have nightmares when I was young, frightful terrors about fire raging through the house. But there was another dream which was quieter, but far more deadly. I dreamt that my mother had died. I woke in the grip of loneliness and a numbing, dull despair, unable to tell her in case it hurt her feelings. Eventually, thank goodness, I overcame this mistaken childish tact, and her loving reassurance took my fear away. But for me, as for every child once the basic need for warmth, food and shelter is met, there was only one thing that mattered to my wellbeing. My parents.

Children crave security. We all do. Unlike the rest of us, though, their craving is very simply met. They need an environment that makes them feel safe, and we, their parents, *are* that environment. Little children don't care whether they live in a two-up, two-down tenement or a fifty-bedroom chateau. If their parents love them and love each other, are consistent and kind and reliable and *there*, the children know they are safe. It is difficult to overestimate the importance of this. To the rest of the world this ordinary couple may be quite insignificant. To their children they are as gods.

And the security we give our children stretches far into the future. A few years ago I was facing a nerve-racking experience. It was about eleven o'clock on a Thursday night, and I knew that all the morning papers would be mentioning me because of something I had said in a brief broadcast. A number of journalists had been downright beastly to me over the telephone: how much worse would they be in print? I assumed (wrongly, as it turned out) that most of Fleet Street would be giving me a pasting. It is foolish to feel frightened by such an ephemeral threat, but frightened I was.

Then I thought of my father. Before he retired as the headmaster of a high-profile school he had been guarded in his dealings with the press and kept his pupils out of the papers as much as possible. I dreaded his dismay at seeing his newspaper the next day, so I rang him up to warn him. The conversation probably lasted less than five minutes. I don't know quite what I was expecting. Worry, anxiety, perhaps even a rebuke? Instead, he told me immediately how proud he was of me, and said he had experienced exactly the same scorn, ridicule and hatred when, as a conscientious objector over half a century earlier at the age of twenty-one, he had refused to bear arms. He firmly exhorted me not to take back a word of what I had said. When I put the telephone down I felt six inches taller. I also knew I could cope with anything. Why, what did it matter what the world thought? *My father* believed in me.

Most of us probably feel that there were occasions when our parents didn't affirm us enough or said the wrong things. We are always being told that when they withhold love and approval it sometimes has a negative, even devastating, effect throughout our lives. This can be true, though let's face it: we can move on from their mistakes. But how often are we reminded of the reverse, which is even more evident and far more important? When we know our parents adore us and support us, when we have known them endorse our decisions and cheer us on even when they don't agree with us, we can be free, courageous, confident and loving – even long after they have left us.

Parents matter. That is why this book, about child rearing, starts long before children even appear. The story begins years earlier, before the children are born. Many of our parenting skills were formed long ago, when our parents were parenting us. Clearly, it would not be helpful to go that far back. We cannot rewrite our childhoods. But we can start from where we are now.

Parents in good spirit

'If your parents do something unexpected, it's as if they've been taken over by aliens. Do you suppose this is worse for people with autism?'
Alexander

'No. I think it's the same for everybody.'
Bink

If we are to take care of others, we need to be in a fit state ourselves. This may sound obvious, but you would be surprised how many parents, particularly mothers, forget it. Pregnant women are told to keep well, eat sensibly, rest and exercise, in order to give their babies the best start in life. This is common sense (although, in reality, a baby is a determined little parasite, and will usually take what it needs from its mother whether she looks after herself or not).

But revisit the same woman a few years later, and you will find she hasn't slept the night through for as long as she can say, the last item she bought for herself was a maternity bra (now grey, and in the dog basket), and if you ask her whether she remembered to eat breakfast she may say, 'Of course!' somewhat indignantly, and then realize it was three weeks ago. This may sound noble and self-sacrificing. And in some ways it is. But it can also be short-sighted. I know that the worst mistakes I make as a parent – losing my temper and being unreasonable – happen because I am just plain tired.

Bringing up children demands stamina. Quite often, what the child needs most from the parent is simply energy. Much of the time we know what is right for our children; the reason we don't do it is not ignorance or indifference, but impatience, lack of time, or exhaustion. When they are tiny we need physical strength, to keep them fed and clean and clothed;

as they get older they need less of this, but the emotional demands are greater.

I remember, some years ago, getting in late after a school concert. I was greeted by a pile of dirty supper dishes, and had to make an immediate decision whether to thank the children for starting to clear up or to tell them off for not finishing. Tired as I was, I also knew it was the only moment to broach the subject, with one of them, of a month and a half's allowance squandered on a badly organized weekend. This required the tact and skill of a diplomat: an allowance, after all, is there so you can spend your money as you wish, but a teenager doesn't know how to get value for money and needs help. We negotiated this acceptably, and I had just breathed a sigh of weariness and was about to climb into bed when one of the others, exhausted himself from performing in his concert, sat down on the stairs and refused to move. Now, I firmly believe parents should follow their instincts. But my instinct at that moment was to box his ears, smack his bottom, and count up to five through gritted teeth. Why? Not because he needed punishment, but because I needed sleep. He really needed an affectionate cuddle because he was miserably unhappy at school. But an affectionate cuddle halfway up the stairs at ten-thirty at night after a tiring day when every fibre of your being is aching for the Land of Nod needs a parent with stamina.

Since our own health and wellbeing are important to our children, we owe it to them to eat, sleep and exercise regularly.

When we moved house many years ago, I realized I was worn out and overworked. Trying to be responsible about it, I went to see my GP. I told her I suspected I had a lifestyle, rather than a medical, problem, so she told me to describe my week. Before I had got halfway through Monday morning she begged me to stop. She was already feeling the need to lie down.

'Tell me,' she said faintly, 'do you spend any time in the week on yourself? Some selfish activity, which is nothing to do with work or family?'

My face lit up. 'Yes,' I said. 'I go to a Latin grammar class on a Tuesday night.'

She buried her head in her hands in despair. 'I meant', she said with a muffled groan, 'an aromatherapy massage, or something.'

My GP was right. It is our responsibility to look after ourselves. So have a good diet. Enjoy plenty of sleep. Get regular fresh air and exercise. Try to arrange some weekly appointment – a game of tennis, or a film (or Latin grammar class) – which you enjoy and look forward to. Do something more modest on a daily basis if you can, reading or playing the piano for half an hour. Think of it as Enlightened Altruism.

I can see you shaking your head in disbelief. Have I taken leave of my senses? Playing the *piano*? Do I not remember what it is like to have a toddler, another child at nursery school, and a newborn baby yelling for a feed? Yes, I do. I admit, for many of us this ideal may be impossible at certain periods of our lives. But for most of us it is more possible than we think. Sometimes we have to risk thinking ourselves selfish in order to be more or less human. I have known some mothers endure continuous, round-the-clock, self-inflicted slave labour rather than ask their husbands to be useful on a Saturday afternoon or employ a willing sixteen-year-old to push a pram around. And I have to say I don't consider them altruistic, selfless, saintly Madonna-figures. I consider them insane.

A friend of mine had recently had her third baby. I innocently asked her if she was finding it more fun with three, and she looked at me groggily as if I'd just brained her with a rolling pin. 'Are you enjoying it more?' I repeated, forgetting all my mother had ever said about holes and digging and stopping.

'Enjoying it?' she asked, incredulous. 'I'm far too tired to *enjoy* my children.' She had clearly never heard of such wicked hedonism.

Curious, I asked her how she spent her day. Soon I was sympathizing with my GP. My friend's schedule was nonstop from six a.m. onwards. However, there was always a window, between ten and twelve, when one child was at school and the others were asleep. As I saw it, she had two golden hours each day. I was agog to hear how she spent them. When my children were that age I greedily gobbled up that time to write novels, because that was what I wanted to do more than anything else in my spare time. Perhaps she spent it eating chocolates and reading *Hello!* because that kept her in one piece. Or playing squash with a schoolfriend so that she could thrash out her frustrations. Or simply having a cappuccino and ringing her mother. Alas, none of these. She did housework. *Housework*. I ask you.

Now look, if some parent loves dusting and it recharges his batteries, fine. Or if another can't afford help in the house and battles on nobly and single-handed, I admire her more than I can say. But this friend of mine and her husband could afford a car, and foreign holidays. To spend her only free time loading the dishwasher and hoovering the sitting room in order to save a few pounds on a cleaner seemed to me – and still seems to me – completely and absolutely potty. Get a life. And get a little selfish. Not because you are selfish, but because your children would rather have cheaper holidays and domestic help, or even a few dead daddy-long-legs in the corners and cobwebs billowing in the breeze under the chandeliers, if it means a mother who has the energy and enthusiasm to enjoy her children because she has spent her two free hours having a long and lovely bubble bath, listening to Radio Five Live while they were asleep.

Be happy to fail

'For you, Mother, being happy to fail must be
an essential survival mechanism.'

Bink

By and large, there is a correlation between contented parents and contented children. Perhaps, somewhere, there is a Bluebeard of a father who beats his children and locks them up and feeds them mouldy bread through the keyhole, gaining intense personal satisfaction and mental serenity from this activity, but I haven't met him. All the parents and children I meet love each other in their own idiosyncratic ways. So, broadly speaking, when the children are happy the parents are, and vice versa. If this is the case, it is clearly in your child's interests for you to be happy and relaxed, rather than trying to be the guilt-ridden, self-deprecating, miserable parent the modern world wants you to be.

So let me pass on something that I have found most liberating. I learnt it from my mother, indirectly. I can't remember her exact words (I was quite small at the time), but one day she expressed the opinion that she was not a very good parent. She compared herself to so-and-so's mummy, who did baking with her, and taught her how to sew, and made the family's clothes herself, and had all the menus for the Christmas holidays worked out before the end of term, and got her children to ballet lessons on time, and probably organized the army of the Third Reich as well. (She was terrifying. I wouldn't have passed her house at night without checking my pockets for garlic, crucifixes and silver bullets. Though I met her at a Christmas party a few years ago and found that she is now passing herself off as a harmless old granny. She wasn't even nine foot six any more.)

My mother didn't stop there. She mentioned another mother who was as thin as a rake, always exquisitely turned out, and good at tennis. Oh, and she made real apple pie. And custard. With eggs. On an Aga. In a tidy farmhouse kitchen. I mean, really.

And then it came on me like a flash of lightning, and the enlightenment has stayed with me ever since. If my mother was not a 'good' parent, the conclusion was inescapable. *The best mothers are the lousy ones.*

Not only that, but we all consider ourselves lousy at it. Why are the bookshops heaving with volumes telling us how to be good enough parents? Because we believe we are not good enough. Even my own mother (who has never, as far as I know, done an unkind thing in her life), even the best mother in the world thought she was inadequate. My father maintains that the greatest artists are the ones most dissatisfied with their work. The same seems to be true of parents. The worse we think we are, the better we probably are.

We will fail. By our own estimation, we will fall short, do it wrong, be lousy at it. This simple piece of wisdom, arrived at when I was still in milk teeth, has given me more joy and peace than the wisest sayings of Confucius. (Possibly because I can't readily call many of the sayings of Confucius to mind. There you are, proof positive: what kind of parent hasn't got the teachings of Confucius at her fingertips?) Long before I started rearing children, I knew I would be useless. I have not disappointed myself. At break-fast this morning I had two further pieces of evidence. Bink asked me if I could tell Shaun to put her clothes in the wash. I explained that he would be out all day, but I would do her laundry for her.

'No. Thank you.'

'I mean, I'll just put your things in the machine. I won't try to hang them up or anything complicated.'

'No, Mum. Really,' she said firmly. I know she would have let Alexander wash her clothes. She might even have let Serena do it. But me? No. There you have it. As a big-bosomed, starching, ironing mother, I am not a success.

Half an hour later I was encouraging Benjamin to eat breakfast. He claimed he just wanted cereal. I explained that I had cooked him two fish-cakes. He declined.

'But they're shop ones,' I coaxed.

He looked at me sharply. 'Are you sure?'

'Yes.'

'You didn't make them?'

'No. I got them out of a packet.'

'You had nothing to do with making them?'

'Nothing.'

'Promise?'

'Look, it says Waitrose,' I said, gingerly picking the packet out of the bin.

'Way-hey! Gimme, gimme!' he exclaimed at eighty decibels.

Some weak-spirited parents might feel discouraged by such exchanges. Not I. (A couple of hours' sobbing in the bathroom and I was fine.) You see, I always knew I was going to be a failure. I am not surprised, dismayed, or disappointed. I cling to my dictum. *The lousy mothers are the best.*

There is another truth I have discovered, to my astonishment, over the years. Children are remarkably forgiving. I don't mean you can say 'sorry' and they will say 'fine' and you can both forget about it. Though that is true too. I mean they seem capable of being *profoundly* forgiving. You can make mistakes, apparently hundreds and thousands of mistakes, and your children can still turn out to be lovely people. I can remember looking at our eldest as she entered adolescence, thinking of the bumbling parenting she had put up with, and being amazed that the chaos we called her upbringing could have produced anyone so gorgeous.

Obviously this doesn't mean we should give our children less than the best. You wouldn't be reading this book if you didn't want to do well by your child. What I mean is that we *will* give our children less than the best. And they will survive.

The sooner we admit, to ourselves and to them, that we are never going to be perfect parents, the saner, and the happier, we will be.

Be happy to fight

I can't remember who first alerted us to the fact that we would have to fight for our marriage. Perhaps it was an older couple, or our vicar, or several different wise friends. After all, it is an obvious message to offer a young couple in love, in a society where most relationships and nearly half of all marriages break up. Certainly before we were engaged we knew that, if we wanted to get married and stay married, we would have to be pretty resolute and determined in the modern world.

Within a few minutes of a conversation of the 'Sweetest, will you …?' 'Oh, all right Old Fruit', type, we had another debate something along these lines. When? Next summer, after Finals, was the earliest feasible date. But what about his second degree? My training at drama school? His ordination? My career? It would be far more practical, on the face of it, to postpone our marriage for some time – probably five or six years. We could then both get started in the work we planned to do, and not have to juggle student life with weekly rep, or accommodate busy commuting with learning to live together. From the point of view of finances, employment, convenience and personal fulfilment, a few years' wait would have made far more sense.

There was another consideration, however. If we each put our respective vocations before our relationship we would be making an unmistakable statement about our priorities. Work first; a wedding when we can make time. But marriage cannot survive this kind of treatment. Certainly not in modern society, which is already so biased against a lifelong, unconditional commitment. Marriage must come first, or it will come apart. Obviously it doesn't always come first chronologically: you may not meet the person you want to marry until you are well established in your career. But it must come first in importance. Your future spouse should take precedence over everything else, if you want to hang on to each other. We concluded that if we didn't make our marriage our priority then, we might never learn to make it a priority later. And if it wasn't our absolute priority, it could never withstand the pressure of modern life.

(Of course, the other factor that helped fix the date was the little matter of the Good Book, and the dim view it takes of any pre-marital slap and tickle. Why do Christians walk down the aisle so much younger than their non-Christian friends …?)

Who knows what would have happened if we had chosen differently? I have often wondered. When single friends of mine had their big breaks at the National Theatre or on film or in television sitcoms, I wondered. When other young clergymen were invited on prestigious speaking tours, when my friends were living in London and getting auditions every other minute, I wondered. And when other people's relationships ran aground because they were living and working in different towns, or their marriages broke up under the pressure of their careers, or they had difficulty having children after they had left it too late, I also wondered. And, however hard I found unemployment and however boring it is being broke, I never, even for a fraction of a second, regretted that decision. I knew then and know now that a failed marriage causes far more heartache than a failed career. I also knew that, if we wanted to be married at all, we had to make marriage our most important project.

This sometimes demands a brutal single-mindedness. Some years ago I was performing with an actor I liked and admired greatly. We worked well together. The opportunity came up to do a first-rate two-hander. But part of the reason we were good on stage together was because of an unmistakable sexual chemistry between us. The play would have involved going away from home. Now, it is likely that nothing would have happened. I value my marriage highly, I have no reason to be unfaithful and no intention of being so. He too was happy in his private life and had considerable integrity. It would probably have been all right. *Probably*. But you don't allow your toddler to cross a busy road alone on the grounds that he will probably survive. If anything had gone wrong, it would have been my marriage at stake. The relationship which is more important to me than anything else. The commitment to the person I vowed to love and honour in good times and bad. The man I want still to be with when I'm sixty-four. How could I run such a risk, on a mere probability of safety? It simply wasn't worth it. Much as I would have loved the job, my marriage is too valuable to hazard.

It is the same with bringing up our children. Indeed, it is true of anything which is both important and demanding. There is no seriously worthwhile activity I know of which doesn't demand a certain setting of the jaw and a readiness to fight. Yehudi Menuhin didn't become a renowned violinist through an attitude of *laissez faire*. Laurence Olivier didn't achieve greatness by not minding much one way or the other. Even a genius can only succeed by being determined and disciplined, by putting his one passion before everything else: in short, by bloody-mindedness and ruthlessness. And these men were simply entertainers, prepared to dedicate all that effort just to giving the rest of us a good night out. By contrast, we are talking about creating a new human being, shaping a character, moulding a destiny. If something is really worth doing – becoming a great footballer or ballerina, preserving a marriage or bringing up children – we need to have resolution, a hidden steeliness, even a militancy in our attitude in order to see it through.

Imagine the young musician. It is six a.m. Time to do his scales before going off to school. But it is cold, the rest of the household is in bed, and no one will know if he stays under the covers, skips his practice, and doesn't get up until breakfast time. No one except himself, and his audience twenty years later when he is merely a good performer, rather than a great one. It needs a pretty stubborn little trouper to get up, get dressed and get going.

It takes the same indomitable spirit to be a parent. Picture the young father. It is three p.m. At four o'clock his son and heir is playing the third angel from the left in the back row of the nursery school nativity play.

He said he would try to be there, but his boss has just called an emergency departmental meeting, he will miss out on some important decisions, and may not be the one at the cutting edge of the project if he sticks to his plans and leaves, after facing the embarrassment of explaining why to the others in the office. No one will know if he slips in during tea at the end of the performance and pretends he was there all along. No one except himself … and his son who, years later, still retains an unshakable confidence in all circumstances because he always knew his father considered him more important than his employer, his colleagues and his team at work. That takes a fighter too.

It is a great help to realize, before we embark on having children, that we will sometimes need the determination of a campaigning general in order to preserve our priorities, support our children and be wonderful parents to them. Being prepared is a great asset. If you have not yet, or have only recently, become a parent, buck yourself up with these two truths. You will fail. And you must fight. If you are anything like me, knowing this in advance will help you to stay sane later. Over and over again in later years, as the rubber goes on hitting the road, you can console yourself that you always knew it would be so.

Parents in charge

> 'Many adults think that if you ask them why, then you are
> challenging their authority. You're not: you're just asking why.'
> **Bink**

Something which gives children, indeed anyone, an unshakable sense of security is knowing that someone else, someone competent and mature and capable, is in charge. In our present egalitarian age there is a temptation to behave as if everyone should be involved equally in all the decisions of running anything. We even extend this principle to children and families.

It's understandable. Once upon a time, we all had the experience of knowing that our opinions and wishes were being passed over. I can remember being appalled at what my parents wasted their money on. Bricks and mortar? *How* many tens of thousands of pounds? Didn't they *know* how many lifetimes of chocolate and bubble gum that could have supplied? (Bubble gum being a penny a packet at the time.) What profligacy … But they ignored my fiscal prudence and squandered their money as they pleased. I imagine yours did too. Presumably, somewhere in the depths of each of our emotional memories we can all still remember that feeling of being of no consequence. And because we love our children we want to spare them this humiliation. So we institute a generous, undiscriminating democracy, in which everyone has an equal say.

But this is what they neither want nor need.

A tyranny, not a democracy

> 'Children don't need to know the reason for everything.
> But they do need to know that you know the reason.'
> **Alexander**

Democracy is an overrated form of government. Families, in particular, were never designed to be democratic. A monarchy is not a bad model for a single parent, since a monarch is one who rules alone. Aristocracy offers a good prototype, meaning, as it does, government by those who are best at it. But perhaps the most appropriate of all is the model of a benign tyranny, since tyrants are strong, their power unaccountable and beyond question. What you are not, absolutely not, running is a democracy. Or, if you must think of your domestic unit in politically correct terminology, at least remember that all decent democracies are run by *senate*, government by the oldest.

Imagine what democratic family life must feel like for children. Suppose, the next time you are travelling in a jumbo jet over the Atlantic Ocean, the pilot abandons his post and comes into the passenger section. 'Ladies and gentlemen,' he begins, 'I think you're all as important as I am. I don't have any truck with this elitism which excludes some people from being in charge of planes just because they haven't yet passed any flying exams. So I would like to invite anyone who fancies it to have his turn at the controls.' This would be bad enough. But believe me, it could get far worse. 'You, sir (or madam),' he continues, turning to you. 'Where would you like to land? Take over, and put us down wherever you like.'

How much more comfortable we were when we were being competently flown by someone else, and could complain with gay abandon about the slow service and the ghastly food. How relaxed we seemed, expressing our annoyance when the pilot didn't take off because he wasn't satisfied that the weather conditions were right or that the instruments had been checked properly. How confident we felt, kicking up a fuss, secure in the knowledge that no pilot in his senses would ever take the slightest bit of notice. We knew he wouldn't start the engine before he was ready. Imagine how terrifying it would be if he did; if he took our objections seriously, and went charging off down the runway before he had refuelled, because he couldn't bear to hear us complaining a moment longer.

This is what we sometimes do to our children. How often have we given in, and agreed to something just to stop the whining? This is not fair on them. We are at the controls and, like a polite pilot, should listen to them and respond graciously, but not take undue notice of what they say. Fly the plane. Take control. Allow them the luxury of being passengers for a few years … and of having a good old moan about us without it mattering two hoots.

Respected, not liked

Some years ago, one of our children wanted to share a party with my niece of the same age to celebrate the end of GCSEs. The trouble was that some months earlier my parents had invited all of us to an open-air concert and picnic, and I had accepted. Unfortunately, modern life being as busy as it is (or me being as disorganized as I am), I hadn't yet told the rest of the family. And it was the only night the friends could all come.

It is the kind of decision which faces modern parents every day of the week. Etiquette dictates that a previous engagement must be kept. But my parents are very understanding, they could easily find others to use the tickets, and what is the point of a treat which the children don't want to have? So it was decided that the adults would go to the concert and the children would have a party, the condition of our largesse being that the other siblings must be included, as always.

Well, we had a terrific evening. The concert was witty, sparkling and superb, the picnic delicious, the gardens gorgeous, the fireworks over the midnight lake spectacular, and my main regret was that the children weren't there to enjoy it with us. We got home in the small hours, and found the cliché that had been waiting to happen. Admittedly they had shown a considerable amount of sense: one guest had not been allowed to leave because the others considered him not fit to do so, but this meant he had deposited all over my study sofa what had incapacitated him in the first place.

There then followed a painful weekend. Damage had to be paid for out of meagre allowances. House rules were drawn up where none had existed before. It is always uncomfortable when guidelines are tightened, rather than relaxed. And it was all because I hadn't wanted to be unpopular. I hadn't wanted to lay down the law and tell them to do as they were told: I wanted to be the kind, understanding parent. I promise you, I was a lot more unpopular by Sunday afternoon than I would have been if I'd made a tougher decision in the first place. (And every year since, we have all been to the concert together, I have remembered to announce it in advance, and it has become a highlight of our summer.)

But at least I learnt my lesson. A few months later our daughter was invited to the opening of a nightclub. I rang the club in question to find out more, and was told no one under twenty-one was allowed in. (She was sixteen at the time.) Sorry, I said, permission refused. But her friends were all going. Then their mothers can ring me and we will all discuss it together, I replied – co-ordinate taxis; share lifts. Nothing happened. So when she telephoned me that evening at nine o'clock to find out whether she could go, permission was still withheld. I felt incredibly daring, as if I were abseiling over a cliff without a rope, or exploring virgin territory unaided and alone in the modern world. Would some policeperson of the Liberal Establishment find me out and curse me with dire warnings of the trauma I was causing my offspring? Would my children rebel horribly, and everyone say 'I told you so'? Pondering these terrifying consequences, I daringly stuck to my guns.

The next day it turned out that all her friends had indeed gone, been allowed in, and had a good time; no one had been raped, murdered or kidnapped. But that was all. She just mentioned it in passing. No fuss, no resentment, no problem. How different from the Weekend of the Awful Party, when we'd had to be so beastly and authoritarian because we'd been too lenient first time around.

Parents are supposed to lay down the law. Children expect it, and depend on it. They are not obliged to keep thanking us for doing it, any more than they thank a teacher who makes them work for their exams, or we thank the pilot who won't take off in a dangerous blizzard. But we know what kind of pilot we'd like to fly with. And they will know which teachers they owe most to, thirty years on.

A parent, not a friend

A particularly unnecessary hurdle we modern parents put in front of ourselves is the idea that we should *befriend* our children. Almost as soon the midwife said, 'It's a girl,' I started dreaming of the confidences we would share together over an espresso, the way we would swap lipstick and ball-gowns, the secrets she would giggle to me about her latest beau, and how I would reciprocate by telling her about her dashing father in a previous era and century. Dismal. How sad would my teenager be, if she had to confide in me? What did we give her a sister for, for goodness' sake?

I never confided in my mother. Did you? I would have died rather than tell her about the latest boy I had a crush on, or what kind of jokes my friends told in school. But I never for a moment wished for a different mother. I never once said to myself, 'How I long for a young, sexy, leggy Mamma whose make-up would suit me.' It never occurred to me that my life would be better if she were more like a chum and less like a parent. Why should it? I had plenty of friends at school. Whereas she was my only shot at having a mother. What I needed from her and my father were qualities they, and they only, could give. High moral standards, so I could measure myself against people I respected. Consistency, so I knew how they would behave and what they would think of certain actions or people. Honesty and truthfulness and faithfulness, so I always had a model at the back of my mind of what I should be aiming for. But total, uninhibited intimacy? The need never crossed my mind. Chumminess is great fun for the parent, but not necessarily the most important quality for the child. And now, because I respect my parents, I confide in them all the time.

I am aware that this is not what the new, dewy-eyed parent wants to hear. Of course we all want to be friends to our children, to be liked by them, to be the kind of parents they boast about at school because we're so funky and relaxed and cool. Naturally this gives us terrific job satisfaction, and makes the whole parenting process seem much more what the doctor ordered. And with a bit of luck and a fair wind behind us, many confidences and much closeness may – indeed, probably will – be shared eventually, some of the time at least. But this will only happen incidentally, as we are trying to do something more important. Being liked by one's children is a smashing bonus but a rotten goal, rather like happiness itself. Aim to be happy and you may well end up selfish and frustrated, going around in self-defeating circles. But aim to be good, kind, dutiful, and the chances are you will often wake in the morning with a sense of your own great good fortune, and wonder how you came to be so blessed.

And just for the record, incidentally, we do now swap clothes. That is to say, Bink pinches all Shaun's sweatshirts. And if there's something of mine that I haven't been able to find for months, it invariably turns up under a dog in Serena's bedroom.[2]

Repeat this mantra. Write it on your bathroom mirror. Hang it by your bed.

> I am not a friend, but a parent.
> They don't need to like me, but trust me.
> This is not a democracy, but a wise, loving,
>   on-the-whole-benign tyranny.

Parents in love

> [Dr Benjamin Salk] turned to the camera, looked millions
> of viewers in the eye and said, 'The greatest thing you
> parents can do for your children is to love each other.'[3]

I don't know how to write this section without causing offence. When it comes to the wellbeing of children, the evidence in favour of marriage is overwhelming. But many parents are bringing up children alone, often through no choice of their own. To enthuse about marriage is to be like the Irishman who, when asked the way, replied, 'To be sure, you don't want to start from here.'

We *are* here. Some people reading this book will be single parents. You are already fighting uphill, as it were. The last thing I want to do is stand at a different vantage point, and tell you how much better the view is from where I am. It will hardly encourage you in the battle. Nevertheless, having just extolled the virtues of truth over popularity, I feel a duty to state the facts as they are. And everything else being equal, there is no doubt that it is generally better for the children if there are two of you. It is a two-person job. It also tends to be easier if both biological parents are involved, and married to each other. But of course there are many people who don't fit into this category, either by choice or accident: stepparents, adoptive parents, widows, divorcees, the unmarried or separated, those who have been abandoned, or whose spouses are in prison or ill or at war, and so on.

These instances are more widespread than ever, and this affects every modern child, not just those whose parents have split up. I can remember exactly where I was in the kitchen, loading the dishwasher, when one of ours, aged eight, asked me a question which I imagine now occurs to every boy or girl in the land, sooner or later. There had been no arguments in the house immediately beforehand (which must be a record in itself) and no particular incident which might have prompted her concern. She simply said, 'What will you live off, when you and Daddy get divorced?'

I stared at her for a moment, then asked her what she meant.

'Well, you don't earn much,' she explained. 'I just wondered how you're going to live.'

I try to imagine what had been going through her mind in the months leading up to that question. Earlier that year we had moved house. She had lost her schoolmates, her teacher, her church, neighbours, garden, bedroom and almost every familiar thing. Most of her world was now alien.

Only one thing was constant, and that was her family. She had the same parents, the same brothers and sisters, the same uncles and aunts and grandparents.

Many children cope with all sorts of upheavals, and always have. If the core of their lives, their family, is unchanged then the ballast of their lives is stable and they can absorb frequent knocks without capsizing. But in our daughter's new class there was another phenomenon. As she looked around her and learnt how other people lived, she was forced to a certain conclusion: the very centre of her life was not safe from change either. Just as she had moved house, many of her classmates had moved family. Some of them had new fathers or mothers, new brothers and sisters. Presumably, therefore, nothing in her life was fixed or guaranteed. Moreover, she had younger siblings: she felt responsible. How would her mother live, without a house or an income? Happily she voiced her concern, so I was able to tell her it wasn't going to happen.

A neighbour and I were recently discussing levels of anxiety which children face today. I was surprised when she said they must now feel far more secure, because we live in more prosperous times. As she put it, 'They don't have to worry where their next meal is coming from.' Oh, but they do. I grant, modern children do know they will get a meal – and a new pair of trainers, their own colour television, and access to the Internet – but they often don't know where it will come from.

When I was a child and family breakdown was still the exception, my father was visited by a couple who were worried about their son's lack of progress in his school. He spent a long time listening to their concerns about the boy's poor academic work, lack of social integration, and various other setbacks. They seemed genuinely baffled by his unhappiness, and my father promised to do what he could. As they were leaving, they happened to say that the school would have to post any correspondence in duplicate in future, as they were going through a divorce. He still refers to this conversation with utter incredulity: they were quite unable to see any connection between their actions and their child's difficulties.

Not much has changed. A few years ago I was taking part in the Duchess of York's first attempt at television presenting. (And yes, since you ask, she was charming, and doing quite well at a difficult job.) It was one of those studio debates in which parents – goodness only knows why – turn up with their problematic teenagers and describe what an awful time they are all having together. Drugs, sex, rebellion, truanting, stealing: you name it, they were doing it. Fergie turned to me and asked for my comment. Any fool could see that these gawky, acne-covered, unhappy people all had one thing in common. Some were rich and some were poor, some one colour and some another. But they had each lost a parent. I started to say so. My dear, you'd think I'd accused all those single parents of being serial murderers. I was cut off mid-sentence. We don't want nasty little views like that, thank you very much. Silly me: I should have remembered the Duchess's own domestic arrangements.

Presumably it is for reasons of political correctness that the difference between having one parent and two is so thoroughly obscured. It certainly isn't because we are unaware of the impact family breakdown has on children. Considerable research has been done into it, and the findings are remarkably consistent. Children in separated families are more likely to be aggressive, delinquent, and have other behavioural problems. They generally perform less well academically and get fewer educational qualifications. On average they will leave school at a younger age, become sexually active younger, form a cohabiting relationship sooner, and are more likely to parent a child outside marriage. They are also more likely to drink, smoke and use drugs, and they display more depressive tendencies. They will typically achieve less as adults.[4]

This much we might expect. However, children whose parents have split up are also more often admitted to hospital, and more likely to swallow poison, have an accident or even die.[5] It is hard to think of any areas left in which they might not be disadvantaged. Those from broken homes underperform significantly in maths, general knowledge and arithmetic.[6] Boys brought up without their fathers are more than twice as likely to end up in court.[7] These trends cannot be put down to financial discrepancies between broken homes and intact ones (though children with only one parent are also likely to be worse off materially), since economic factors are usually taken into account. For instance, children of single mothers have been found to have a higher death rate than children below the poverty line.[8]

Sometimes the differences are staggering. One study showed that children are thirty-three times more likely to be abused if they live with a man who is not their father. Even more alarmingly, perhaps, their own father is twenty times more likely to abuse them if he is not married to their mother.[9] And we say marriage is just a bit of paper. Not to the children it isn't.

Now, you and I are not planning to abuse our children. So what is the relevance of all these alarming statistics in bringing up our own children? To return to the Irishman and his travel directions, how we use the map rather depends on where we're coming from.

For the single or divorced

If marriage is such an advantageous environment for children, what hope is there for those of us who cannot supply it?

Well, sight is an asset, but David Blunkett hasn't done badly, has he? And none of us would have heard of Louis Braille if he hadn't injured himself as a child. Hearing is conventionally considered an advantage for a musician, but Beethoven's track record is pretty impressive, as is Evelyn Glennie's (the profoundly deaf percussionist). A handicap doesn't mean you are out of the race.

I know, it is deeply, shockingly un-PC to say any of this. I'm supposed to reassure you that single parenthood is just as natural and serene and apple-pie-shaped as any other: it's all the same, really. But it isn't. I will not lie. Bringing up children on your own is not ideal and not easy. This doesn't mean it can't be good. It helps, however, to start by being honest. You have a considerable disadvantage, but it is a disadvantage that can be overcome.

When my talented, clever, easy-going cousin was twenty-one he went on holiday to France. One day he went swimming with friends in a river. The next day he woke feeling stiff. By evening he was paralysed, from head to toe. Shortly after he came home his speech went too. For years I prayed for him to be healed. He never was. But something else, arguably far more important, happened instead. He used his disability to become an inventor: first he made a car which could be driven by one hand; then a machine which could write, and then speak, for him. He now has his own business, employs numerous people, and has twice won a Queen's Award for Export. My ordinary cousin has become a most extraordinary success. No one would ever have wished his fate on him, but it is also hard to wish it undone, given his achievements and the benefits he has brought to others.

Being a lone parent can be similar. We should no more choose it as an option than we would choose to inflict any handicap on our child. But no decent person would dream of wishing your children unborn, any more than they would wish any child with a handicap unborn. If you are already there, the rest of us must give you all the support we can. You have a more difficult job to do. It isn't fair and it isn't a doddle. But it's possible, and it's worth it.

So be encouraged. *Statistically,* it's true that children in single-parent families are disadvantaged. But there is nothing to dictate that your child is going to be part of these statistics. The *average* child with two parents does better than the average child with one. Your child is not average.

It is perfectly possible to bring up your children better than many couples do. After all, I wouldn't choose to bring up my children in poverty and deprivation, but many poor parents do a better job of bringing up their children than vast numbers of rich ones.

Sometimes living with one parent alone is better than the alternative: living with violence, alcoholism or infidelity, for instance. Almost always, the children will respect the one who has had to make the hard choice. Admittedly, when they are young they may find it hard to accept (though, if the situation was bad enough, they may be relieved). But when they are grown up they will realize what you went through for them, and should be profoundly grateful.

Divorce is a terrible pity, but it is not the end. A friend of mine was determined not to let his children suffer because of his divorce, if this was humanly possible. So he and his wife agreed never to argue about the break-up in front of them, and never to undermine one another to them.

Because our society heavily favours mothers and because we now have no-fault divorce, it was a foregone conclusion (despite the fact that she was the one who had been unfaithful) that his wife would be given custody of the children and the marital home. This was grossly unfair and nearly broke his heart, but he didn't fight it. He could see that she would do a good job of it, and the effect of a legal wrangle on the children would have been devastating. He bought a house within walking distance. He kept on scrupulously good terms with his ex-wife, and consequently, throughout their teens, the children stayed with him two or three nights a week. His efforts have been amply rewarded, and his children are gorgeous.

Finally, there is one category of single parent that is unique. I am aware that we are not allowed to make such distinctions, but the children themselves do (consciously or otherwise), so we might as well own up to it. Some lone parents are single wholly involuntarily. Widows are not the same as divorcées. Parental death is cruel and wicked and sometimes deprives children at their most pitifully vulnerable: they are entitled to be angry and they often are, sometimes with the parent who has deserted them, sometimes with the parent left behind, sometimes with God, sometimes with everyone. But the bottom line is that they know, in their hearts, that they were not abandoned deliberately.

One of the loveliest friends I had as a child was brought up by one parent alone. Her mother had a beautiful character, which she had clearly succeeded in passing on to her children. When I was young I put this down (rightly or wrongly) to the circumstance that caused them to lose their father. He drowned, rescuing someone else's child. I remember my mother telling me that he had plunged into an icy river to save twin babies, pulled one out successfully, went back in for the other, and both their lives were lost. I always believed this must have given my friend such pride in her father that it enabled her to overcome the sorrow of living without him. Children seem capable of understanding, from a very early age, the background of certain circumstances, of knowing something is not your fault, and of respecting you and loving you all the more for it.

If children are valued by how much we suffer for them, yours may be even more precious than anyone else's. Love them, and they will know it.

For the married

*'Everyone needs a daddy. In summertime anyhow:
otherwise, who will get rid of the spiders for you?'*
Bink

The implication of all this research for those of us who are married is clear, and rather sobering. Presumably you are reading this because you wish to be a good parent. Most of us do. I can't think of any of my acquaintances who don't want the best for their offspring. Many of us would say we would lay down our lives for our little ones.

So we must take the evidence seriously. Clearly, the first and most obvious service we can perform for our children is quite simply to *stay married*. It is insultingly simple. Get married and stay married, and we are giving our children the best possible advantage in life. We are offering them a hand up academically, socially and economically; their chances of good health are better, they are less likely to be in trouble with the law, less liable to have underage sex, less likely to truant now or face unemployment later, less likely to have to cope with divorce or separation themselves. We are even improving their life expectancy, for goodness' sake. It is awesome in its straightforwardness.

Loving our spouse is the most important thing we can do for our children, once their physical needs are met. We often don't realize how much we are doing simply by putting food on the table and tucking our children up into a warm bed each night. If we are also sustaining a stable marriage we are almost there. There will still be much fine-tuning we want to do – learning to appreciate their company, teaching them to cope with failure, developing their self-discipline – and if we care about the work of child rearing we will go on improving these skills all our lives. But we can rest assured that, even if we never get any of these details quite as we want them, we are good, even great, parents already. Definitely time for the KitKat.

(Brace yourself, however. Don't think they won't censure us for the details we do get wrong: forgetting the crucial football match; not encouraging the playing of the Uillean pipes or the career as a topless model;

moving to Scotland just when the girl next door had become indispensable to happiness. The social climate in which we live demands that they tell us all the little things we have left undone that we ought to have done and vice versa. But they will do so from a position of strength – provided we feed them, cuddle them and love their other parent, they will criticize us ... and *survive*.)

Your bedside table is no doubt already weighed down with manuals about Staying in Love, Preserving the Magic, and Men Being from Outer Space. (If it's not, it ought to be.) So I won't bother you with the Four Languages of Love (or is it five?) and exhort you to remember the wedding anniversary, be romantic and spontaneous, and overwhelm her with sex and red roses (though not simultaneously – you might hurt yourselves). What follows is not a marriage manual. This isn't the time or place. But there are three simple principles for your marriage, which will therefore also greatly enhance your children's sense of security.

Commitment

'Never mention the "D" word. Never use it. Never think it, nor even contemplate it as a solution. It is not part of the vocabulary of your relationship. Murder maybe: divorce never.'[10] Such was the gist of our marriage preparation. And quite right too. It has stood us in good stead ever since.

Every marriage has its ups and downs. And whatever the compassionate reasons for easier divorce – the hard cases, the examples of suffering which have led us to this point – the truth is that nowadays, when we encounter marital obstacles, divorce beckons like a cream cake to a dieter. However thin you want to be, it's much easier to give in than to persevere. Be kind to yourself and don't allow cream cakes in the house in the first place. Give your marriage a chance, and rule out divorce right from the beginning. Then you can use your resources to find another solution.

Every long-term happily married couple has had to fight for its marriage, one way or another. The family friend who made my wedding dress said to me, 'Have beautiful photographs of the day, Annie. Then, when you hit a bad patch – *and you will* – it's good to remind yourself how lovely it all was.' I remember feeling slightly shocked, even prurient, to think that a friend of my parents had been through bad times with her husband. I'm sure I thought we would do better. And yet, when she bravely succumbed to cancer a few years ago, her husband was so heartbroken that he died soon afterwards. 'Do better' indeed. They died as they had lived, like turtledoves. But presumably they had times when they felt like hurling frying pans at each other.

Fortunately it doesn't happen to me often, but I can remember a bleak evening in mid-winter a few years ago when I sat at the kitchen table and couldn't think of any reason to stay except that marriage is for life. And yet, at the risk of sounding quite revoltingly soppy, being in love (including the result of it, our children) has brought me more happiness than anything else in my life, many times over. If we are conditioned to think of divorce as an answer in a difficult time, it is much harder not to turn to it. Thank goodness we were never offered such poison.

I'm not saying divorce is never the least bad option. If there is dangerous violence, repeated and deliberate adultery, or serious criminal behaviour, it's hard to see how the other partner can bat on alone for long. Happily, this is not the case for most of us. For the ordinary, run-of-the-mill, selfish creatures like you and me, marriage is sometimes glorious and sometimes ghastly, but always worth fighting for. But because it is hard work and divorce sometimes seems much easier, solutions to marriage problems will not be audible whilst we allow ourselves to be battered and confused by the deafening racket coming through the open 'Divorce' door. Shut the door, get used to the peace and quiet and listen hard. After a while we will hear them, the little voices whispering secret solutions. What do they say? 'Compromise'; 'Apologize'; 'Give in'; 'Be more realistic'; 'Don't let the sun go down upon your wrath'; 'Talk about it'; 'Change career'; 'Get help'; 'Leave him alone'; 'Say sorry'; 'Buy her a present'; 'Make love'.

But 'Divorce'? Don't even think about it. Marriage is for life.

Priority

Children are not made to feel secure by being treated as the most important people in their world.

When Serena was a few weeks old some neighbours took charge of her for the evening, and gave us money to go and have a meal *à deux*. I was grateful but bemused, not seeing the significance of the gesture at the time. A few children later, I do. Children are the most wonderful and natural result of their parents' love for one another, but they must never replace it. We are lovers first and parents second. We forget this at our children's peril. If either of the parents is so besotted or busy with the baby that the other one starts to take second place, trouble lies ahead.

Imagine yourself three foot high again. Would you like a universe which revolves around you? Your parents were due to go out this evening, but you had a bad day at nursery school (Teacher confiscated your spud gun and broke it while trying to play with it; and as if this weren't enough, Sophie Holsworthy-Jones spilt squash all over your Masterpiece in Poster Paints, then said it was your fault for pushing her over) so you feel cross, tired and upset. You decide to have a good old scream, assuming your parents will put you to bed anyway and tell you to behave because the babysitter will be along soon. You know that you can yell a bit and throw your toys about, and after they have left the house everything will calm down and you can go to sleep, honour satisfied.

But for some reason, tonight this doesn't happen. Because you are complaining vigorously, your mother comes into your bedroom and frowns somewhat. Your father tells her to hurry up. She says you seem so unhappy she doesn't want to leave you. He comes in and looks at you, wondering whether he should appear worried too. You spot a good delaying tactic, so you ask for various things you don't want, and when they bring them to you, tip them on the floor. Soon your mother is agitating that they are late now and what should they do? They both ask you if Mummy and Daddy can go out and enjoy themselves, because they've been looking forward to it for so long. So you cry a bit more, and say, 'No!' because it seems to be expected of you. Father sighs and rings the babysitter. Mother cries and goes downstairs. The whole evening has turned into a disaster, and the worst of it is that you seem to be responsible. How much safer life was when you thought you had entered a stable universe and could tiptoe about, awe-struck, or stomp about chucking things, and either way not do much damage. The world was always there and always stable, and your parents always came home again when they were ready.

Grow a few more feet and lots more spots, and ask yourself whether you want parents who are more interested in your love life than their own. OK, fine when they show a mild curiosity in the girl you met last week or the boy you are seeing tonight, but suppose you suspected they hadn't had any romance in their own lives since before you were born. Ugh … perhaps then your mother's questions would seem prying and intrusive. You might actually wonder if your father was ogling Katie when you brought her home. How much more liberty you would have knowing they had their own, vibrant love life (though of course it's yuck because they're old, so you groan when they don't keep it to themselves). But at least you know they don't depend on you for exciting romance.

A few years later you want to leave home. But imagine the kind of mother who has given up twenty years of her life to wait on you hand and foot, and has nothing in common with your father any more. The minute you leave you know she will pine and mope and have nothing to do and no one to talk to. What a burden of guilt you carry. How much you would prefer to think that, much as they love you, they love each other even more. To imagine them taking up where they left off two decades ago, holding hands and strolling by rivers and going out to pubs together, just the two of them. How reassuring it would be to think they had a life before you arrived on the scene, and that their business would continue after you had gone.

Give your children space. Set them free. Love each other more than you love them.

It's a good idea to set the tone right from the beginning, which was why our neighbours' kindness was so shrewd. Reserve moments for the two of you, alone. Put them in your diary. Guard them jealously. Children absorb all the hours and energy you can spend on them, so preserve your time together without quarter. I know a couple who regularly go out and spend Friday night alone, leaving the children with a baby-sitter. Other friends of ours make sure their children are always in bed by six, so their evenings are just for the two of them. When our children were small my parents kindly took care of them from time to time, so we could take a week's holiday without them every year. It's not because you don't love them, but because you love them so much that you are going to stay together.

To paraphrase Lovelace:

> I could not love thee (Dear) so much,
> Lov'd I not Mummy more.[11]

This is one of the many reasons it is easier for children to be living with both their natural parents. After all, they obviously won't mind Daddy putting Mummy first if they think Mummy is the most important person in the world too. But suppose she isn't Mummy, but Amanda, Daddy's new girlfriend. Are they still happy to come second in their father's affections then?

When I was writing my column in the *Telegraph*, I received a letter from a young woman who was near despair. The man she was in love with had two pre-teenage daughters who were giving her a horrible time. She had done everything she could to be affectionate and understanding, but in return they were rude and unkind to her at every opportunity.

I could see their point of view. They had lost their mother, and now feared losing their father too. Even though they would still have a home with him, they were being usurped in his heart. I told her I was going to say something she wouldn't like: in my opinion the girls had more right to their father than she had; they were first on the scene; they had not chosen the mess their parents had made of their marriage. I believed that their father should defer to them, and ask them what they wanted. They should genuinely be given the choice as to whether he should marry again.

Not only would it be a huge risk, but it would be a very humble thing to do. And we grown-ups are not usually good at being humble with children. I expected her to reject my suggestion.

I always loved it when a correspondent contacted me again to let me know the result of my advice. It was a couple of months later. She wrote to tell me that she and the girls' father had done exactly what I suggested. And once they were given the dignity they deserved, his daughters changed completely. They decided they would like to have her as their stepmother, the date was fixed, and they were now the best of friends. As soon as they knew they were not being supplanted in their father's eyes – that they had more claim to him even than his new love, and were, in the first instance at any rate, more important in his eyes – they were able to judge my correspondent on her merits, and realized they loved her too.

Though, once they were married, of course, he should go on to show her the loyalty essential to husband and wife.

Loyalty

Never let your children drive a wedge between you.

'Mummy, can I go to the cinema?'

'Not until you've done your homework.'

That's torn it. Never mind, let's wait until she's out of the room and give it another shot.

'Daddy?'

'Yes, dear?'

'Is it all right if I finish off my homework tomorrow?'

'S'pose so.'

'So I can go out?'

'Uh.'

'And c'n I have a fiver?'

'Mmm.' Daddy turns to sports page. Daughter and fiver make hasty exit. Re-enter Mummy. Explosion.

Mother and Father are an item. You see the world as one. You do not disagree. Yes, well, of course you disagree over the war in Iraq or how to solve the world energy crisis or whose father farts worse at Christmas time. But on *important* matters – whether or not you are allowed to turn your fork upside-down to eat your peas – parental opinion is united. You can be as disunited as you like afterwards or beforehand, as you hammer out these principles in the privacy of your bedroom, but you absolutely do not say to your beloved, in front of the children, 'Actually, I think you're being a bit strict on that one.' Or, if you do, you must immediately make it crystal clear to the children that they have to do as they're told anyway, even though you may be negotiating these matters between you. But under their noses is seldom the best place to do this. You are whisking the carpet out from under each other's feet and dealing a devastating blow to parental authority. And other mixed metaphors. So back one another up, through thick and thin. After all, if you don't think your spouse has good judgement, why did you marry him in the first place? You chose her: you have only yourself to blame.

I'm not saying you must never argue in front of the children. Rows are beastly, and I wish we inhabited a world where we all lived at peace, but we don't. Opinion is divided as to whether it's worse to know that your parents are having a quiet and deadly ding-dong through gritted teeth in the bedroom, or to see them hurling things at each other in front of you in the kitchen. The advantage of disagreeing in private is that it is generally more considerate and polite to keep our unpleasantnesses to ourselves. But be assured: your children will know if you are fighting, however well you think you've hidden it. The advantage of arguing in front of them is that they know how bad it is, aren't tempted to imagine it's much worse, and as long as you retain dignity and consideration and respect, they are learning how to handle disagreement themselves (and stay married) later on. But if we disagree in their presence, we *must* make up in their presence as well. I don't care how embarrassing it is. It's only fair. You called her a stupid cow in front of them, so you can jolly well give her a cuddle and say you're sorry and tell her she's beautiful in front of them too.

Best of all, learn not to argue too much anyway.

But do not, however much you row, ever undermine each other to the children. Never seriously criticize your partner to your offspring. Never complain, or moan, or disagree behind her back. Do not, in fact, tell tales about him to your best friend or your mother. It can be the beginning of the end.

And if one parent has proclaimed, then that is the law. The other will not rescind it.

'If your father has said the Lycra bicycle shorts and the see-through crop-top are unsuitable [why, oh why, did he pick this particular battle?], then you know the answer. They are not suitable. Yes, I know the party is at my parents' house, not his [silly old fool], and I may have said last week those shorts were fine for school [did I?], but this is different. It just is. That's what we've decided. Yes, I do mean we. If one of us has decided, we both have. I daresay Granny did think they were lovely, but she didn't know that your father had said ... oh, for goodness' sake, where is he?'

Back each other up. United you stand.

'The most important thing a father can do for his children is to love their mother.'

Parents need to be strong. They are the rock on which their children stand.

Don't take the experts too seriously. *You* are the expert. As Benjamin Spock said, 'Trust yourself: you know more than you realize.' It used to be said that every parent needed a copy of Spock, if only to biff his child over the head with when he was naughty.

Let's face it, great though the doctor was, that may have been the best thing to do with his book – along with every other child and baby manual, including this one.

············· Action Page ············

Make your child feel secure:

1. Affirm yourself

a. Don't be too critical of your failures. Don't take it to heart if others criticize. And don't try to impress anyone: good parenting doesn't really show till years later.

b. Rest and eat properly.

c. Give yourself regular treats. Pour yourself a glass of wine. Put your feet up.

2. Take control

a. Trust your judgement, not your child's. Nor, incidentally, your neighbour's, GP's, health visitor's, or even your mother-in-law's.

b. Don't give in just because your child disagrees.

c. Next time she asks 'Why?' say, 'Because I say so.' You will feel very wicked. But it's hard to improve on it, as a one-size-fits-all answer. (And sometime, when you've got a couple of hours to spare, treat her to your thesis on the destabilizing of the whole fabric of society once parental authority has become weakened – so you can go on saying, 'Because I say so'.)

3. Love one another

a. Get married.

b. Stay married.

c. Put your spouse before your child.

d. Don't undermine each other.

e. Make love. Now, if you like. Why not? The next chapter isn't *that* interesting. (But finish the wine first. Otherwise you'll find it tomorrow morning, all vinegary, or spilt all over the carpet.)

Self-worth
'I am lovable'

'Self-esteem comes from being of use to others – but I think
most people don't realize that. It's important to give children jobs
to do: they want to know they can help their parents.'
Bink

'That's right. If there's someone you love more than anyone else
in the world, the one thing you don't want to hear is that you're
no use: go and play in the garden. Well, obviously you do,
because it's better than laying the table. But it's not what you
really want to hear.'
Alexander

I used to believe I had one friend who was truly self-confident. She is one of the most charming people I know. She puts everyone at ease, exudes feel-good factor by the bucket-load, and always somehow convinces you that there is no one else in the world she would rather be with. If there's one person in the world who oozes assurance, I thought, it is this friend of mine. And yet quite recently, after I'd known her for nearly twenty years, she admitted that she has always felt inferior in the presence of most of her friends because she never went to university.

After that I came to the conclusion that we are all in the same boat. I can think of a few people in their eighties who don't seem to worry about self-image any more, but under the age of retirement, there we are, all wandering around like Woody Allen, tortured by self-doubt and making jokes about other people's inadequacies in order to disguise our own.

An individual's self-confidence benefits all around him. It allows us to be more positive about everyone, as we don't need to bolster ourselves up by doing others down. Someone who feels she is achieving what she wants in her own life won't feel diminished by other people's accomplishments.

Self-esteem also helps us to be more open-minded. Those who are confident of their own opinions can genuinely listen to and take an interest in different ones, since they don't threaten their own. My grandfather-in-law, a wise old bird, tended to be suspicious of views that were too emphatically expressed: when the lady doth protest too much, it may be because she believeth too little.

Most attractive of all, being confident makes it easier to accept criticism: if we know we are valued, we can cope with being imperfect. One crucial factor in being able to maintain healthy and happy relationships is a readiness to say sorry. Nothing is more disarming than a sincerely meant apology; few things more aggravating than the inability to offer one. But it takes self-assurance: when we are feeling insecure the last thing we feel able to do is accept we were at fault. It feels as if it might lead to rejection. It won't, of course. But when we are confident in ourselves, we find it much easier to say, 'I was in the wrong. Forgive me.'

This ability to hear and make use of constructive criticism gives a further advantage: being able to listen when his weaknesses are pointed out to him, the confident person can learn from them and correct them. Success breeds success.

And you guessed it, the key to our children's self-confidence lies in how we, their parents, first treat them.

Unconditional love

One of the most precious gifts we ever give our children is the knowledge that they are unequivocally loved. They should feel that, however hard they try – even if they set out deliberately to be as obnoxious as possible – there is absolutely nothing they could do to stop us loving them.

You know the scene. Some revolting specimen of the criminal classes has at last been apprehended by the boys in blue, and his shortcomings are being reiterated during the nine o'clock news. He is a multiple murderer, serial rapist, crack dealer to little children, and microwaves kittens as a weekend hobby. After we have heard the full inventory of his sins, the camera pans in to his mum, in her front room, being interviewed about her tearaway.

'He's got his little faults,' she says, tutting a little, 'like anyone. But he's a lovely boy really. Wouldn't hurt a fly.'

Presumably Jack the Ripper was a lovely boy to his mum.

And quite right too. She should adore him: she's his mother. He may have revolted twelve good men and true in a jury of his peers; he might have caused Mr Justice Bloggs of the Bench to consider bringing forward his retirement after the trauma of presiding over his trial; he may feature large in PC Plod's memoirs as the most depraved criminal the worthy constable ever came across. But his mother is still his mother.

There are many ways in which parents are like God, whether we are aware of it or not. He gives life. He then sustains it. He provides the moral map to tell us right from wrong. He exerts authority when necessary. But the most surprising and affirming aspect of the Christian gospel is that God's love is not diminished by our failures. He loves us because he loves us, however low we sink and whatever we do wrong. And that is exactly what parents do too: we go on loving our children even when there is nothing left lovable about them.

Obviously, it is quite easy to love them when they are lovely children. The girl who comes top of her class and has beautiful blonde curls and a clean smocked frock on, who does as she's told and gets distinction in her violin exam and is kind and considerate and courteous and passes the cucumber sandwiches before helping herself ... well, she offers no particular tribute to parental love, because even the stranger in the street thinks she is divine.

It is when this little madam has thrown a tantrum, got a dreadful school report and deliberately bitten another child – or has grown up and started smoking pot, playing foul music, staying over at her boyfriend's without ringing home and dyeing her hair the colours of the Ruritanian flag to show solidarity with his country of origin – that she sees the true extent of her parents' love. The times when our children are horrible are, in this sense, far more important and precious, because it is only then that we are able to show them quite how much we care. That is the time when we must grapple them to our souls with hoops of steel. That is when they will get the message.

> There was a little girl who had a little curl
> Right in the middle of her forehead.
> And when she was good she was very, very good;
> But when she was bad, she began to realize how tough and
>   enduring parental love really is, when they cuddled her and
>   told her they loved her and tucked her up in bed even after
>   a row that had been particularly torrid.

This is when your child learns to be, and to value, herself, because it is then she discovers that it is she herself, not her good behaviour, that was the object of your love all along.

Let them fail

One way we can show unconditional love is by allowing our children to make a complete mess of something.

I have a friend who is a terrifically committed mother, makes a point of spending what is known as Quality Time with her children, and affirms them over and over again. So much so that I'm sorry to say she is something of a byword. If any of her three offspring – who are, of course, the most beautiful, talented, accomplished and extraordinary children the world has ever seen – so much as blows her nose or combs his hair, their mother will comment on the wonderful way he or she has done it. She somehow turns everything they do into a great achievement. I believe she does this with such enthusiasm because she herself is lacking in confidence:

2. Self-worth: 'I am lovable'

she felt her own parents didn't affirm her enough, and she wants to do better. And three cheers to her. It may be laughable to her friends, but it is also noble.

However, I do think she is making one crucial mistake. She always seems to praise them in response to some laudable action on their part. Daniel has finally, after years of persistence, won the st custard's mrs joyful prize for rafia work: celebrations all round, and isn't Daniel *clever* everybody? Or Angela has at last passed her ballet Grade I, so Angela (and everyone in the neighbourhood) is told how brilliant she is. This is all very well, but it carries a price. Angela and Daniel are inevitably picking up the message that their doting mother dotes on them *because of* something. This begs the question, would she love me if I failed? All three of her children are motivated almost to the point of mania. I wish my children worked half as hard, but not at this cost. A friend of mine who had a similar upbringing told me that the reason she was so industrious at school was because she was, quite simply, terrified of failure.

It is essential that our children don't get the impression that we value them chiefly because of what they can do or how much they can achieve. We must love our children whatever their achievements, or lack of them.

Between the ages of six and ten, one of our children went to a wonderful school called Finton House, in South London. Finton House has an integration policy on disability: every class of fourteen or so has two or three pupils with special needs. One of the numerous advantages of this was that our son was educated in an environment where every child was a success, from his best friend who was a boffin in maths and swept the board of scholarships to senior school, to his classmate with Down's syndrome who wrote a movingly beautiful two-line poem about a tiger.

One day I went to a swimming gala organized by the school. There were all the usual races and somersaults and feats that all parents other than the obsessively enthusiastic find yawningly dull. But Finton House had something else that afternoon: a star performer. There was in our son's class a short boy called Tom. Everyone else had done some flashy dive or other, identical to the one before, and received the same obligatory, perfunctory clap from polite parents who were thinking longingly of the office. Then

Tom, all two foot six of him, approached the diving board. I can't now remember quite what it was about his dive, but somehow it was obvious how much effort it had cost him, how difficult it had been, and in particular what an achievement it was. Clearly, it was a major triumph for him simply to go head-first into water. It was the most spectacular accomplishment of the afternoon. We all burst into tumultuous applause and I'm sorry to say I burst into tears.

That is the kind of affirmation our children deserve – or rather, that they should be given, whether they deserve it or not. You shouldn't need to compete with anyone else in order to be the light of your parents' life. You are beyond compare as you are.

Let them be naughty

Central to the Christian faith is the doctrine that we don't have to be good to be loved. Jesus was constantly shocking his contemporaries by his choice of friends. Look, respectable people said, he eats with crooks; he fraternizes with whores; he was executed with common criminals, one of whom he welcomed into the Kingdom of God that very day. The message is unmistakable. He loves us anyway.

Paradoxically, we need to affirm our children when they are naughty. Obviously this doesn't mean we approve of or encourage the undesirable behaviour. But we have to let them know that we love them even when we don't like what they are doing. In traditional Christian teaching this has been expressed as 'hating the sin while loving the sinner'. Like most great truisms it is easy to ridicule, but it is a wonderfully liberating concept once it is properly understood. God always loves us, even when he hates the wrong we do. Similarly, our children need to see and believe that we, our parents, love them even when they are being horrible.

A friend of mine was coping with his daughter having a tantrum. Suddenly, the little girl screamed out, 'I hate you, Daddy'.

Stung and deeply wounded, her father retorted without thinking, 'Well that's fine, sugarplum, because I hate you too'.

I don't want to make a big thing of this, because we all say frightful things to our children, and frankly they get over it. Yes, all right, they remember one phrase thirty years later and tell us they still mind and it still hurts – but the very fact that they can be honest enough to say so proves that the occasional ill-expressed phrase hasn't done too much harm.

Nevertheless, what he said was totally and utterly untrue. Whatever negative emotions he felt in that split second, he didn't love his daughter any the less (nor did she him, actually, whatever she may have said). It's always easy to be wise about someone else's event afterwards, but with hindsight it would have been more accurate to say, 'Well, hard luck darlin', because I still love you.' Or the even more infuriating, 'Do you dear? Well, I'm glad you felt in a position to discuss it with me openly.' After all, she had also just paid him the compliment of knowing that their relationship was robust enough to withstand such an outburst.

This may be all very well when children lash out by mistake, being rude or disobedient before they have had a chance to think about what they are doing. We know we should forgive such youthful lack of control. But what about when they deliberately flout our authority, openly rebel, and do something they know they are not allowed to do? Are we still supposed to be accepting of them then? Yes, absolutely, we are. They are still our children, and they still need the security and self-esteem that comes from knowing they are loved even when they are being as horrid as they can be.

As we see in the next chapter, discipline should properly be conveyed in a calm, objective and thought-through manner. One of the great advantages of this is that it is much less acrimonious and personal. If the parent is able to say, 'Right, Johnny, you've done so-and-so, and the punishment for that is such-and-such,' it is much clearer to Johnny that it is merely the *action*, rather than the person, that is being disapproved of.

It is also perfectly consistent with good discipline to cuddle a child who has just been punished or told off, and to assure him you still love him. Modern, rather sloppy assumptions about subjective, emotive disciplining don't understand this, and think it confusing or contradictory. But it isn't at all. You *do* still love your child (I sincerely hope), even when he has just been unspeakably naughty. Indeed, that is why you punished him. So you might as well tell him so.

When Shaun was a small boy, he and his friends got up to some mischief in the street. He can't now remember what crime they had committed, but he clearly remembers – and still values – what happened afterwards. His father called him inside and spanked him for his misdemeanour. Shaun challenged his father's apparent unfairness. 'You didn't punish any of the others,' he protested, 'and they were all doing it too.'

'That's right,' his father replied. 'You're my son. I love you. So I care when you're naughty. I don't care about the others.'

We discipline our children *because* we love them, not *despite* our love for them. So they should know that, though we don't like them being difficult or disobedient or unkind or downright impossible, it doesn't make the slightest impression on our love for them. We don't want them to be naughty. But we do want them to know they can be, without fear of jeopardizing their status as our children one iota.

After our son contemplated suicide at the age of ten, he and I discussed various alternative courses of action, in case he ever felt that desperate again. Better to get on a train and come home, I said; it might not be the best solution, but it is a considerable improvement on suicide. A few years later I happened to telephone his mobile one afternoon when he was a hundred miles away at school, and heard a mysterious ringing in the house. Teenagers can do all sorts of clever things with machines, so I thought nothing of it. But when I went into my study and found him at my computer, I thought even he probably couldn't have conjured himself up with holograms.

He had remembered what I'd said, and had come home because he hadn't been able to complete a particular piece of work that was due for a rather strict teacher.

I rang his housemaster, who agreed that the prodigal could return to school the next day. Then just before hanging up, when he might have been expected to send my son the message that he was a blasted nuisance and he hoped he felt ashamed of himself, he said, 'Tell him we still love him.'

How much more valuable is such a statement at such a time, than if he had just won a glittering prize or brought credit to the school?

Let them be different

'This family is full of weirdos.'
Serena

Even as a teenager I considered one of the most obvious tributes to my own parents' parenting was that all four of us ended up in such different fields. My eldest brother has a self-sufficient smallholding in Wales, my next brother is an Oxford professor, while my sister trained as a teacher for the handicapped and then became a missionary. We were each free to pursue our own interests without feeling we had to conform to a family pattern.

My father extended this outlook to his work in education, and I have now discovered, sadly, how rare this is. For nearly twenty years, he ran a prep and choir school of two hundred boys (and, after a long battle on his part, girls too). And a more motley collection of individuals you never saw in your life. When the pupils from the other choir school in the city walked in a crocodile down the road, they went two by two in the proper manner, socks all pulled up to the regulation height, caps on at the same angle, shirts tucked in and ties hanging straight. They were a picture of orderly conformity. Whereas when my father's pupils were seen in public they looked more like enterprising Ancient Britons on a skirmish than Roman soldiers on an orderly march.

On one occasion a headmaster from a well-known public school came to visit for the morning, so my father naturally asked a boy who was destined for his establishment to show him and his wife around. Afterwards my father asked the other head how the tour had been. Very interesting, came the reply. The boy had conducted the entire expedition in his stockinged feet, carrying his shoes the while and singing a Bach aria (both habitual with him, though of course the visiting headmaster was not well enough acquainted with him to know this), and had shown him the boiler room, the latrines, and the pig swill buckets twice. And that was all. 'Which is fine,' he concluded. 'But I have made a note to change his housemaster when he comes to us.'

It was not until the time came for our own children to attend school that I realized most teachers don't take such a liberal attitude to their pupils' idiosyncratic behaviour. Such individuality is often barely tolerated, let alone encouraged. It is as if most people employed in education think their job is to run an impressive and uniform establishment rather than to enhance the life of each individual child. (How often have you heard a teacher say, 'We can't allow that: it would set a precedent.' Who *cares*?) One striking exception was the school I have already mentioned, Finton House, where our son went for three years. Because there were children in every class with handicaps, differences were very visibly and positively welcomed, accepted and appreciated. If one child runs the race on Sports Day on his crutches, and another follows in her wheelchair, there is simply no question of measuring every child by the same standard. Each is a unique person in his own right, and loved as such.

This is one of the many privileges that the disabled bring to the rest of us. They force us to approach them as unique, because they are so obviously different. They demand that we treat them as individuals – as, indeed, we should treat anyone.

What is true of disabled or handicapped children is just as true, though less visibly, of us all. We are each different, but much of the time we are made to feel as though our differences are defects.

When our son was first diagnosed as having special educational needs there was one aspect of his differences – and only really one – that mattered to him personally. This was the fact that, despite being an ardently academic child, he was quite unable to pass exams. This was a real handicap, because it stopped him doing what he wanted to do. At twelve he very much wanted to go to a certain liberal-minded, highly intellectual and individualistic school, where he would have been blissfully happy. Consequently, he particularly wanted to overcome the difficulty he had and pass their rigorous entrance exam.

But the professionals, the consultant who diagnosed Asperger's and the psychotherapist who tried to make him 'normal', did not seem interested in this at all. For us to care about his exam results was frowned on by them as being pushy or – worse – middle class. Their focus was on his social eccentricities. But it was his lack of conventional academic achievement that was compromising his happiness; his social individualism – all right, let's be frank: what some might call his complete and utter battiness – didn't matter to him in the slightest. Yes, he sometimes comes out with loony comments at a formal tea party. So what? Why shouldn't he? They make him far more interesting than many people you are likely to come across at formal tea parties.

What right has anyone to pressure one person to become like others? If some unusual characteristic is preventing your child from doing what he wants to do, by all means address it and give him the power to change if he chooses. But if it simply makes him different and he doesn't mind, why shouldn't we leave it alone?

Bullying sometimes happens at school because a child is different. As parents we will be tempted to persuade the child to conform. I don't believe we should. Children need to be affirmed, as positively as possible, for being who they are. If she is the kind who buries herself in a book on the playground bench every lunchtime, she should be loved for it. If he collects Guatemalan stamps and everyone else in his class plays football, he should be praised and encouraged to enthuse about the stamp collection. If she is the only eleven-year-old in the school who doesn't care about her appearance, good for her.

Naturally, any of these things may cause a child to be teased by more conventional friends. And if this should happen the parents owe it to their child to visit the headteacher and ask for the problem to be addressed. It is always totally unacceptable for any child to be bullied, and to be picked on simply for being different is iniquitous. Any decent teacher will do everything possible to put a stop to it. Being realistic, however, it may continue. Some staff are lazy, others are incompetent, and even the best sometimes do everything possible without necessarily managing to remove all teasing or ostracizing behaviour.

When this happened to our daughter when she was seven, I explained the cause and effect to her and told her she had a choice. She could continue as she was, ignore the bullying and wait until she reached an environment where everyone was as interested in books and indifferent to frocks as she was. Or she could stuff her book in her bag and take more trouble over what she wore in the hope that she would make more friends. But the choice was hers, and it was not a moral one. It was simply a question of her preference. If she had asked my advice, I would have suggested she continue to be herself and let the others take her as they found her. (I didn't need to, though, because she decided this for herself.) She was who she was, and who she was, was great.

But whatever the child decides, the important thing is that her parents appreciate and encourage her however she decides to be. It won't really matter if she feels she has to conform at school, provided she knows that, at home, she can be exactly who she is, and be loved for it.

Unconditional time

'The only dilemma parents need advice on – the only thing they can't work out instinctively – is how to balance work and children. Obviously if you spend too much time at work you won't see enough of your children; but if you spend too much time with your children you'll get stressed because you won't have enough money. Most people should be advised to spend less time at work and more time with their children. You're the opposite. You really don't seem to do very much work.'
Alexander

Children need unconditional love from their parents, and one of the most effective ways of expressing it is by giving them unconditional time. It has been said that love, for children, is spelt T-I-M-E.

A great deal of contradictory theorizing has been done over recent decades about the kind of time parents should spend with children. First came the idea, to ease the guilt felt by many hard-working parents putting in long hours at the office, that Quality Time is what matters, and that five minutes – after you've toiled away since seven a.m. to bring home the bacon, surfed the world markets and chaired the board meeting and dashed off the tube and run all the way to get home before bedtime – that five minutes spent focusing with puckered concentration on playing chess, or listening to some rambling anecdote about what happened in the playground at lunchtime, is worth more than five hours of the occasional grunt while cleaning the house or making the supper.

Then came the counter-claim, to support parents who were slogging away at home, that children know of no such concept as Quality Time and only recognize Quantity Time, pure and simple. According to this theory, it is only when a child knows the round-the-clock reassuring presence of a parent pottering around in the kitchen that he feels secure, knowing that his parent is there at that one significant moment when he grazes his knee or discovers the Second Law of Thermodynamics and wants to share it with her. This is the only kind of parental time that cuts any ice.

Clearly this debate has been fuelled more by ideology than common sense or pragmatics. For one thing, there seems to be a general assumption that the mother's time is more important to the child than anyone else's, including the father's, which is insulting to both sexes and contrary to reason, experience, and Judaeo–Christian Scripture. For another, it seldom affirms the importance of earning a living as an essential aspect of parenting: after all, it is pretty vital to the little blighters' sense of security that there should be tea on the table when they are hungry. When you are at work, earning the means whereby to support your children, you are spending time on them every bit as much as – and sometimes far more sacrificially than – when you are at home teaching them advanced basket work. Finally, the discussion almost always ignores the fact that the issue is a very modern one. Before the Industrial Revolution, work was so intricately bound up with home that earning a living and rearing children were done simultaneously, generally by both parents, without any obvious delineation between the two.

I find the whole debate rather a red herring. My guiding principle is to ensure I *enjoy* my children's company. Then I will spend as much time as I can afford revelling in their society anyway. (In fact, the opposite problem has developed in our house. I find it very difficult to do any work at all, because it is always more interesting to sit around the kitchen table listening to the conversation.)

There are numerous ways in which we can take pleasure in spending time with our children. Here are a few ideas.

Spontaneous time

Every so often – probably many times a day when the children are young, if you are at home for enough of the day for this to happen – you will be asked to drop what you are doing to come and participate in something. This can be surprisingly difficult to do. There you are, just at the crucial stage of making a roux sauce or getting a breakthrough on *The Times* crossword, sorting the company accounts or enjoying five minutes of a buttery Australian Chardonnay and the next chapter of the thriller that you've been looking forward to all week, and somebody wants you to show interest in Mr Blobby's Day at the Park, or how the computer blows up aliens, or something else equally gripping. Unless you are mentally defective, it is usually the last thing in the world you want to do.

In which case, it helps to bear the following in mind. First, in terms of actual time, very little is probably being required of you. At moments like this, five or ten minutes, or even less, will often satisfy. And spontaneous minutes are the currency equivalent of planned hours to your child. Time when he actually asks for you, at his convenience, is far more valuable to him minute for minute than time that you had previously arranged to give him, at yours.

Second, the opportunity may not come again. Today, she wants you to read *Clarence the Cat Comes out of the Closet* as her bedtime story. Next week, next month, whenever you next think of it, she will not only be sick of Cuddly Clarence, but of bedtime stories altogether. You will offer to read to her at a time that suits you, and she will look at you as if wondering what sad planet you have just fallen off. Bedtime stories? How could you be so patronizing? Now she reads to herself at bedtime. Soon the time will come when you would love to read to her. When you wish she was still around to be read to. When you long for her to ring home, or even have a moment spare to read your last five emails to her. You don't need to be a slave to your children, obviously, and always answer their beck and call. But it's worth bearing in mind that the chance may be now or never.

When our eldest was nine she had to spend ten days in hospital. One night I had just finished work, had my bath, got into bed and opened my longed-for book to read for a few minutes before dropping off to sleep, when she telephoned. It was about eleven o'clock. 'Will you come and see me?' she said. 'I'm lonely.' I took a deep breath and chatted to her for a minute or two, trying to decide how important this was and, more to the point, how to make myself get up again and bicycle the twenty minutes to the hospital in my pyjamas without being arrested.

'Just a minute, Mummy', she said. 'The nurse wants to talk to you.'

'Mrs Atkins?' the nurse asked, and then said the most welcome words I could have hoped to hear. 'You don't need to come in. She'll be fine in a minute, I promise you. Besides, she'd be asleep long before you got here.'

Do you think I have ever heard the end of this? 'The one time in my life when I asked you …' 'All I wanted was a bedtime story …' 'When you're dying in your old people's home and you call me begging for a drink of water …' She'll probably quote it when she gives the speech at my funeral.

For an hour of my time when she wanted me I could have saved myself a lifetime of recriminations when she doesn't. Believe me: I've been there. Don't do it to yourself.

Go on, get out of your comfy armchair and go and play Scrabble. You know you'll be glad you did.

Planned time

Children, as well as being spontaneous creatures, also love routine. So do most grown-ups. If you plan time with your children into your schedule you will find it much easier to safeguard it.

When our sons were eight and ten they embarked on a couple of years' boarding at a prep school twenty miles away. In addition to coming home at the weekends, they also had every Wednesday afternoon free. The school was near to a field with a river and Ben had long shown an interest in learning to fish, so we got into the habit of making up a picnic every Wednesday, setting off after lunch and spending a couple of hours with them. Many were the blissfully relaxed and happy afternoons, usually sheltering under a bridge from the rain, watching Ben knotting himself up into tangles of fishing tackle, threading worms or maggots or other tempting titbits onto a hook, and never, in all the time we spent over two years, ever catching anything. Every Wednesday I packed gloopy, mayonnaisy egg sandwiches (Alex's favourite) and sticky, get-on-everything chocolate cake (mine) and the Volcano (an outdoor Kelly kettle) and a teapot and tea and milk into a huge wicker basket. Every Wednesday we scoured the river bank for twigs for the kettle while Ben's dog annoyed all the rowing eights from the nearby senior school by chasing them along the bank urging them to go faster. Sometimes Serena and Bink would come with us, and recognize a friend among the eights, and make him blush in front of all his friends by calling out to him as he tried to concentrate on his stroke.

A few days ago, Shaun asked me if I remembered the house on the bank opposite, where a golden retriever used to run up and down along the river barking, while we imagined who lived there and how lovely it must be to have tea on the smooth lawn running down to the water. Do I? I suspect I shall remember those afternoons for ever, presumably long after the boys have forgotten them (if they haven't done so already).

But if we hadn't put them into the diary weeks in advance, booking up every Wednesday in term-time, Alex and Ben would simply have kicked around with their friends longing for the weekend. If, one Wednesday morning, I had said to Shaun, 'Shall we go and see the boys this afternoon?' we would both have found that we couldn't possibly spare the time. And that would have happened week after week. But because it was a fixture, it always happened, we always had time for it, and soon looked forward to it more than almost any other event in the week.

There are numerous ways in which you can plan events like this, depending on your lifestyle, your child's timetable, and your individual preferences. Try to pick something that you will both enjoy. From time to time, Serena has asked me to take her shopping. She has strong views about the correct way to do this, and it includes not only extensive use of my credit card and long hikes up and down Oxford Street on sweaty summer afternoons, but also protracted sessions in Starbucks over several thousand calories obtained at considerable expense, revelling in successful purchases and having girly talk while watching the passers-by and imagining their private lives. It is a delightful theory. Only trouble is, I loathe shopping with an antipathy I find impossible to disguise. I can't stand Oxford Street. Trying on clothes bores me witless. I have an unshakable conviction that sweltering afternoons are for spending comatose in the garden, or for the really energetic, sitting in a punt. I have made an effort, honestly I have: once we had an extremely successful twenty minutes in Cambridge in which we bought everything she needed for a wedding all within fifty yards of the marketplace.

It hasn't done me any harm to have tried; perhaps it's even right that I should continue to do so. But taking it all in the round, this is not necessarily the optimum activity for us to do together. I get the sneaking suspicion that Serena does not look to me any more as the ideal shopping companion. (Don't worry about me: I will get over the disappointment somehow.) I sometimes wake up in the middle of the night with the mysterious but unshakable conviction that we both have more fun when we go out on horses and gallop through a muddy field. But if you both like shopping and have no desire to get treatment for your condition, then by all means make it a regular Saturday morning fixture. Or perhaps you are even more peculiar and enjoy football matches. Book up a season.

Maybe you could always spend the last ten minutes before bedtime playing the piano together. Or perhaps you can make a point of getting home in time to watch *The Simpsons* (I mean with your child). The point is to find an activity that you both enjoy, and a time that suits you, and stick with it. Once you've done it half a dozen times it will be a habit. When my godchild was younger and lived nearer, I would try to read her a Bible story for a few minutes once a week before she went to bed. Again, if I'd attempted one occasion of an hour, I probably would never have managed it. But because it was semi-regular it was not only easy, but a real pleasure (for me, anyway).

Individual time

'I wish you had been more enthusiastic about my extracurricular
stuff. Like playing football. You didn't do it with me.'
Benjamin

'Ben, I don't think she would have been much good at it.'
Serena

You will notice that I have started to refer to 'both' of you, not 'all' of you.
Naturally, planned time is not always one parent with one child, but there
is great value in singling out each child for individual attention for him
or her alone – particularly in a larger family.

This can be anything from a regular few minutes once a week, to a
weekend treat once in five years. When Serena was fourteen I was asked
to write a travel article for a newspaper about going on holiday with my
daughter, and the two of us had the fortnight of our lives, camping and
riding in Australia. We both came up with the same idea independently
of each other; I was terrifically excited, because I remembered my own
mother telling me, when I was a child, of her father taking her camping
in the Australian bush during her teenage years. It remains one of the most
memorable experiences of my life, that sunny October springtime; particularly the afternoon when the two of us cantered through wild eucalyp-
tus forest for mile after mile, jumping fallen trees, spotting a lyre bird,
straining our eyes for koala or other less familiar wildlife, and eventually
reaching the clearing and ancient stockman's cabin with its billycan and
matches left ready for any passerby, where we lit the fire and collapsed
in the sunshine by the stream to wait for the rest of our small party. Those
distant few days in the 1930s, which a busy Melbourne businessman had
set aside to spend with his daughter, had reverberated down the generations to the late 1990s, from my grandfather to Serena ... and, who knows,
may also enter the family folklore and be imitated by her descendants in
years to come.

We were extremely fortunate to have such an opportunity, which I shall
always treasure, but I've also greatly valued much simpler activities. When

Alex was five or six, I went with him and a couple of girlfriends to the New Forest for a weekend. The best day I've ever spent with Ben was when he signed Shaun and me up for a charity walk one Sunday in the country-side around his school. It was a blustery, sharp spring day, and the walk encompassed half the villages in Hampshire. It went on and on and on. When we eventually hit the lunchtime pub stop sometime in the late after-noon we could hardly walk to our table. By evening we needed crutches. And yet I cherish it now as the extremely precious day when Ben hon-oured me with hour after hour of his lifetime's plans, the work he intends to do, the girl he will marry, the eight children he is going to have and how he will pay for them all.

Family time

Perhaps the most enjoyable aspect of having children is the moment when all of you are together as a family. There is, quite simply, nothing like it. And the larger the family and the more opinionated the children, the more fun it is. The conversation flies back and forth, the arguments range from the correct use of a comma to the nature of black holes, and Shaun and I, out of our depth since the children were out of nursery school, won-der where it all comes from and where it is all going. And I think, It was worth it: the broken nights and endless nappies, the school run, even the school reports. They may have been unspeakable. (The reports certainly were. What do I mean 'were'? They still are.) But they were a small price to pay for this.

But family time also has to be arranged in advance and fought for, and sacrifices have to be made to render it possible. As your children get older they may start to question why they should turn up for supper at all when their friends have a take-away on their laps in front of the telly, or why they should go on a family holiday if their contemporaries are all sharing a pot-fugged villa on the Costa Lot. But if you have captured their imagination when they are young and made such occasions fun and pleasurable, it will be second nature to them.

When ours first started school we pinched an idea from the dining habits of our alma mater, and instituted a weekly Formal Hall. I realize this must sound more pretentious than a soirée with Hyacinth Bucket, but they were a real laugh. Every Saturday, at about six p.m., our dining table was decorated with silver candlesticks and linen napkins and numerous items of cutlery, and even a vase of flowers if we were being really serious about it.

We also had rules of conversation, though I don't think we can have insisted on the traditional avoidance of politics, theology and the portraits on the walls, judging by the extraordinarily raucous ding-dongs we seem to have on these subjects today (though the portraits on the walls still get off lightly). Presumably we gave guidelines, instead, on hearing each other out politely and not interrupting, and the phrase 'engage in polite conversation' still sounds oddly familiar, as if I have spent years telling them to do it. And we did attempt to civilize matters by instituting a procedure favoured by the Amish: if you want to say anything, instead of shouting everyone else down you should raise your hand and wait patiently; if you see another raised hand you raise your own; eventually everyone in the room is holding up a hand, ready to listen, and you can speak. It's a great theory, and works a treat for the Amish. It doesn't work at all for the Atkins because we quickly learnt to raise our hands but never learnt how to stop talking, so you get a roomful of raised hands with all of us still shouting at the tops of our voices, and you are rather back to square one. (Serena has recently suggested we stick our tongues out instead as it would then be harder to talk, but I don't suppose it would really stop us and would be somewhat disconcerting to guests.)

Anyway, the children were supposed to take it in turns to choose a selection of courses, the theory being that they would also help buy and cook them. Of course this was way beyond our organisational abilities, so the same idiot who didn't have time to synchronize it ended up cooking it all instead. And the Latin grace we attempted on the first occasion fell apart at the *Benedictus benedicat*, before we reminded ourselves that it is a thing plainly repugnant to the Word of God and the custom of the Primitive Church, to have publick Prayer in a tongue not understood of the people. And though I say we did this 'every Saturday', I find it hard to believe that we were anywhere near that methodical.

However, I do remember one occasion vividly. Clearly, if you are going to do anything in today's rat race of a world you have to make it a priority, and Saturday night Formal Hall was no exception. We knew that, if we were going to spend the evening with our children, we would have to eschew other entertainments. And by and large we did. Inevitably there were some offers that were harder to refuse than others, and one day a letter arrived inviting us to a dinner party one Saturday evening with friends whom we liked inordinately and hardly ever saw, and I would have loved to accept. I must have left it on my desk waiting for the moment when I had the time to reply and the willpower to refuse, but before I managed either, Alex (then about ten) sent the hostess an answer on my behalf.

'Shaun and Anne always spend Saturday night with us,' he explained. 'But you can invite all of us if you like.'

She didn't. (Nor, alas, was the invitation ever repeated.) Naturally, we could have made an exception for that one evening, as no doubt, we must have on other occasions from time to time. But I'm glad we didn't do it often, because the benefits from those Saturday evenings far exceed any sacrifices.

One evening a week

Try it. Set aside one evening a week. (Friday or Saturday is often good when the children are small; Sunday might be better when they are teenagers, as their Fridays and Saturdays become more precious.) If shift work or some other commitment simply doesn't allow it always to be the same, then at least make it clear to everyone in the family, each week, as far in advance as possible, which night it is to be.

Make it a priority, but be stricter on yourself than on the children: it doesn't matter so much if one of them misses it as if the adults do, and you want to make it enticing, not oppressive. Obviously if your daughter is invited out to a birthday party she should accept, but you might suggest she avoids that night for a casual trip to the cinema if another would do as well.

Eat together. Yes, you should be doing this every night anyway, but on this particular evening you could cook it collectively, or eat something special, or have more courses than usual; indeed, the meal can be the entire activity, if you manage to spin it out for as long as we seem to. Or you can have more simple food, leaving time for some other activity afterwards. This can be almost anything – playing games, making music or going for a ramble in the dark – but go easy on the television. Occasionally hiring a video is fun, but if you just switch on the box you will kill the evening stone dead. Again, when choosing your activity the children's preferences are more important than the adults'. One evening Shaun suddenly decided we were going for a midnight picnic. We all piled into the car with a huge jug of Pimm's, a couple of big bags of Kettle's chips and some dips. He found a deserted stretch of river in the middle of London that felt as if we were in the depths of the countryside, where we sat on the river bank until way past our bedtime, under the dripping trees, in the pouring July rain.

And here's your money-back guarantee. Within a few years (possibly one or two, almost certainly not more than five) you will start to see the benefits.

First, you will begin to realize quite how interesting your children are. You have taken the trouble to talk to them, so they have become worth talking to. One fine day you will accept an invitation to dinner, go through all the obligatory motions, do your hair or find your cufflinks, buy a bottle of wine or bunch of flowers, get in the car, find the place on the map, be introduced to half a dozen people you have never met before and will probably never meet again, negotiate the first course, then, as you find yourself nodding through the umpteenth question about where you live or how you know the hostess, suddenly wake up and realize with astonishment that you have left far more interesting company at home. Your baby-sitter is probably having a more stimulating time than you are. Why did you bother to go out? (Though before we are completely carried away with smugness, we should still make the effort, otherwise our families will become impossibly self-satisfied and introverted. But it is worth reminding ourselves that the people we are with on all the other evenings of the week are just as rewarding to be with.)

Second, because you have bothered to spend time with them, your children will bother to spend time with you. I was recently with a friend of mine who is in her forties when she arrived home to find a message on her answerphone from her father, asking her to ring him as soon as possible. After she had spent the best part of the evening ignoring it, I asked when she was going to return the call. She shrugged with indifference. 'He never talked to me when I was little,' she said. 'Why should I talk to him now?' Happily, the reverse is also true. A year or two ago we had a barbecue to celebrate something or other, and after all the guests had come and gone and we sat down with a drink to savour the memory of the party, we realized the people we had been most pleased to see had been my parents. Our parents have done so much for us that it is a real pleasure when we can do some little thing for them, even if it is only lunch. And you don't have to wait till your children are in their forties. Teenagers whose parents have clearly enjoyed their company are far more likely to return the compliment.

The greatest need a child has is to be loved, unconditionally. Whether gifted or handicapped, short or tall, clever or kind, in sickness or in health, he or she must know that parental love, acceptance and commitment are non-negotiable.

If we spend time with our children, they will know they are loved. And once they know they are loved, any problems they encounter are manageable, somehow. It is an awesome claim to make, I know. But if both parents spend time affirming their children when they are little, when the children are older they will know where to turn for help.

As the advert says, they will know they're worth it.

• • • • • • • • • • • Action Page • • • • • • • • • •

1. Say It

a. We could do a deal: if I promise this book is not going to be full of embarrassing exercises, will you tell your child you love him? Today. Not next week, next year or on his wedding day, but now. I know it's hard when he's seventeen and he'll squirm horribly, but it won't do any harm. And if he's only seventeen months, you have no excuse. Tell him every day, and when he's got a beard he still won't have found the right moment to tell you to shut up.

b. Next time she does something badly, tell her how much you love her. You can tell her that her artwork is rubbish if you like, but tell her you love her. Praise what she does well, by all means, though there's no need to praise things she does indifferently: she will see through it and feel patronized. Just tell her you love her.

c. Next time he is really, really naughty, after you have punished him, make sure you tell him you love him.

I think we've got the message. Now do it with hugging too.

2. Do It

a. When your child next asks you to drop what you are doing and come and see, think of me. When Alex was ten I was planning a novel about millennial computer fraud, so he led me to his old BBC computer that a kind teacher had given him, and tried to talk me through a programme he had designed which involved coloured spectacles and three-dimensional images. You could actually see things coming out of the screen towards you or going on behind it. It gave me brain-ache for a week and I've never managed to understand anything on a computer since, but my IQ went up several points over the course of an hour. Give it a go. You never know what you'll learn.

b. Pick one of your children at random and ask her what she would like to do for a whole Saturday afternoon with you sometime this year.

c. Institute your equivalent of Formal Hall for the family once a week (or month, if you prefer).

Significance
'I matter'

'I was three, maybe four, and you and Dad were asleep in bed
with the door closed. We were all up. I'd gone downstairs to get a
jar of honey, and I was back upstairs, with the honey, and Serena
said, 'I'm going to tell on you.' So I said, 'No, no, I won't eat it then,'
and every time she got up to tell you I became frightened and
stopped eating it. I didn't think there was anything wrong with it;
I was just frightened.

'So eventually Serena told you. And you went nuts, obviously.
And you asked me what on earth I was doing, being so naughty.
And what I said, in my defence, was that I didn't think Serena
would tell. I really thought that was an adequate answer; that you
wouldn't be cross. I didn't think there was anything wrong with
what I was doing, as long as you didn't find out.

'To a child, there is no guilt. There are just parents.
If they aren't there, there's no right or wrong.'
Bink

As well as safety and love, children also need discipline.
Once they are comfortable with their external environment (knowing it is reliable) and their internal selves (knowing they are valuable),
children should see that these two – the world out there and the world

within – interact. And it is a two-way process. They don't simply depend on others: they affect them. They have an impact on their surroundings. They matter. So all the time, as they grow in awareness and size and influence, they are assessing this process. Is it better to be kind to others, or focused on one's own needs? Should they do as they are told, or think for themselves? What happens when they break something belonging to another child, or kick the dog, or get up after they've been put to bed, or befriend an unpopular playmate whom everyone else is bullying?

This is what makes them significant. They are not irrelevant flies on the wall. They are players on the stage. They help to shape the plot. And the people who show them how to do this are, first and foremost, their parents.

This aspect of parenting, because it is far more consciously taught than the first two, is more talked about and consequently sometimes thought more important. 'How we should discipline our children' is a frequent topic of debate and disagreement, and has a much higher profile. But I don't believe it matters nearly as much as making one's children feel confident and loved. In my experience, those whose parents have made them feel thoroughly safe in their surroundings, and unequivocally worthwhile in themselves, can cope well with most of what life throws at them. I have known horribly 'badly brought-up' little brats who answer back, disobey their parents, generally run riot and eat their peas off their knives, who eventually grow up to be quite delightful teenagers, because they are secure in themselves and know that their parents love them inordinately even though they didn't discipline them very well. Looking back, I think my parents were quite absurdly lenient with me, but I seldom wake up in the morning and wish they had caned me every day before breakfast. (The fact that my friends regularly regret this omission is neither here nor there.)

So if you were to put those other two principles fully into practice and stop reading at this point … well, I was going to say I'd be delighted, but being honest I suppose I might be a little miffed, considering all that effort I made to write the rest of the book and all. (Though if, instead, you were to recommend it to at least a dozen friends, your local library, reading club, bookshop, and every other parent in your area, I would probably learn to live with it.)

3. Significance: 'I matter'

Nevertheless, discipline is well worth the investment of parental attention – for a number of reasons.

The first is that we inevitably shape our children's behaviour one way or another, whether we intend to or not. If we don't think the process through systematically we may embark on it in a haphazard fashion, and not get the result we want.

Consciously, for example, you might decide to teach little Bertie that, if he pinches his sister's sweets, he will not get any pocket money that week. Which is a perfectly reasonable, upright, old-fashioned lesson in the propriety of personal property, the ultimate fallibility of Marxian philosophy, and the wisdom of thinking through the consequences of one's actions – thus keeping him out of the juvenile courts and saving Her Majesty the trouble and expense of maintaining him at her pleasure at a later date.

But if you don't work the principle out thoroughly and apply it consistently you may also, without realizing it, be teaching him that it's better to filch things on a Monday because by Friday you will have forgotten and you'll cough up anyway. Or that tooth-rotting junk food must be more valuable than fresh fruit because you don't make a fuss when he takes apples but only when he pilfers chocolate. And so on.

I knew one mother who seemed consistently to give her children messages she didn't intend, because she hadn't clearly worked out the ideology of what she did intend. She believed, in a rather muddle-headed but alarmingly tenacious way, that overt forms of discipline were morally abhorrent. Unpleasant punishment for bad behaviour and positive praise for good behaviour were alike anathemas to her. I could never really get to the bottom of *why* she believed this. She simply said it was wrong, as if it were obvious. 'You shouldn't hug and make a fuss of a child for doing what you want,' was the nearest she got to an explanation. 'You should be hugging and making a fuss of him anyway.'

Well, yes.

Indeed, I said as much in the last chapter. But the trouble was, she was a real human being living in the real world with the normal stresses and strains of life weighing upon her: inevitably she both rewarded and punished her children, without even realizing it.

Like all children, they were demanding, rewarding, noisy mixtures of good and bad who frequently wore their mother out. So at the beginning of the day Mummy was sweetness and light, and all their behaviour, good and bad, was rewarded by smiles and cuddles and reinforcement. The little boy kicked his sister. His mother, full of patient endurance, told him he shouldn't, but nevertheless gave him his favourite cereal for breakfast.

But by the end of the day she would be shattered and at the end of her tether, and all their behaviour, again good and bad, was rewarded with martyred sighs and escalating shouts. The same child who maliciously kicked his sister in the morning, in the evening absent-mindedly forgot to ask for the potty. His mother, utterly exhausted and not knowing how she would find time to finish preparing supper while she stopped to change his trousers and mop the floor, told him he was an absolute pest and grabbed him roughly when he squirmed. So being foul to his sister was rewarded, but having an accident in his underpants was punished. Tomorrow, however, it might be the other way about.

These children looked to their parents to learn what was acceptable and unacceptable behaviour, as children do the world over. But because their parents never took the trouble to work it out, the children couldn't work it out either. Not surprisingly, they became very confused and insecure – and quite quickly also extremely badly behaved.

Their daughter had the misfortune of being an exceptionally clumsy child. On one occasion she was playing at our house when she broke a cup and cut her hand. Shaun asked her whether she had hurt herself and she vigorously denied it, so we left her alone because we had no reason to doubt her word. Much later in the afternoon, however, we discovered not only the broken cup but also the hurt hand, though she was still doing her best to disguise it. We concluded that the poor child must frequently have dropped things when her mother was tired and couldn't cope, and had been shouted at because it was the last straw.

Her mother had shaped her behaviour, without a doubt, but not in the way she had intended. She didn't believe in reward or punishment, but she had been rewarding her child nevertheless – for lying. Or rather, even more distressingly, punishing her for telling the truth. If the little girl broke something and came clean about it, she would be told she was a nuisance. The lesson was that she should lie. She dutifully learnt it.

So the first motive for working out how to discipline our children is because if we don't, we may teach them all sorts of things we don't intend, and even undermine the security and self-worth we have been enthusiastically building up elsewhere.

Second, it makes life a lot more pleasant while they are still children. As I say, I have seen children grow out of the most shocking lack of discipline – but the intervening years can be pretty gruesome, it has to be said. And unnecessarily so. Some children are not much fun to have around, because they have not yet learnt how to relate to their environment in a way that will be as pleasant for that environment as it is for them. If they can be dissuaded from throwing tantrums, snatching, fighting each other and cheeking grown-ups, and instead be induced from time to time to do as they are told, hand the fairy cakes round rather than throwing them on the floor and jumping on them, and refrain from breaking all the family china in a fit of pique, it is generally effort-effective from the parents' point of view.

It also makes life more rewarding for the children themselves. Others will tend to enjoy their company more, they will be more popular, more welcome, and likely to have a more agreeable childhood.

So don't despair if discipline is a struggle and never seems to work out quite the way you intended, because the chances are it will be a short-lived problem. But any time you invest in getting it right will soon be paying you dividends.

There are three tools to good and effective discipline: patience, reward and punishment. But before even considering these it is worth noting how to make it as easy as possible for them to do our bidding in the first place.

Make discipline easy

'I don't think adults appreciate that it's not a question of conscience, or feeling guilty. It's much more a case of learning the facts of life. Do this, and that will happen.'

Bink

The best example of parental instruction is the account of God directing Adam in the Garden of Eden at the beginning of Genesis. 'You are free to eat from any tree in the garden,' God says, 'except from the tree of the knowledge of good and evil. When you eat from that tree, you will certainly die.'

Before anything else, God is positive. What excellent psychology this is. Look, he points out, at all the trees you *can* sample. What a selection ... What delicious fruit is all around you, and what freedom you have to enjoy it! It's much easier for children to do as we say when we tell them of all the things they may do before we emphasize the one or two things they may not; or when we praise them for all the achievements we're proud of before we point out the one aspect of their behaviour that was disagreeable.

Then God gives Adam a clear instruction. Don't, however, eat from that one particular tree. There is nothing ambiguous about this. He doesn't say, 'You can eat from any tree in the garden, but don't be too greedy about it,' which would have left Adam in an invidious position. How greedy is too greedy? Children like to know exactly where the line is that they are not allowed to step over. If it isn't obvious, they will often push the parent to clarify it.

When my niece was small my sister-in-law told her she was not to overturn a certain wastepaper basket. 'No,' she said, every time she did it; and when she persisted, gave her a gentle smack on the back of her hand. Her daughter thought about this. Then she looked at her mother and crawled in the direction of the bin. No response. She put her hand towards it. Nothing. She touched it. Again nothing. She turned it upside-down and scattered the contents on the carpet. Smack. As her mother was recounting this to me, I rather stupidly thought my niece was 'trying it on', as they say, being naughty for the sake of it to see what she could get away with. Not a bit of it, my sister-in-law said. She simply wanted to know *exactly* what was forbidden. Touching the basket is fine; turning it over is not. As soon as she knew this, she tottered away and never touched it again.

God also allows Adam the freedom to do wrong. This has been the subject of endless theological witterings down the centuries, the profundities of which I suggest we skip for the moment. From our point of view, it's simply interesting that the forbidden tree was right bang there in the garden without a fence around it or anything. Most modern baby books tell parents to remove temptation altogether, rather than have the trouble of teaching the child what he can or can't do. Why not confiscate the wastepaper basket and put it out of reach? Well, you can if you want to, though I think this approach is patronizing and ultimately insulting: do we think they can't understand the concept of leaving it alone? Besides, we can't remove every evil for ever, every electric socket, every bin in every-body else's house, each forbidden item. Sooner or later he has to be taught the difference between 'Yes' and 'No'. Isn't it simpler to do it straight away? It's surely more convenient than keeping all the wastepaper baskets on top of the piano.

God also gives a good reason for the prohibition. If you eat it, you'll die. This is doubly important. Not only is this command undoubtedly in Adam's interests: however much he didn't want to hear it, it would have been most unkind not to tell him that the effect of the fruit would prove fatal. But also, and as an adjunct to this, if he takes no notice, there will be consequences. Nothing undermines discipline so quickly and effectively as a lack of consequences. If my sister-in-law had done nothing when my niece overturned the bin, she would have gone on overturning it all day long – and so she should. It is most dispiriting to see parents threaten their children with punishments if they do so-and-so, only for the pun-ishments not to be forthcoming.

God's clear, caring, easy-to-follow instructions are then illustrated all over again in reverse, like the negative of a photograph. When we see how the serpent subverts all the original aspects of good discipline, we see even more vividly how wise the initial instructions were.

'Did God really say, "You mustn't eat of any tree in the garden"?' the snake asks disingenuously. God hadn't said anything of the sort, as we've just seen. He said Adam could eat from all of them but one. But the snake deliberately confuses Eve to make God seem a spoilsport, never wanting the couple to have any fun at all; who wouldn't disobey such a parent? She manages to correct him, but goes on to make another mistake instead. 'We're allowed to eat from all of them except this one,' she says, 'but if we eat this fruit, *or even touch it*, we'll die.' Hello? Where did that spring from?

God didn't say so. Perhaps Adam didn't pass the message on to her accurately; perhaps she didn't listen carefully. Either way, she hasn't got the instruction clear in her mind, which is the beginning of the end.

'You won't die,' the serpent says. 'God knows that when you eat, your eyes will be opened and you will be like him, knowing good from evil.'

Clever. This commandment is not in your interests, he persuades her. God really is a killjoy. And there won't be any consequences if you disobey. (How wrong he was, as the rest of history relates ...)

It is a beautiful piece of writing. Here are all the ways in which a good parent makes discipline simple and easy for the child, illustrated again in reverse through all the ways in which the voice of temptation subsequently confuses and muddles the instructions up again afterwards.

How should we put this into practice? Let's take a hypothetical, everyday request: say, for your child to be in bed by six-thirty. (I hasten to add that I'm not suggesting that any particular bedtime has anything to do with discipline, or that one time is better than another. When I visited Africa a few years ago, I noticed not only that the children were exceptionally well behaved compared with European children, but also that they never seemed to be put to bed at all, but fell asleep wherever and whenever they wanted at the end of the day. Bedtime is simply a matter of cultural differentiation and parental taste. Put your children to bed when you like. I simply pick it as a random issue because it makes a handy example.)

First, *be positive*. Which would you rather hear: 'You've got to be in bed by half-past six,' or, 'You've got from now until six-thirty to play downstairs, read a book, listen to a tape, choose a game, or do anything you like'? Yes, they have to be told that the playtime will have an end, but it will be much easier to accept in the context of what they are allowed, rather than what they are forbidden.

Next, *make your instructions clear*. Assuming they are old enough to read the time, we should make sure they know the allotted appointment with the bedroom is six-thirty, not sometime after tea, or safely before Mum hits the Rioja at eight, or jolly-well-before-your-father-gets-in-that's-all. Not only will they find it easier to comply, but they will certainly know if they have not done so, and so will you.

Children, like anyone, feel more secure when they have clear boundaries. Suppose your parents don't tell you exactly when bedtime is, six-thirty comes and goes without warning, you are happily still playing with toys in the sitting room, when suddenly *wham!* The dinner is burning, the telephone is ringing, someone is coming round in twenty minutes, and Mummy is furious because you aren't in bed yet. Wouldn't you have preferred to know what you were supposed to be doing? At least then, if you decide to disobey, you know what is coming to you. And you can choose to avoid trouble next time if you prefer.

Third, *be consistent.* If children always have to be in bed by six-thirty, they will be in the habit of it and there will not be a daily struggle. But even if this particular six-thirty is a one-off, be consistent about that. Tell them at four o'clock. Remind them at five. At half-past five tell them there is still an hour till bedtime, and sound the warning again half an hour later. Don't move the goalposts. If you keep giving an extra five or ten minutes under pressure, they will naturally keep applying the pressure. The bedtime is six-thirty, and that is that.

(This doesn't mean there should never be compromise. Compromise is helpful in teaching children to reason and negotiate. But that is the point. It should be in response to rational argument, not a weary capitulation to endless whining and moaning.)

Fourth, whenever possible, *explain that it is in the child's interest* to do as you say. To have to go to bed because tomorrow is a school day, you need sleep, you will be much nicer to know if you have a decent night, I am more likely to read you a story if I'm not too tired, is far easier to comply with than being told to go to bed because we've got really interesting people coming for dinner and we don't want you in the way. (Of course, this latter may occasionally be the real reason ... but in that case try to swing it so that it is still in their interests. For instance, let the children down for ten minutes to meet the guests once they arrive, on condition that they go back up again as soon as they're asked; explain that if they manage prompt obedience this time, you will be happy to let them do it again next.)

Lastly, for goodness' sake *enforce* all instructions. If these are given and then ignored, they quickly become meaningless. If she is in bed by six-thirty, she gets her bedtime story. If it's twenty-five to seven, she doesn't. It is as simple as that. But it's extraordinary how difficult we seem to find this straightforward principle. Up and down the land, in every supermarket, you can see harassed parents of young children bribing and (far more often) threatening them and then doing absolutely nothing about it. No wonder the children are not taking any notice. Actually, they are taking notice, as children always do. 'If you do that one more time, you'll get a smack,' says the exasperated young mum. The child then does it again, giving the impression to the casual observer that he has just ignored his mother. Not a bit of it. Watch carefully. He knows perfectly well that what she is really saying is, 'If you do that again, I'll raise my voice a bit more, threaten to smack you again, and then give you a sweet if I think it might stop you.' Bang on cue, predictably Pavlovian, he does as his mother prompted him to do. And bang on cue, she gives him his sweet.

Children are quick to learn. If they know that the consequences of their actions will be pleasant, they will repeat them; if they are unpleasant, they will stop. Make your actions cue the desired response.

We can make discipline easier by using these five simple techniques: making instructions positive, clear, consistent, in the child's interests and invariably enforced.

Once we have done that, there are three vital principles to training our children in the way that they should go.

Understanding and tolerance

'A lot of things that children do wrong, they do out of ignorance or thoughtlessness. In that case, you should just explain. Punishment is only relevant if you know they've done it on purpose.'
Bink

'The crux of it is that you should see it from the child's point of view.'
Alexander

Seeing the issue from the child's point of view is probably the most important, and certainly the most difficult, quality to cultivate. Without this, it is frighteningly easy to punish the wrong thing.

Which is worse: for your child to push his sister on purpose because she has annoyed him, or for him to push against a table in a museum by mistake because he loses his balance, breaking a Ming vase worth a quarter of a million quid? Well, obviously breaking the Ming vase from your point of view, especially if it's not insured and you are liable. From the *child's* point of view, though (whether he has worked this out yet or not), the deliberate act of unkindness was morally culpable, whereas the accident was simply unfortunate and he wasn't really to blame.

But which is more likely to get him into trouble? It would be a rare parent indeed who would not tell a child off in a moment of such acute embarrassment – if only for the benefit of the curator of the museum. But is this reaction appropriate? Assuming the child wasn't being careless or larking about, he did nothing wrong. He was simply unlucky. So chastising him cannot possibly do any good. After all, the action wasn't one of his choosing, so he can't change his behaviour in future to avoid committing the same mistake again. It's not that rebuking him will have no effect. It will. It will upset him, undermine his confidence, make him feel helpless, and alienate him from his parent. But is this the effect we want?

And yet, being human and fallible, we do this all the time. A child does something by accident, and gets a frightful dressing-down. The clichéd example is when he wets himself. In fact, it is such an obvious cliché that most of us manage to avoid it. But how often do we punish children for dropping things, spilling food, getting excited, forgetting something, or even – heaven forbid – failing exams or underachieving at school?

When we sat the eleven-plus, various other girls in my class were promised all sorts of rewards and incentives for doing well. One was due to get a new bicycle, another some special outing. Diana Swan, tall, blonde, gorgeously glamorous and enviable in every way, was even offered a pony if she passed (though to be fair her parents also promised her a kitten if she didn't). My mother would have none of this. When I got home on the day of the exam itself (my parents were so relaxed about it I hadn't known I was sitting it, or that it carried the slightest importance, or even what the eleven-plus was anyway), there were various presents waiting for me and a special tea as a reward for 'doing my best'. My mother had no idea whether I'd done my best or not, but she is a generous-hearted person and always gives everyone the benefit of the doubt. And that was all. When the results came out they would be their own reward. (Diana's, I still remember vividly, was the kitten.)

This is a tradition we have continued, with considerable embellishment, into the next generation. An Exam Tea is about the most lavish spread you can be offered in the Atkins home (even more than a Birthday Tea), and it is served straight after the exam – no nonsense about waiting several weeks for the outcome. (Though I'm afraid we rather lost our heads when Serena got into university, and opened the champagne at breakfast the moment the letter arrived. Well, not quite at that moment. We waited until I'd finished screaming.)

The point is this: exertion, not attainment, is within the child's power to change. So it is more logical to reward the effort than the result. Similarly, disobedience, unkindness and spite are subject to the will and can legitimately be punished. But clumsiness, tiredness, an inability to govern the bladder, or forgetfulness, are all things that – though we hope the child will eventually be able to regulate them – are not necessarily immediately within her control. So patience, not punishment, is the most constructive parental response.

Now, clearly, some of these issues are ambiguous. Did he deliberately forget to do his homework? Probably not, but with a bit more effort he might (indeed, must) learn to remember it in future. How voluntary was her temper tantrum at the end of a long day in which she didn't have her usual rest and she's not feeling well anyway? Again, probably not very, but she must still eventually learn self-control even when she's tired and the world is against her. Both of these are examples of behaviour that should be discouraged, even though it's not really intentional. So do we punish it or not?

3. Significance: 'I matter'

I believe, if there is any doubt at all about the child's volition, it is better to be lenient. Like my mother, always give the benefit of the doubt.

For one thing most of us parents are, sometimes at any rate, tired, grumpy, fallible human beings who are liable to fly off the handle with insufficient provocation. We are far more likely to be cross with our children when we should be patient, than kind and understanding when we should be strict.

Second, there will never be any shortage of issues over which the child will unequivocally and deliberately have overstepped the mark. We do not need the grey areas in order to teach a child right from wrong. She will disobey you on purpose often enough, believe me, to give you opportunities to correct her.

Finally, if the misdemeanour was not intended the punishment will be utterly fruitless. Most unfortunately for him, our son's special needs had the superficial appearance of deliberate and wilful laziness. Though he could understand some of the most complex and intellectually challenging concepts often better than his teachers, he was unable to deliver even the simplest written assignments. In fact, the simpler they were the more impossible he found them. He could never finish them. He couldn't even get his shoes on for playtime before all the other children had been out for half an hour and come back in again.

I won't even touch on all the pointless and distressing punishments his first school put him through to try to make him conform. Suffice it to say that, as parents, we tried everything. Every carrot or stick ever devised was used, to no avail. He often couldn't get dressed in less than two or three hours, for instance. Like the best of them, I had read Dr James Dobson (an excellent writer on child discipline) and one morning, completely bankrupt of ideas myself, I took a leaf out of his book. I had given my son repeated and ample warning over a period of at least an hour and he had still failed to put any clothes on at all. Serena and Bink were expecting me to pick them up after a dancing class; soon they would be waiting for me on the pavement. It was summer and the weather was warm. So I bundled him into the car in no clothes at all. It wasn't until I saw an elderly couple tutting at him in the altogether and obviously contemplating ringing the police that it dawned on me that this might not be such a good idea after all. Dr Dobson had obviously been writing for a less vigilant and interfering generation. It's a miracle we didn't lose him to social services that day. And it never speeded him up one jot.

In the end I had to conclude that, contrary to appearances, his eccentricities were involuntary. (Luckily, it was soon after this that he was given a place at a school that recognized this and let him be. They understood that he wasn't doing it on purpose, because of their training with disabled children: there's no point in punishing a child in a wheelchair for not running faster.) It was a watershed in our relationship. He needed patience and understanding, not reward or punishment. I have spent the ten or twelve years since, explaining this to every teacher who ever has dealings with him: the greater ones have understood it and the lesser ones have not, but even the best have sometimes needed a while to see it for themselves before they would believe me.

His trait was an exaggerated version of what most children suffer from to a much smaller degree: their involuntary behaviour may seem deliberate. Before punishing a child in any way, including raising your voice or showing irritation, ask yourself whether your response will do any good. Remind yourself how young he is. Is she deliberately shouting at you because she wants to be rude, or is she just tired and upset? Will he be able to change his behaviour if you give him sufficient incentive? Is she really in need of patience and understanding, rather than reward or punishment?

If you are in any doubt, give him a cuddle, a listening ear, and as much tolerance as you can muster.

Children need more patience than it seems possible to give, and then some.

Reward

'Children are like dogs. You have to reward or punish them straight away or it doesn't work. I know: I can remember.'
Alexander

There are some very odd ideas currently passing muster with regard to child rearing. One is that rewarding children for good behaviour is an inferior way to bring them up.

I potty-trained each of our first four with a jar of olives, a picture book and a novel. At the age of around two they were plonked on the potty, given the picture book, and expected to sit there for twenty minutes or so while I read the novel. Perhaps if they were very lucky I occasionally took a glimpse at Diffy Duck and made a quacking noise, but I tend to find two-year-olds' books jolly boring so I doubt if I did it often. They got one olive for a wee and two for a poo. (I don't know why, since poos are easier to put in potties. But then, they're a lot nastier when they're in the nappies, so I had more incentive to get that side of things in order.) It never took more than one jar to learn the ropes. (With our fifth, Rosie, I miraculously rediscovered what our grandmothers knew all along, that even a tiny baby a few months old would rather use a potty than a nappy as soon as she can sit on it, so doesn't need either any incentive or ever to put a poo in a nappy. Or to wait till she is two. But that is another story, and the subject of another book ...)

But hey, you say. This breaks all the rules I've just laid out, above. Children can't necessarily control the movement of the digestive tract. Isn't it contradictory to reward them for something which, certainly the first few times, is a mere haphazard matter of luck? Well, yes and no. Or rather, yes. Yes, it is contradictory, but let me explain it anyway.

Whereas I would never recommend *punishing* a child for undesirable behaviour if you're not sure whether or not he can help it, *rewarding* him for desirable behaviour, even if there is the same ambiguity about his intent, is not only perfectly acceptable but a jolly good idea.

If you penalize him for something he didn't mean to do it might discourage the behaviour, but it is just as likely to undermine his confidence and fill him with resentment. Actually it will probably do both. Clearly, the disadvantages of this course of action are likely to outweigh the advantages.

Whereas, if you reward him for something he didn't intend it may make him feel he's just received an unexpected bonus for something he didn't mean to do, or it may encourage the behaviour. Again, it will probably do a bit of both. From his point of view it will certainly be worth working out what he did and whether he can repeat it. Good news all round, both for you and him. Certainly worth the price of an olive, for goodness' sake.

Which brings us back to the potty. Sorry, but there it is. Now the odd thing is, if ever I told friends or neighbours how the children had learnt to use the loo they would look shocked and superior, and say, 'Ah. Bribery and corruption, eh?' as if I were a member of the Mummies' Mafia and had persuaded them to control their bowels by giving them crack cocaine.

It is a mystery to me why rewarding children has such a bad name. A system of incentives is a superb way to train children. Or indeed dogs, horses, grown-ups, performing fleas, or fund managers. Make a certain action, any action, result in a predictably pleasant outcome, and we become motivated to do it. Repeatedly. Why else would we bother to get out of bed on a Monday morning and put in an appearance at the office?

It is said that a young actor, fresh from drama school and full of idealistic Stanislavskian zeal, was playing a minuscule role in a Noël Coward play opposite the great man himself. One day at a rehearsal, seeking pearls of wisdom from his hero, he asked the playwright what his motivation was in the scene he was playing.

'Your motivation?' Mr Coward asked. 'Your motivation is your pay cheque at the end of the week, dear boy.'

So if your child finishes her homework quickly, let her watch her favourite television programme and it will encourage her to do the same tomorrow. If he clears the table without being asked, lavish him with praise and he will want to do it again. If you would like her to tidy her room, you could offer her extra pocket money. The only thing that really matters is that you pick something convenient enough for you to stick with. You know, don't offer her twenty quid for picking a pair of tights off the floor, or anything daft.

My children are *still* berating me for the currency I used when they were little.

'If we did our violin practice,' they say,

'And Latin homework,' chips in another,

'And cooked the dinner,'
'And washed it up,'
'Put it away,'
'Laid the breakfast,'
'And walked the dog ...'

'Then you would give us,' they all chorus together, 'a RAISIN. A *raisin* ... Just the one.'

'And we all thought you were being so generous.'

'Yes, until we discovered that all the other children got a whole box of Sun Maid in their lunchboxes every day. For doing nothing.'

So? It meant my children appreciated it all the more when I upped the stakes to half a banana.

Of course, reward doesn't have to be tangible, if you are even meaner than I am. Praise, affirmation, enthusiasm, even showing interest in your child's activity, are all ways of rewarding and encouraging good behaviour.

You can, if you are organized enough, have star charts for everything. I can remember extraordinarily complicated grids and graphs that I pinned up in the kitchen for almost every task and chore imaginable. Teeth-cleaning, one red star. Face-washing, another. Getting up, going to bed, breathing. Five red stars equalled one silver, five silvers a gold, five gold stars, and I expect – bearing in mind my legendary generosity – they got some improving book or other, or a pair of wool-mix socks, school uniform issue. Not that we ever got nearly as far as that because the system always collapsed under its own weight long before anything had added up to anything. But, as I say, if you're that way inclined, it can be spectacularly effective. So I'm told.

When my children were a little older I was in charge of running the music group in our church. I had two reasons for wanting them to turn up. The first, of course, was that it was greatly improving for them, helping them to sight-read, play in ensembles, improvise, learn to co-operate with others, develop mathematical potential and all the other beneficial things that they are always discovering music does to the young brain. And so on and so forth. The second reason was that I couldn't get hold of any other musicians at nine-thirty on a Sunday morning.

Now, presumably Serena, Alex and Ben turned up each week with no problem, but I can distinctly remember having to cough up fifty pence for Bink to be there.

'How lovely that she plays her violin every week for us all,' one well-meaning lady in the church said to me. I stupidly let slip my secret, that it was only because I'd paid her. She looked absolutely horrified. How sordid it all was; and in *church*, I could see her thinking. On a Sunday, too.

But the truth is that, after only a few weeks, Bink got into the habit of coming, discovered she rather enjoyed it, and the bribery was quietly dropped. By the time she was in her teens she was our lead instrumentalist, and held the whole group together for nearly two years. And all for an initial outlay of a pound or two.

So reward your children for anything and everything you want them to do. But take my advice and keep quiet about it.

Punishment

'Anyone who thinks it's acceptable to lose your cool and shout at a child to relieve the adult's feelings, but it's not all right to punish him calmly and on purpose because he's been naughty and you love him, has obviously never been a child.'
Bink

Punishment is not in vogue. It has been an essential part of all decent parenting (and much good teaching) since the year dot. But sometime in the 1960s mankind suddenly came of age, reinvented children, and since then all self-righteous parenting gurus (at least those too ignorant to have learnt from Rousseau's *sauvage noble*) have been preaching that punishment is a Bad Thing, and an indication that we have failed in our parenting, but we-mustn't-mind-because-we-all-make-mistakes. It isn't and we haven't.

Punishment, used properly, is proof that we love our children enough to be unpopular with them.

Why?

> 'If you don't want your children to take the law into their
> own hands, you have to be the source of law and justice. When
> two children disagree, you can't just say, never mind.'
> **Alexander**

> 'That's absolutely true.'
> **Serena**

> 'Yes, it is.'
> **Bink**

> 'I agree. It's really important.'
> **Benjamin**

Skilful parents don't need punishment often. Nonetheless, its occasional use is not only advisable but indispensable as part of good child rearing.

It is *advisable* because it *works*. Just as we all need incentives to encourage us to do right, by the same token we need disincentives to discourage us from doing wrong. In this regard (as in most others too) children are not much different from adults.

We turn up at work for two reasons. The first is Friday night and the little brown envelope full of cash; or, if you are very lucky, job satisfaction, fulfilment, significance, status, camaraderie, Being Your Own Person and all that 1960s feminist stuff. The second is the threat of the sack: imagine the humiliation of having nothing to say at parties when asked, 'What do you do?' Not to mention how you would pay the gas bill. It's lovely to have the positive incentive on a fine sunny day when we're looking forward to having lunch with an appreciative client; but it's also quite important to have the negative disincentive when the rain's chucking it down and there's a football match at home on the telly and we're dreading the backlog of paperwork on the desk.

And yet I noticed, when reading all the latest puppy books a few years ago after getting Serena a Great Dane for Christmas (what should you never give children for Christmas?), that the second string of the discipline bow has completely gone out of fashion, even when it comes to dogs. It is all carrot and no stick these days.

'Never punish your puppy when he does wrong,' the books gush. 'Simply lavish praise on him when he gets it right, and he will get the message.' Yeah, right. How many years later? Given the combined life expectancy and brainpower of your average Great Dane, probably just before he retires to all those pussycats that need chasing and lampposts that need weeing on in the sky.

You try training a ten-stone cerebrally challenged adolescent dog to walk quietly to heel without ever rebuking him for pulling. Promising him little titbits of dried liver if ever he manages to walk by your side for more than two seconds is a great idea ... until he spots a poodle the other side of the park. In fact, all Hamlet needed was one almighty yank on a professionally placed choke chain, and you could see the notion gradually sinking into that soggy mass between the ears that tugging Serena over the road and under an articulated lorry might not be such a good idea after all. Thereafter, he never pulled again. Cruel? Not at all. For one thing, a Great Dane is so strong it is almost impossible to hurt him. (Except his feelings. I admit he has a permanently baffled expression, as if wondering how he has offended this time. Though this could just be the markings on his face.) But more to the point, in exchange for a moment's surprise he is now having a lifetime of pleasant walks. The bottom line, with a dog that size living in a crowded country, is that if he isn't properly trained he can't go out.

People are not very different. (I mean, when it comes to the learning process. I can think of a number who go out without being properly trained.) Unpleasant disincentives work on us to discourage undesirable behaviour, just as pleasant incentives do the opposite. Use both, and use them correctly, and discipline will be twice as fast and more effective.

Punishment, however, is not just advisable but occasionally *indispensable*, because *it defines who is in charge*. The less often it is used, the more pleasant for all concerned, and some happy children only need it very rarely. But all need to encounter a real reprimand once in a while to know that their parents are competent to bring them up. (I think I only experienced it once. It was enough.)

Sooner or later, every child in the world is going to do something naughty. On purpose. That she knows is naughty. And when she does, if we don't take decisive action we are letting her down.

Take a trivial example. She is throwing her food on the floor. Mummy and Daddy are keen to do what the contemporary parenting guides tell them to do, so they politely ask her to stop. She doesn't. So, following step number two in the trendy instruction manual, they explain why. 'Don't put your food on the floor, darling, because it's a waste.' Plop. Another glob of yoghurt hits the dog. 'And we have to buy the food, sweetheart ...' Splat. The dog is getting the hang of this ... 'And Mummy and Daddy have to go out to work to earn the money to buy the food ...' Slop. Fido now has his mouth strategically open under the chair ... 'And it's an awful waste, not to mention the bother of clearing it up ...' Clonk. Having got bored with yoghurt, she has aimed the jam pot. Fido is stretched out, concussed ...

Mummy and Daddy, with commendable patience and self-control, move on to step three of the manual, which is to remove everything from their daughter's orbit. If they can't control her with reason and argument, there is nothing else they can do. Poor child. She has won a victory, but it is a dreadful, Pyrrhic one. If Mummy and Daddy can't make her do as she is told, it must be because they aren't strong enough. And if they aren't, who is?

The reason children challenge our authority is not because they are horrible. It is sometimes, as with my niece and the wastepaper basket, because they need to know what the boundaries are. But it's also because they need to know who is in charge. If they push us and we give in, they learn the awful message that they are more powerful than we are. This is a terrible thing for a child to learn, because she knows she is not particularly tough. If we are weaker still, who will fight for her when the chips are down? We have gone to all that trouble to build up our children's security and self-worth, but now we are giving them the message that they are not important enough for us to discipline properly, and we would not be capable of doing it even if they were.

Whereas, if our children have to obey us even when they don't want to, they know we are stronger than they are. If we make them pursue a course of action that is good for them, they know that we love them. And if they are in the hands of strong people who love them, what could be safer than that?

When?

> 'I think all children should have a good caning every day whether they need it or not. Alex, give Hamlet a cuddle.'
>
> Serena

There are two situations that call for punishment, in my view.

The first is when children challenge their parents' authority. Suppose you tell her to come and she runs in the opposite direction. What are you going to do? That is what she wants to know. Do you change your mind and pretend you didn't really want her to come anyway? If you do, you will be telling her you are less competent, less capable of achieving what you want, than she is. Moreover, next time you ask her to do something, she might as well disobey that too. There is no reason to follow your bidding if you are not going to enforce it. Be kind to yourself and her, and show her you are in charge.

The second is when a child is deliberately unkind, spiteful, malicious, deceitful or wantonly violent and cruel – say, towards another child, or an animal. Luckily some children genuinely almost never are. Don't worry: you haven't spawned an unnatural goody-goody, you just have a normal, decent child who feels happy and confident in himself. He has no need to be rotten to anyone else. Conversely, don't worry if your child seems to be more difficult, more often, than others. It is very unlikely that he is an innately nasty piece of work; for some reason he is probably feeling insecure and unsure about himself. You may be able to work out why, you may not, and you certainly ought to try offering him even more affirmation and attention than usual when he is not being naughty. But you also need to give him the unequivocal message, when he is, that such behaviour is not acceptable.

How?

'You can't reason with very young children.
You have to punish them.'
Bink

There is a dangerous lie abroad at the moment, which has infected child rearing as it has everything else. We no longer live in an age of reason. Ours is an age of emotion, not intellect; of feelings, not convictions.

As I write, one item is featuring regularly in the newspapers. The so-called liberal Anglican Church in America is following a course of action that more traditional members of Anglicanism consider morally wrong. (In brief, the American Church has appointed a man as bishop who has been unable or unwilling to honour his marriage vows.) Over and over again, the papers have said that traditionalists are 'angry'. Or 'furious', 'incensed', what you will. There is no evidence for this at all. They believe the liberal Church is wrong. But modern journalists are apparently incapable of imagining anyone disapproving of anything without engaging an entourage of negative emotions. Do you believe shoplifting is wrong? Almost certainly you do. Are you angry about it? Probably not. Do you think shops should try to stop people nicking things from them? Assuredly. Do you need to be furious in order to think this? Of course not.

It is the same with the disciplining of children. Modern commentators never imagine parents punishing their children without being angry with them. But angry is the last thing you should be. For one thing, anger clouds judgement. If you are irritated with your child, you probably have his misdemeanour out of proportion. Wait until you have calmed down and can view the matter objectively before imposing sanctions. The old adage 'count to ten' is a good one (though I find I often need to count for a day or so before I realize that my reaction is over the top, or my behaviour more unreasonable than my child's).

More to the point, anger is dangerous. When we are angry we are far more likely to lose control, punish our children too severely, or react in a way we may regret. Why do we feel embarrassed when we see parents shouting at their children in public? Because shouting is not appropriate.

Yes, I know we all do it. (Everyone except my mother: she has never shouted at anyone.) As with all the mistakes we make when we are bringing them up, our children will probably recover. Nonetheless, yelling at children is unnecessary, unpleasant and wrong. Strictly speaking, you should never need to raise your voice to your child at all unless she is in danger. Punishment should be administered calmly, kindly, and for the benefit of the child.

It is crucially important to distinguish between reacting to something subjectively because we feel cross about it, and taking action about something objectively because we know that it is wrong. Nowadays, when childcare campaigners talk disapprovingly of punishment, it is obvious that they are thinking of the former: an emotional, personal reaction. It is almost as if we are losing sight of critical judicial punishment. Some years ago, when Jill Sayward, a vicar's daughter, was brutally attacked and gang-raped at knifepoint, one of the reasons given for the lenient sentences meted out to the perpetrators by the judge was that Miss Sayward had a supportive church and family and therefore didn't seem too traumatized. So if she had coped less well, if she had been less commendably restrained, if she had kept her raw emotions on the boil for the many months leading up to the trial, if she had burst into tears or bawled at a policeman in court or pummelled the judge with her fists, would the crime have been more serious?

Such an approach is not only dangerously subjective, abandoning as it does all fixed measures of good and evil. It also takes a dreadful toll on our nerves, if we can't condemn anything as being wrong without an extravagant display of emotion.

Notice, too, that we have forsaken self-control. We have road rage, computer rage, now even wrap rage (prompted by those violent orange cartons and bacon packets that fight back when we're trying to open them for breakfast). Small wonder, when our children annoy us, that we fly off the handle. Like many trends in modern society, lack of control and emotionalism have gone hand in hand with secularisation. When we remember God's wrath, we know (I hope) that he isn't jumping up and down and swearing horribly, stamping holes in the clouds and chucking the plates around while the angels hide for the afternoon. He simply asserts that wrong is wrong and he can't tolerate it. Parents should be similarly dis-passionate and self-controlled.

'Susie, if you kick Robin again you will be sent to your room,' you warn. Susie kicks him again. So what do you do? You pick her up and take her to her room. That's all. You don't need to scream and shout. You don't need to be cross. You don't even need to be mildly irritated. You may be in the middle of an amusing anecdote to a friend that you continue the minute you get back. All you need to do is to ensure that the threat is carried out. The less it takes of your temper the better, both for you and your child.

I know, I know. Easier said than done. Tell me about it. Some time ago I heard some women being self-righteous about male domestic violence, and I thought, hang on, sisters. Add up all the female domestic violence done by mothers towards their children using their voices alone, and we wouldn't look quite so smug. *Mea maxima culpa*. For a while I used to pray with two other friends, also both mothers of young children. Every week we would repent at losing our tempers, and ask for more patience with our children, and every week we would come back and confess to having shouted at them again. If I could do one thing differently in the way I have brought up my children, I would rear them all over again without raising my voice. And yet, do you know what? I'm still doing it …

What?

'People who oppose smacking are wrong, but they have got one thing right. They're right that it's very easy to smack your children or shout at them because you're annoyed, to make you feel better. You have to make sure that you never do this, that you only punish your children for their good.

'With corporal punishment you have to be even more careful because the children might feel they have no control. If you're given a choice of punishment, obviously you will choose a smack; but if you're not, it could be frightening.'

Alexander

To be honest, it doesn't matter much what kind of punishment we use, as long as it is fair, proportionate, and does no damage to the child. Oh, and unpleasant, of course. Otherwise it isn't a punishment.

Make sure it isn't too inconvenient for you. If you threaten something that you would find a nuisance to carry out, you'll find yourself making endless excuses rather than imposing the sanction. 'Do that again, and you won't go to Sophie's birthday party this afternoon.' Really? Despite the fact that you've accepted the invitation, bought and wrapped a present for Sophie, and offered a lift to Deborah next door. Are you seriously happy to change all the arrangements? I don't think so. In which case it was a silly thing to say. Don't punish yourself along with your child. 'Do that again and you won't get any sweets after lunch,' is far easier to follow through. Though of course you shouldn't be giving her sweets anyway because they're bad for her.

The spell on the Naughty Stair, the banishment from the room, the cancellation of a treat ... And what about the despised, unfashionable, disapproved-of, now-almost-illegal smack? Do we dare?

When Bink and Alex were aged four and five, they smashed up a door with a claw hammer. To be fair, the panels were already broken and it was a job crying out to be finished off, so the temptation must have been considerable. Nevertheless, when I found them red-handed, one of them still holding the smoking hammer, surrounded by splinters of wood and what had once been part of a house that didn't belong to us, and asked them whether they had known what they were doing was wrong, they both nodded and said yes.

'I think that deserves a punishment,' I observed. 'Do you agree?' Commendably, they did. 'Right,' I went on. 'You have a choice. You can be sent to your room for an hour, and not be allowed to come down and play. Or you can have a smack that will hurt, but be over immediately.' I even went to the trouble of specifying that, as the family of smacks went, this would err on the side of being a Big Daddy of a one. 'Which would you prefer?' They conferred for all of five seconds, then opted for the smack.

Sometimes, when asked to debate the rights and wrongs of smacking, I have mentioned this episode to those who would criminalize parental corporal punishment and asked why they would deny children this choice. They have always been completely flummoxed, because it never occurs to opponents of smacking that a smack could be given as a fair, considered and calmly administered disincentive for the benefit of the child. It is always thought of as an expression of anger against a defenceless victim for the relief of the perpetrator. (And, seeing it as self-indulgent as they do, some think it even more sadistic if it is given with composure, as if it were a murder in cold blood instead of a *crime passionel*.) When I was debating this issue with Claire Raynor, for example, and quoted this instance, she ignored the question of punishment altogether and became sidetracked by her righteous indignation that any mother could be so awful as to leave a claw hammer where children could get hold of it. For goodness' sake, it's hardly Semtex. The conversation has remained with me ever since as a chilling symbol of all that is bossy and interfering about 'liberal' Britain: I'm not even allowed to bring my children up within reach of a toolbox any more.

Simple, effective and above all over immediately, a smack is one of the least acrimonious punishments on the statute books. Threaten it, explain it, give it, supremely forget about it as soon as it is over – even have a good cuddle straight away afterwards. Children usually accept it with far less fuss than other forms of punishment, because, if administered dispassionately, there need be no nastiness about it at all.

When I first drafted this chapter I intended to advise that smacking isn't appropriate for a child under two, and that generally by the age of eight or so it is rather humiliating so older children usually prefer other punishments. But as I reread, I had to rewrite. If we watch and listen to children we learn all the time, and I have recently learnt something new and, to me, highly significant.

Rosie is now ten months old. Living in a hectically busy household, we often put her down on our large kitchen table to dress her or put a fresh nappy on her, and as she grew she learnt to twist around and grab anything within reach. Conditioned as I am by the fashionable theories around me, I moved the pepper pot because I wasn't convinced she would like it sprinkled in her eyes, and prised the mustard spoon out of her little fingers to spoil the fun of flicking it at the wall.

Her sister, however, has never read any parenting books so her approach is far more infallibly instinctive. Recently she has taken to bringing me flowers on her way home from school, and these sit in a vase in the middle of the kitchen table. Or rather they did, until I kept moving them out of Rosie's reach. But her sister refused to do this. One day, as Rosie was sitting on the table, she reached out to grab a flower and shred it in her little razor teeth. Her sister didn't move the flowers, she simply said, 'No.' A second later Rosie must have done it again, because she smacked the back of her arm. Hard? No, of course not: she was seven or eight months old. But hard enough for her to notice. Her little mouth turned down at the corners and she reached out for a hug. 'It's all right,' her sister said, scooping her up and drying her tears. 'I'm not cross with you; I'm just telling you you're not allowed to do that.'

Since that moment, Rosie has understood two things: that you don't pull flowers out of a vase and munch them up, and that 'No' means you aren't allowed to do something. She didn't need to be told again. I don't need to move the pepper and mustard any more. She doesn't chew flowers any more. If she's about to touch a hot cup of tea we just say, 'No.' We don't need child-proof clips on the cupboard doors: we tell her she's allowed to open them, but she mustn't take anything out. Obviously we wouldn't leave bleach or sharp knives in there in case she decided to do it anyway, but now she knows she shouldn't and is generally quite happy not to. There is no other way she could have been taught this so young. And this simple, natural, instinctive act of love is now a criminal offence in some parts of Western Europe.

Why is there such a campaign to make this illegal? A campaign which, though it has certainly failed to persuade the vast majority of parents that we need legislation on the subject, is undoubtedly succeeding in making us feel more and more guilty about an integral part of the parenting process – and incidentally is repeatedly trying to insinuate that there is a link between controlled, loving punishment and sadistic child abuse.

It is undoubtedly partly because, instead of being understood as objective, fair and based on external concepts of right and wrong, discipline is now seen as personal, preferential and springing from what I may or may not like. Not so much, 'Lying is wrong so I have to punish you in order to teach you that it's wrong.' More a case of, 'Whining is irritating so I'm going to lash out at you because that will relieve my feelings.' Seen in this light, a large person smacking a smaller one in a fit of selfish annoyance is clearly an appalling and terrifying abuse of the weak by the strong. This is why those who want to abolish smacking insist on calling it 'hitting', because hitting is what we do when we are angry and want to hurt. No wonder corporal punishment is so shocking, if this is what we think is going on.

But this is not what punishment is about at all. Punishment is part of discipline. And discipline is for the benefit of the person being disciplined. Every child has a right to moral as well as intellectual education, to be trained to do good and avoid evil. The punishment can be as gentle as a rebuke, the reward as subtle as a smile, but one way or another effective parents are reinforcing good behaviour and discouraging bad behaviour all the time. And if, as part of the armoury of disincentives, you find smacking helps you and your child, you should be free to use it as and when you need to.

The objection is made that smacking 'doesn't work'. Yes, it does. Though only – as they say on the packets of slimming products – if it is part of a diet of good discipline, not just if you randomly wallop your kids because you feel like it. A fairly given and adequately explained smack is about as effective as it gets.

Or there is the claim that smacking makes children violent. Of course it doesn't. Smacking children for misdemeanours does not make them aggressive, any more than kissing them because we love them turns them into sex offenders. To argue that it will teach them brutality is as illogical as claiming that we shouldn't detain criminals because it will teach them to kidnap people.

Or there is the allegation that smacking is an assault, proved by the comparison that if you crossed the road and slapped someone else's child, you would be arrested for it. Yes, and if you crossed the road and undressed someone else's child, or wiped his bottom, or even kissed and cuddled him, you would probably be arrested for that too. Certain things are appropriate between a parent and child in certain circumstances that would not be acceptable in any other relationship or circumstances.

Now, of course we could bring up our children perfectly well without smacking them, just as we could bring them up without pocket money if some bizarre dictator decided that fifty pee a week would turn them into fascist capitalists and made it a criminal offence. But why should we? If the state were to criminalize a parent's smacking his child, in one sense it would not matter at all. Loving, imaginative parents can find plenty of alternative disincentives. And many wonderful parents bring their children up perfectly well without laying a finger on them.

In another way, however, it would matter very much indeed. Such a law would be the most symbolic manifestation of all the anti-parent 'professionalism' that is so undermining of child rearing today. It would be saying, in effect, that the state knows more about the child, and has more of a stake in his welfare, than his own parents do – a pernicious and perilous lie. And it would go further. It would intrude right into the home, the centre of expertise for child rearing, with the force of law, to overturn that expertise and go even further to destroy the authority that parents have had, in all truly free civilisations since the dawn of time, to bring up their children as they think best.

The state that does this is a state that has gone too far.[1]

Children need and want their parents to guide their behaviour. To do this effectively, we have to be clear in our own mind what we want that behaviour to be. Then we must communicate our expectations unambiguously.

But communication alone is rarely enough. Children, like anyone else, need encouragement. We should give it enthusiastically and unapologetically, whether it is a hug and a smile or a multiple-figure bonus. Sooner or later they will work out that goodness is its own reward (or at least that working hard will pay off the mortgage), but we ought to give them a bit of help for the first twenty years or so.

And every child occasionally needs chastisement. They seldom need it as often as we think they do: much of the time, if they are being obnoxious, rude or irritating they are probably more in need of understanding, patience and explanation than a clip round the ear (or, indeed, that far more destructive modern equivalent, an earful of abuse). If the bad behaviour persists after a child knows it is wrong, however, then we owe him a reasonable and effective disincentive. It should only be in response to deliberate defiance or unkindness, and it should always be fair, calm and considered. But we shouldn't feel guilty on those (happily usually rare) occasions when we have to make life momentarily unpleasant for our children in order to give them discipline.

Good discipline will last them, and help them, for life.

Action Page

1. Decide:

   What kind of child do you want? How do you wish to shape his character? It doesn't do any harm to ask some hard questions. If you *had* to choose, would you like your child to achieve all A grades, get into Oxbridge, and earn megabucks in the City? Or would you like him to be kind to his wife, attentive of his children, and happy?

2. Remember:

   Cast your mind back to when you were the age your child is now. If she is too young for you to have any memories from that age, simply go back as far as you can. Make a real effort to remember what you found difficult or upsetting: did those older than you fail to understand or listen to you? Did they make unreasonable demands? Were you told off for things that were not your fault?

   Try to get into the habit of seeing the world through your child's eyes, if only for a minute a day. Then, when she is naughty or difficult, stop for a moment and try to remember. Is it tiredness? Distress? Confusion? (Or is it just rather fun to throw a bottle of ink at the wall? Try to remember that too.)

3. Forgive:

   Again, think of your own youthful misdemeanours. I can remember lying to my mother about whether I'd washed my face, but when one of my children lied to me I was incensed. If I'd remembered my own sins, I might not have overreacted quite so much.

4. Teach:
   a. Clarify. Agree between the two of you (I mean yourself and your spouse, not you and your child) exactly what is allowed and what isn't.
   b. Communicate. Make the rules crystal clear to your children.
   c. Confirm. Reward the behaviour you want, keep sanctions to a minimum and always carry out threats and promises alike with scrupulous reliability.

   Discipline should be proportioned like a vinaigrette: at least three parts reward to one part rebuke. *At least.* It doesn't matter if it's more. Go over the events of today and see whether you had these in the right balance.

part II:
Building
the House

'Your family are the only people you know you can rely on.
Your friends might really care about you, but you can always
depend on your family . . . if only to drive you nuts.'
Serena

All children have always had and still have these three vital needs: they need to be safe, loved and disciplined. Happily, our parental instinct usually enables us to provide these without even thinking about it.

We rarely have to make a conscious decision to feed and clothe our children and provide them with a warm home to live in. We also know intuitively that they need a loving environment, preferably with both parents deeply committed to one another.

It is also instinctive for us to love them whatever they are like. The caricature of the adoring mother – disposed to see her wrinkly little squished-up newborn, which to the objective eye may look more like a traffic accident than a human being, as lovelier to behold than the Archangel Gabriel – typifies the proper parental inclination to dote on one's children regardless of their faults. This provides them with a sense of their value and worth.

Lastly, we all have an innate sense of right and wrong, and an urge to pass this on to our children. Provided we have not been bullied and befuddled by too much psycho-twaddle about his expressing his creativity by pulling his sister's hair, or her having the freedom to throw her greens on the floor, we know that children need to be rebuked when they are being objectionable and rewarded when they are sweetness and light.

So the key to parenting that is rewarding, easy-going and enjoyable is to harness the inherent parental instinct, and have the confidence to trust in it. We may need occasional reminders that we are doing the right thing: it is helpful to have a compass to reassure ourselves that we are not going off course. But usually, most of us are going in roughly the right general direction on each of these three essentials.

And they are essential. These are the non-negotiables, the three legs to the stool of childhood. Weaken any of them, and your child will wobble. She will probably right herself again sooner or later, especially if she isn't subjected to counselling telling her that her early experiences were life-scarring and have left her with permanent problems. But the more strongly and confidently we can meet these needs, the easier we will find the child rearing process and the more agreeable it is likely to be.

Part II: Building the House

Aside from these, however, there are still plenty of issues we parents worry about. Where should they go to school? What time should they be in bed? How much television is too much? Is it still rude to put one's elbows on the table? There are also weightier matters such as how many children we should have and when it is safe for them to play unsupervised in the park. And whether it is better for your children to be looked after by a professional nanny or by their grandparents, to go on the family holiday or be allowed to do their own thing, to attend a day school or to board ...

Unlike security, self-worth and significance, these are all, ultimately, matters of taste and opinion. Perhaps you go out to work to provide for your children while your neighbour stays at home to care for hers: you are both doing the 'right' thing. Or rather, there is no such thing as right and wrong: there is only what suits you. These differences in child rearing are far more visible, and in some ways far more individual, but they are not nearly so crucial. After all, there is a right way to lay the foundations of a house. If you neglect this aspect of your building work the house will always be weak and liable to cracks, subsidence, damp and goodness knows what else. But where you put the windows and how you pitch the roof is down to personal taste.

What follows in Part 2 is a matter of individual preference. It is not random: there are reasons for all the choices offered here. But you may have other choices and other reasons for them. Fine. Disagree with it all, if you wish. Simply raising the issues, I hope, may enable you to come to your own conclusions, even if you don't see eye to eye with me on any of them.

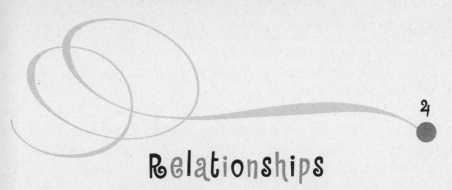

Relationships

'There are two things I care for: people and music. Work, achievements, money, all the normal things that people worry about, are only useful if they enrich your relationships with people. Or enable you to buy music. There's not a lot of point in working all your life, if you don't have time to spend with people.'
Alexander

'Hang on, Alex, what about your cat?'
Serena

'That counts. People means relationships. Girls and cats and suchlike. And music means any of the arts, anything beautiful or aesthetically pleasing. You know, girls again.'
Alexander

In the end all human life comes down to this. The happiness of our existence largely lies in the happiness of our relationships. (Unless you are a hermit living alone on the windswept slopes of a Tibetan mountain. In which case the mind boggles as to how you got hold of this book ... and *why*.) Health and wealth, fame and success are great as far as they go. As my mother says, 'Money can't make you happy. But it can allow you to be miserable in comfort.' Relationships, however, bring genuine contentment.

The story is told of a contraceptive campaign in India, presumably funded by some do-gooding Western aid agency or other. The idea was to put out an advertisement illustrating the attractions and advantages of having fewer children. The poster showed two families side by side. One followed the model of the prosperous, developed-world nuclear unit: mother and father and pigeon pair of offspring surrounded by material trappings, fridge, television and so on (this was some years ago). The other showed parents with half a dozen tumbling children and no possessions at all. The advertisement backfired spectacularly. Why? Because when the targeted people saw the pictures, they interpreted riches in terms of relationships, not possessions: they saw the poverty of the couple with only two children, and the wealth of the pair surrounded by offspring, and commented on the good fortune of the second family compared with the first.

They were absolutely right. Money is like vitamins. If you genuinely don't have the minimum requirement, you will find yourself fairly wretched. Try to survive without enough iron and you will feel tired, lethargic and lacking in energy. (Yes, I know iron is not a vitamin, but you know what I mean.) As soon as you start taking your daily supplement, however, your health quotient shoots up and everything is fine again. Your iron level is back to normal. You might be tempted to think that, as one pill has made you feel so much better, two pills will make you feel twice as good, and five make you almost supersonic. But this is not the case. Ten iron pills will give you no more of a feel-good factor than one. And you will end up very constipated.

Money is similar. If you don't have the basic minimum to survive comfortably, life is pretty grim. Constantly worrying whether you can afford to go to the supermarket for food or buy the next pair of shoes for your children is no joke. If the Lotto fairy were to visit in the night and top up your income to the amount you need for food, clothing and a few other essentials, your quality of living would increase exponentially. Research and common sense both tell us, however, that after that, increasing your wealth further does not make a great deal of difference. From poverty to subsistence is a vast and important step; from subsistence to wealth far less so. (Consequently, lottery wins of several million do very little for the sum total of human happiness.)

So, provided we have enough money to live off, enough health to get up in the morning and meaningful work to do, our sense of wellbeing is likely to be measured, largely, by the welfare of our relationships. Conversely, it doesn't matter how successful someone is: if his relationships are not functioning well, you can be sure he will not be happy.

And the place where relationships happen first and foremost is the family. This is why it is so important.

Parents teach their children all sorts of things: how to read and write, or ride a bike; how to play the violin or sail a catamaran. My mother even – goodness knows why – taught us how to knit. But above all, we teach our children how to relate. This is one of the reasons why it makes so much difference when parents stay together. Why are children of still-married parents more likely to stay married themselves? Or, to put it another way, why did the Princess of Wales fail in the one overriding ambition of her life, to have a happy marriage? Her own parents having separated when she was small, she presumably never had the chance to copy and practise the necessary skills. In forging our own relationships, our primary resource is the relationships we were brought up with. If we don't have a role model of marriage to draw on, it is much more difficult (though of course not impossible) to stay married ourselves.

Nor does the family we grow up in just teach us how to understand families. It enables us to relate to the whole world. Are you finding your boss impossibly aggressive and superior? Your brother was surely worse, wasn't he, that Christmas when he settled on becoming a surgeon and amputated your new Barbie doll at the knee? You miraculously refrained from stabbing him in the eye with his fifteen-blade Swiss army knife then. That early restraint has given you hidden resources.

After all, in learning how to relate to other people, the most significant people in your child's life next to you, her parents, are usually her siblings. (If she has any. If she hasn't, and never will have, you might want to skip this next section … though you never know, you might change your mind.)

Siblings

'I think if you have children you should have lots.
You have to have siblings because they are your best friends.
And to stop your parents driving you around the bend.'
Bink

'Er, Bink. Why is it better if it's your sister driving
you around the bend?'
Alexander

Important though our children's relationship with us is, in some ways their relationships with each other are even more so. After all, they will usually last longer. Long after we are gone, we hope, our children will still have one another: we want them to establish something that will outlast us. In addition, they are equals: it is right that they should be able to enjoy confidences with each other that they might not want to have with us. Most important of all, it is essential that children sense that their parents' love for each other takes primacy even over their love for the children themselves: you will inevitably have things that you share only between the two of you. I have almost no secrets from my children at all; nevertheless, I wouldn't want them to overhear every conversation Shaun and I have together. Some things are properly private just between the two parents.

This being the case, it stands to reason that we should want our children to be closer to one another even than they are to us. Siblings can sometimes help an ill or disabled child in a way that their parents never can. They can say 'no'. We, her parents, instinctively put a sick child's welfare even before our own, if necessary allowing our work or health to suffer in order to care for her. After all, if we didn't want to make sacrifices we wouldn't have had children in the first place. But her brothers and sisters should not do this. They have their own lives to live. So they can challenge without threatening and help without patronizing.

I am constantly amazed at the potential that is neglected when it comes to siblings. I often see parents going to considerable trouble to find playmates for their children, ignoring the fact that they have provided them with a permanent playmate at home. It is as if the estrangement between the generations that we now take for granted in Western society has extended even to children two or three years apart. So, for instance, a neighbouring mother to us, with girls aged six and eight, expected her nanny to organize friends to come and play with each of them, separately, after school several days a week. When I asked her whether her two daughters didn't enjoy playing together, she sighed and said, 'I wish. No, they don't spend much time with each other.' Well, of course they don't, if you keep shipping in other playmates for them instead.

Children pick up how they are supposed to behave from their parents' expectations. Adults who believe that children are interesting, well-meaning creatures usually find that they are. New mothers who expect their babies to sleep easily and put up with noise and bustle tend to have babies that do; others who think their newborns will be sensitive and liable to cry at the tiniest disturbance will also usually find their expectations fulfilled. It is the same with sibling relationships. It works in subtle ways. If you believe that your children will be each other's best friends, you will not feel the need to provide alternative companions for them. They will turn to each other. If you expect them to find sustenance from one another, you will encourage it in all sorts of ways, subconscious as well as conscious.

But we can go further and institute a positive policy. We had a rule that our children were not allowed to exclude one another from games. I vividly remembered my sister having a friend to play (who, ironically, was my age not my sister's; and later became, and remains, my closest friend) and the two of them always used to cut me out. I found it such an upsetting experience that I was determined my children should not do it to each other, and never allowed it. So because their birthdays are all at the same time of year, they had joint birthday parties when they were small. As they have grown older and have had individual parties for one event or another, they have always been organized at times when they could all be there.

I have been hugely gratified when, as teenagers, they have stood by each other. On one occasion they were all invited to a birthday party in a pub. Their teenage hostess had not worked out that, at thirteen, Benjamin was not allowed in, and when he was asked to leave Serena left the party too and sat outside on the pavement with him for the rest of the evening while the other guests were inside. I was proud to be her parent. That, I thought, is real friendship.

Her boyfriend recently told us of the first date he ever took Serena on, two and a half years ago. He invited her to the cinema, thought he had scored bingo when she accepted and, being an organized sort of chap, bought two tickets. But when he went to pick her up she said Benjamin was particularly interested in the film too. Not only did he have to pay for her younger brother to go on his first date with her, but he also had to sit at the back of the cinema on his own because he could no longer get three seats together. (I suppose he ought to be grateful that she didn't simply send Ben in her place.) It is over a week since he recounted this story, and I'm still laughing …

All of which begs the question, how many children is the optimum number? Of course there is no right answer to this. Most people either know how many they want, or have no choice in the matter. Some want large families and find they can't have them. Some stop at one, and are blissfully happy pouring all their energies into an only child who grows up with all the initiative and energy that so much adult attention gives. Others want lots, and are surrounded by noise and chaos for two or three decades. Some have one or two more children and a rather noisier house than they really intended.

If you have already played your innings and drawn stumps, undoubtedly you will have chosen the right number for you; if you had no choice, assuredly you will be grateful for what you have. Nevertheless, many couples are often unsure, or not in agreement, or wondering whether to have more, or still deciding. If this is true of you, here are a few things to bear in mind.

I concede that many parents have small families, either through choice or necessity, and it works extremely well. I know a couple whom I admire enormously, who stopped after one child because the mother suffered severe postnatal depression. I have no doubt they made the right decision. Their child is one of the most charming I have ever come across. And it is said that most of the world's greatest leaders have been either eldest children or only children, while families with only two children are invariably tidier, more organized and certainly quieter than larger families. They also have more time for homework and other achievements, because they don't invest so much time in relationships.

Nevertheless, I have a number of friends who have regretted not having a bigger family. I have never yet met any parents who wished their families were smaller.

Kathryn and George had already been together for some time before they considered having children. George had always resented not being well off as a child, and was determined to have enough money before having children of his own. He eventually estimated that they could afford one, so they had Toby. By the time I knew them, when Toby was about five, they had a house worth a million pounds and two good incomes. And still only one child.

'I wish we'd had more,' Kate confessed a few years later.

'Why don't you now?' I asked her.

'I'm too old,' she said. 'It's too late.'

It was said with such wistfulness that I could never forget it.

I also know a number of people who have restricted themselves to two children because they 'couldn't afford any more'. What is interesting is that they are all, without exception, comfortably off. So presumably what they mean is that they couldn't easily afford private schooling, Mediterranean holidays, summer camps, and debt-free university for more than two children. I rate education very highly, but I've never yet come across a school that could make as much difference to anyone's life as having another sibling (or certainly not in the West, where everyone is educated anyway).

In vivid contrast to Kate's, Jenny's story is familiar. I don't know her well, but I have several friends who have had similar experiences. All of them had four children already, and had always planned to stop at four. All of them, like Jenny, became pregnant by mistake with a fifth.

'I was beside myself,' Jenny told me, 'throughout my pregnancy. It was the last thing I wanted, I had no idea how I was going to cope, and I became quite depressed.'

'And now?' I asked her.

'It's the best thing that ever happened to us,' she glowed.

I don't take offence easily, but I confess I find it offensive when people ask whether a child was a 'mistake'. No child is ever a mistake. God plans them, even when we don't. And sometimes the ones he plans in spite of us are the ones who give the most pleasure. (Our family, of course, was meticulously planned: Shaun planned the first, I planned the last, and the ones in the middle seem to have planned each other.) Having said that, I have frequently wondered, during more than one of my pregnancies, what on earth we were doing and why, and whether the whole *idea* of having children was a mistake, even if that particular child wasn't. Pregnancy can be a terrifying time, and I can understand why some women feel they can't go through with it. But I have never known any who have regretted it once they have. (And if there is a stable marriage, enough money to live on and no ill health, I can't imagine the woman who would.) Being reminded of it again so recently, seeing the way everyone's eyes light up as soon as Rosie grins at any of us, the laughter she gives us all, the therapeutic effect on the illness we were coping with, the fun one child can bring to so many, I find it inconceivable (so to speak) to think of any child – even one the parents might have been unsure whether or not to have – as being a mistaken idea.

So if you are in doubt, have more not fewer. If you are not in agreement, go with the parent who wants more. It is not uncommon to wish you had more children when it is too late; it is unthinkable that you would ever wish you had fewer. My brother-in-law once said to me, 'Your sister wanted four, I wanted two, so we compromised and had four.' That's what I call a compromise.

Many years ago I read a magazine article interviewing families of all different sizes, from one child to ten. Obviously it was a tiny sample, and the findings hardly representative. But I found it so striking I have remembered it since, so I repeat it here for what it's worth. The children of families with fewer than four children tended to want to have more children themselves: the only children, and the children from families of two or three, all said they would like large families, or certainly larger than they had grown up in. But children in families that were larger than four had mostly decided to have fewer when they grew up. So the child who was one of six, or eight, said it was great fun, but he would only have two children himself. Only the children who were one of four wanted families of the same size.

Since then I have noticed a similar trend in friends of mine. One who was a child of six was determined to stop at two, and did. But many who were one of four go on to have four themselves. It is a kind of magic number: enough people to have fun with, without going mad.

I have to say, though, that for many years we had four – both of us, true to form, being one of four ourselves. And I always knew, deep down, that it was not quite enough …

Perhaps the best answer is that you can never be too rich, or too thin, or have too many children.

Grandparents – and wider family

'Children need to have responsibility for others,
to shield them from apathy and depression. If you just have
responsibility for yourself it's easy to lose sight of your purpose.
But if you need to keep going for someone else that won't happen.
That's why it's important to have younger siblings.
You need responsibility within the family.'
Bink

As I write, my father is shopping for lunch and my mother is doing maths with Alex; my brother is out sailing with Ben and Shaun and my niece's boyfriend, while my niece herself revises her chemistry; Serena lies on her bed reading a novel, and Rosie is sleeping in the garden, waiting for someone to pass and wake her up to give her a cuddle (which happens a lot, as she is the only baby here). This afternoon a bunch of us will swim and boogie-board before tea while Bink does Greek with my father, and tonight we are going to the theatre with cousins who have rented a house nearby.

We are by the seaside. My parents keep an alarmingly small terrace house in north Norfolk, within spitting distance of the beach, which my grandfather bought for exactly this purpose, and every August about eighteen members of the extended family squeeze into it somehow, sleeping all over the place, all higgledy-piggledy and luckily not usually all at once … and this is what we call a holiday.

At the end of the month my parents will go back to Cambridge, where they live for the other eleven months of the year, and where they continue to work, in their mid-eighties, to pay for this wild extravagance every summer. And some bright spark among their contemporaries may ask them, as they have asked them before now, 'Don't you think you have earned the right to stop work, put your feet up, and pamper yourselves instead? A nice little Saga cruise to Turkey, for instance, just the two of you?'

My father will chuckle over this comment for months to come. A quiet, relaxing dry martini alone with my mother, in a deck chair overlooking sunset on the Bosphorus, before a four-course dinner and palm court music in the deck lounge and a spot of bridge with a bunch of other old crocks? No thank you. He prefers getting up at six to make me a cup of tea because I've got a BBC car coming at half past, taking a quick dip in the sea before any other demands are made on him, shopping for milk before breakfast because half a dozen teenagers drank it all the night before, helping someone with Latin A-level before shopping again for lunch, washing up all afternoon, shopping again, doing Greek GCSE with another, then taking several of them swimming before supper. There's no contest, really, is there?

Actually, no, there isn't. It is not the fashion, but I know my parents have made the right choice. And as they travel back home at the end of August, exhausted and broke and longing for a bit of peace and quiet, they know they wouldn't swap it for the world. Why? Because it is more satisfying to serve others than oneself. Because they are giving their children and grandchildren an incomparable heritage. Because the relationships will last for ever: there is no chance whatsoever of my parents having a lonely old age. (Though they might occasionally wish for one …) And because they love it and it keeps them young and they want to give their grandchildren what they were lucky enough to have themselves.

The extended family has been in demise for generations, and the losses are incalculable. We live in Fulham, which in living memory was a working-class area where daughters set up home within calling distance of their mothers. Not much chance of that now: five years ago, little two-bedroom 'cottages' in the street next to ours were selling for a half a million. The nearest that youngsters can hope to live to their parents is a good hour's drive away.

It is a great shame, because intergenerational intimacy benefits everyone. The children grow up with numerous advantages. Wisdom from those older than themselves. Tolerance towards those who are different. Even, if they are very lucky, a smattering of table manners that hark back to a gentler and more civilized age. Today, at lunch, one of my children (loyalty forbids that I should name which) made himself an enormous sandwich, oozing mayonnaise, olive oil, salad and meat from every aperture. We are used to the eating habits of today's teenagers, and hardly registered the sight of him attacking it much as his cave-dwelling predecessors might have taken on the challenge of a raw leg of antelope. His grandparents, however, were visibly shocked. We had to ask him to stop, take stock, wash his hands and consider why the strange invention of cutlery has stayed in vogue.

They may even learn from the example of self-discipline. I have noticed that anyone under twenty now considers it quite natural to get up at any time of day, honestly believing it can be impossible to rise before teatime. From time to time one can even see reports in the press arguing that there are biological reasons for teenagers to sleep around the clock. Such articles could only be written by journalists with short memories and an ignorance of history, since when I was a teenager we wouldn't have stayed in bed beyond breakfast-time unless we were seriously ill. A friend, visiting our house the other day, astonished our children by saying that he used to get exhausted at their age, and wished his mother had let him have a lie in, till eight or nine in the morning, say. I'm sure it does teenagers good to spend a few weeks with people who consider it normal to get up at seven o'clock and do a day's work even when they don't feel like it.

But the younger generation is not the only one to benefit. Just as young people gain maturity, manners and conversational skills from the grandparents, so the older generation gains insight, energy and fun. I would far rather be at a gathering where young and old are mixed together than one that is restricted to my own age group. It is much more interesting. When I am old as well as decrepit I shall much prefer being surrounded by riotous grandchildren and great-grandchildren than fellow senile members of the nursing home.

Extended families also benefit society as a whole. (Well, of course they do, if they benefit families, because society is only as strong as the families in it.) When I was at university I had a friend who was fortunate in living in a house large enough to accommodate various aunts and hangers-on as well as his immediate family. He had an uncle who disconcerted guests by standing a foot or so away from the wall and talking to it at great length, frequently during meal times. It was a sight I found oddly cheering. A family with fewer resources would have abandoned him to an institutional fate; but here, in the family home, he was happily part of the furniture, so to speak – though, admittedly, a fairly chatty part of the furniture. In the years since, when I have come across mental illness first hand, I have thought of Uncle Peter, living with his sister and her children, and smiled nostalgically. Accommodating such eccentricity enriches the lives of all who live with it.

But, you may say, much of this is easier said than done. We do not choose our children's grandparents. You may not have a family 'large' enough, in outlook, commitment or material assets. I'm aware that I am extremely fortunate, through no merit of my own, in the family I have inherited. But I also believe the spirit of the age teaches us to denigrate our parents instead of appreciating them, to blame them for every little fault instead of thanking them for all their good qualities. Nobody has a perfect upbringing, but most of us had a pretty good one, nonetheless. And we should all make the most of what we have.

First, we can include our parents and in-laws from the moment we have children. My mother-in-law came to stay with us for the births of our first two, and was a great boon. If she hadn't been there when Serena was born, there would have been no one to clear up after the dog, who got so excited he was sick all over the drawing room carpet. At Bink's birth, there would have been no one to finish Shaun's 2,000-piece jigsaw puzzle after he was called upstairs by the midwives. And because of her own experiences as a new mother, she knew she'd be far more use doing the shopping and washing up than cuddling the baby.

Next, accept any offer you are given. After Serena's first Christmas, when she was eight months old and no longer breast-fed, my parents offered to have her for a week over the New Year. I can still remember the odd feeling we had as they drove off with her in the back of the car. She was crying, and I momentarily wondered whether we had done the right thing. But of course we had. Parents are not the only ones who have a stake in their children. She is my parents' granddaughter as well as our daughter: they had a right to her company, as well as some responsibility for her welfare. And that week we had to ourselves was one of the best Christmas holidays we've ever enjoyed.

Third, we must trust those who are helping with our children. When we were first married and living in a college flat, Shaun's tutor's wife rang me up in a fix and asked if I could baby-sit for her, as she had to nip out unexpectedly. I said I was very willing but had just sat down to lunch, so she told me to bring it with me. I turned up with my cheese sandwich and half-pint of lager, and the minute his mummy had left, her five-year-old asked me if he could taste my drink. I knew absolutely nothing about children, but I suspected this was not the thing, so I told him I doubted if he would like it. But he pleaded and pleaded, for 'just a tiny sip', till in the end I handed it over. He downed it in one, gave me back the glass, and said proudly, 'Mummy would *never* let me do that.'

Not sure whether he would pass out or throw up, I took his pulse at regular intervals and confessed to his mother in fear and trepidation as soon as she stepped through the door. I will never forget her response. 'If I trust you to look after my children,' she said, 'I trust you to do it your way.' I have frequently repeated this to myself when other people take responsibility for ours.

When children are with their grandparents, grandparents' rules apply. My father has what I consider extraordinary ideas about the constitution of a healthy diet. There I was, handing over children so frighteningly organic they could have been stamped by the Soil Association, knowing that the minute they were in his care they would be filled with so many E-numbers that, if they had died and been buried, they would have been preserved like mummies till Kingdom come. I was faced with a straightforward choice between my dietary faddishness and my children's relationship with their grandfather. You should see me now, the model of a non-interfering parent, biting it all back when he produces a tub of supermarket ice cream or margarine (it's hard to tell the difference) made from industrial-grade North Sea oil, and fairy cakes iced so fluorescent you could see in the dark with them. Their relationship with him is one cemented with refined preservatives.

Our parents are bound to have rules slightly different from ours. What time they go to bed, whether they are allowed to watch television, what they eat at table, is not going to be the same at Grandma's house as at home. This is one of the beauties of it. Our children learn to adapt. But this means we have to adapt first, and back up our parents or in-laws, whatever their rules may be.

There may be times, however, when the wider family simply doesn't work. And when this happens we must, however reluctantly, make our children our priority. A friend of mine believed passionately in the concept of the extended family. When her mother-in-law was widowed, Helen invited her to make her home with her husband and children. To begin with all went well, but as the months went by Helen's mother-in-law became more and more of a recluse despite the fact that she was perfectly fit and relatively young, till she seldom emerged from her room and had, to all intents and purposes, ceased to be a member of the family. Not only was this not doing her any good, but it was giving the children the clear message that family life was something to opt out of, as well as that their grandmother was not interested in them. Chiefly to help her mother-in-law, Helen gently suggested that she should make a habit of joining the family at teatime when the children came home from school, as it would be lovely for them to see more of her. Not only did she not take up the suggestion, she resented it so much that she told her friends Helen had only invited her to live with them so she could exploit her as a free baby-sitting service. In the end, she was having such a negative effect on family life that Helen and her husband had to ask her to leave. This was made the more difficult as the old lady had nowhere to live. Nevertheless, they made the decision that, being an adult, she would have to fend for herself – and she did.

We owe our parents the utmost respect, so this kind of thing is most regrettable. And if we still lived in a society that understood the ties and obligations of the extended family, such conflicts would be far less likely to arise. But when they do, our duty to our children takes precedence even over our duty to our parents. Our children are totally dependent on us for their welfare. Our parents are not: provided they are healthy, they are responsible for their behaviour, and can usually fend for themselves if necessary.

Happily, these conflicts of interest are unusual. So treat your parents well. After all, in this, as in everything, our children will follow our example. If we want to be revered in our old age, we should show our children how it is done.

The first of the Ten Commandments with a promise is that we should honour our father and mother, that it may go well with us and we will enjoy long life. It delivers its promise. When we honour our parents, our children honour us.

Professionals

'Is there anyone apart from me who thinks
Mum should see a shrink?'
Benjamin

'I don't think anyone should see a shrink without a shotgun.'
Alexander

There was a time, not so long ago, when adults always backed each other up. If you came home from school and told your dad that your teacher had boxed your ears, your father might well do it again for good measure to teach you not to get into trouble. Now, of course, he would sue the school, get the teacher hounded out of the profession, and then sell the story to the *News of the World*.

There was something to be said for the old-fashioned solidarity of grown-ups. In some ways life was easier when there was a clear structure and hierarchy. Adults were always right even when they weren't, and you jolly well had to do as you were told and never would waste time playing one off against another. It was not only the children who knew where they stood. I wouldn't be a teacher in this day and age for all the tea in China, with even the most civilized parent as likely to challenge a teacher as back her authority, and the roughest quite capable of beating her up. Now, the parents' first loyalty is seen as being to the child, not the fellow adult.

Nonetheless, though I think we are now too quick to strike this attitude, I believe it is ultimately the right one.

I can still remember the smarting unfairness of it. I was already planning on acting as a career when I was cast as Luciana in *The Comedy of Errors* by one of the best directors in Cambridge, to play for a week in the professional Arts Theatre. Miss Winter wouldn't let me accept the part because she wanted me in a beastly all-girl two-night school production of *As You Like It* ... playing (oh, please) Orlando, and one of the dates clashed. I cried for a week. Why didn't my parents do anything? Perhaps partly because they didn't realize how important it was to me. But also because parents sided with teachers. (Once, my mother challenged the school over my maths teaching. Being a mathematician, she knew they were getting it wrong. But it was only once. And the school took no notice anyway.) How I wished, and still rather wish, that they had told me to say 'boo' to Miss Winter, who, I was too young to know, had absolutely no right or power to make me star in her horrid production or turn down something that would have done me far more good. If only my father had sprung to my defence and told her what he understood so well, that benefit to the individual pupil is what education is about, not the corporate school image.

It is obviously much better if parents and teachers – or parents and any other professionals involved with their children – can work co-operatively. Teachers teach much better if we are backing them up. But ultimately it is right that our underlying loyalty should be to our children. If they really are being treated unfairly, bullied at school or not being taught properly, we should stand up for them to other grown-ups. Nobody else is going to do it. But this should be a last resort. It usually means we have got into the wrong situation in the first place, either by choosing the professionals unwisely, or failing to set limits to their influence, or even, most worrying of all, allowing the wrong adults to have authority over our children.

Choosing professionals

Modern life demands that almost all of us employ some professionals in the child rearing process – most notably teachers, but also, for many of us, nannies, child-minders, *au pairs* or baby-sitters. There is nothing second best about this. If you want to educate your children at home I take my hat off to you; I have done it briefly myself with one of ours (and now believe, in his case, we should have done it far more extensively). But most families find it more convenient and efficient to use schools for education. Similarly, if you would prefer (and can afford) to stay at home with your children rather than turn up at the office and earn a crust, good for you. But most families need some form of childcare.

Success in these relationships largely comes down to making a good choice in the first place. In my experience it is a matter of finding those who will do what we are doing in the way that we do it. Where I live, parents talk endlessly about getting the right school for their children. Some schools are better than others, it is true; but there is no 'right' school. There are those that see eye to eye with you, and those that don't. And when it comes to choosing the professionals to help you bring up your children, what matters is finding those who see the world – and particularly the world of children – in the same way that you do.

It's a bit like choosing a marriage partner. There is a Mr Right out there for you somewhere. But he isn't Mr Right for everyone, or he'd be married already. The reason he's right for you is because he values the same things, laughs at the same things, dislikes the same things, wants the same things for your child as you do. As we know, the parent is always right. So the right professional is the one who agrees with you.

We live in an imperfect world, and it is often impossible to find an exact match. Two of ours went to a school with a first-rate academic reputation, good sport and arts, and superb results. It was a fine school, and we were happy with it. Nevertheless, there was a slight discrepancy between what the teachers believed in and what we believed in. They wanted their pupils to get good scores in their exams and be smartly turned out; we had rather more idealistic notions about developing a love of learning and not worrying too much about one's physical appearance. It didn't matter when our daughter was merely being teased because her nose was always in a book; but it did when she was actively bullied because her school uniform hadn't been ironed and she tended to climb trees in it.

But every so often you find a school, or a teacher, or a head who fits your family and your child so perfectly that it's like winning the jackpot. The school Alex went to at thirteen had a headmaster who was the best thing since sliced bread: he treated every pupil as an individual, never did anything just because that was the way it was done, and had a wonderful sense of humour. Every time Alex ended up in Pontefract by mistake instead of school chapel and had to spend the night in the police station because he had taken the wrong train again, his head found it almost as funny as we did. (Or rather, as I did. Shaun – and the police – tended to find it rather alarming.)

We had an *au pair* called Birgit who stayed with us longer than any other we've had, and became a real member of our family. I realized why one evening when she was getting spruced up to hit the town. In an environment where many young people think they're supposed to latch on to one boyfriend and 'go out' with him, Birgit had lots of friends and went out with all of them (just as I had at her age). Because I consider this a much better way of spending one's single years, I liked the example she was giving my children. We had a similar outlook on life. So we agreed about the children and were not giving out conflicting messages. And we enjoyed one another's company.

Another was Elizabeth. Elizabeth was not what one might conventionally think of as the ideal *au pair*. She was, in short, the most undomesticated person I have ever come across. She refused to wash the milk bottles because, she said, the factory would only have to do it again any-way. I asked her to talk to the milkman about it, partly because I liked the milkman, but also because I found that I was, rather uncharacteristi-cally, embarrassed at the look of our doorstep with its selection of fungal substances in various forms of advancement, distinguished by the differ-ing length of their green and black whiskers. So she collared the poor chap and asked him to justify the three and a half seconds it would take her to swill the bottles out with soapy water. He was utterly stumped, and said rather feebly that he thought it was nicer.

Once we had to call somebody out to fix the oven, so we pulled it away from the wall and found everything you might expect, bits of bacon, fluff and so on, and one or two things you might not, including a dead mouse. After he'd finished I suggested to Elizabeth that we could take advantage of the occasion to sweep some of this extraneous matter up. 'Don't be ridiculous,' she said, slamming the oven back against the wall. 'It never bothered us before, so it won't now.'

We adored Elizabeth. She was taking a gap year before becoming a bio-chemist, and she would sit in the garden studying while Serena tumbled around her feet. She once mowed over the flex of the lawn mower, and at least once a week she would melt another plastic washing-up bowl by putting it on top of the grill and then making toast under it. She always bought a new one, which was really sweet of her because her wages hardly stretched to one washing-up bowl a week. Shaun liked her because her theological challenges were interesting. And it was encouraging to meet someone even less houseproud than I was.

By contrast, we later had a couple of *au pairs* who were prudery per-sonified, and would scream very loudly in German if ever the children went into their bedroom when the two of them were dressed only in bras and knickers. I swear this is when the children started locking the bath-room door and insisting Shaun and I wore dressing gowns – though they say this was part of the normal progression of adolescent psychological development. (In what other way do they show any signs of normal psy-chological development, I ask you?) It may not sound a serious fault, but I found it really annoying.

Most of us entrust our children to other adults – teachers, carers, god-parents, holiday club leaders – for part of their upbringing. The best are generally those who think as we think and value what we value. They may not be better in any objective way, but they are better for us. We visited, and rejected, five housemasters before we found the one who was right for Benjamin … or rather, the one Shaun and I found absolutely inspirational. Others in the school have occasionally suggested he is a tad disorganized and a trifle absent-minded. Good. He esteems the things we consider important: academic learning for its own sake, kindness to others, spiritual truth and intellectual integrity. If this leaves him no time to fill in forms or check the paperwork, so much the better: it will make Ben feel more at home.

By choosing adults whom we like, we will relish rather than dread handing our children over to them. They will naturally and effortlessly back up what we are doing.

Working with professionals

Frequently, however, we have no choice. You may not have much choice over your childcare. Many people have no choice of schooling. We seldom have much choice when our children need medical care. We may not particularly like, and certainly may not see eye to eye with, professionals our children need from time to time, whom we cannot choose. In this case we need to co-operate with and support their work without allowing them to undermine ours – which is, after all, more important.

The mistake I have made is to think they know more than I do and they have more authority than I have. They do not and they have not. Parents know more about their children than anyone else. We, not they, are the experts.

I took one of ours, aged nine, to a hospital appointment. We had not been warned beforehand that this would involve an invasive procedure. The doctor didn't offer me a choice, ask me for a decision, or expect me to take any role other than that of supporting him, so I'm ashamed to say it never occurred to me to question what he was doing. I assumed it was a medical necessity, and that my duty was to help my child endure anything the hospital did. My maternal instincts were screaming at me to intervene; my upbringing, education and social conditioning, however, were telling me that doctors know best and that if they say we have to take the medicine, we have to somehow. It was an extremely traumatic event for both of us.

Sometime later I was having dinner with a friend who was just completing her houseman's training. I was still upset by what my child had been put through, and poured out the story. 'What should I have done?' I asked her, agonized.

She said something that shocked me deeply, though I suppose it is obvious as soon as it is pointed out. 'Most of what we do is just routine', she explained, 'in case it gives us some insight or information. The vast majority of investigative procedures turn out to be unnecessary.' (Call me irresponsible, but since that day I have never had a smear test. I know, I know: they save lives. But the sense of freedom is wonderful.)

I still hadn't learnt my lesson though. Sometime later I agreed to our daughter's missing an eagerly anticipated poetry competition in order to attend a five-minute hospital appointment, at which she was insulted, ignored and treated like a mentally defective three-year-old – by a consultant *paediatrician*, if you please. Shortly after that I told a different paediatric consultant that our daughter didn't like to be manhandled by male doctors, only to watch him back her into a corner to feel her tummy. I gazed, open-mouthed, and said nothing. Why? Because he was a professional and I was brought up to respect them. And so we should, in their area of expertise. But by the same token, they should respect us, in ours.

I know many doctors are wonderful, sensitive, and exhibit common sense and good manners. Even those few who are insensitive, discourteous, or simply too busy to listen have specialist medical knowledge that benefits us. Western medicine has greatly enhanced and lengthened our lives. And a doctor, as I said in the introduction, may know more about our children's ailments and illnesses than we do.

But we know our children.

If your instinct tells you that it is meningitis not the common cold, then go on getting second, third, fourth opinions till you are satisfied that somebody has listened to you. Yes, you probably are a complete pest and the day you move house the surgery will open the champagne at the thought of your making someone else's life a misery. So what? To be utterly brutal, it's better than spending the rest of your life remembering a tiny coffin in a cold morgue, isn't it?

If you think your daughter is dyslexic, or hyperactive, or has attention deficit disorder, or is sensitive to the way the teacher raises her eyebrows when the homework is late, go on, make a nuisance of yourself.

Professionals to avoid

Unfortunately there are some professionals whose effect on a normal, healthy family is so destructive that I would advise having as little as possible to do with them.

Some years I ago I was speaking to Valerie Riches, Founder President of Family and Youth Concern, for whom I have unbridled respect and recognize as having far more experience than I on such matters (and who also, incidentally, is an ex-social worker). I happened to mention a family who had asked for help from social services for one of their children. 'Oh no!' she exclaimed immediately, and said it was the last thing anyone should do. I was taken aback, and considered it a rather cynical reaction. Surely social services are there to help us?

That was then, and this is now, and I'm sorry to say that I have come around to her point of view.

Social services are there to help, yes, but in specific circumstances, notably when the family has failed. This is necessary, even noble: if a child is being beaten by a drunken stepfather, abused by a lecherous lodger or neglected by a mentally ill mother, of course society must intervene. If only we had done so in the case of poor little Victoria (Anna) Climbié, whose guardian and her boyfriend tormented the poor child for months before they killed her, she might still be alive today. But think about it. You know if your child is being beaten, starved or tortured. If she were, you wouldn't be wasting time reading this book. But other people do not know for sure, and if their remit is to protect children it is their duty to assume the worst. So if there is even a chance that any abuse is going on, social services have to step in and pull the family apart in order to rescue the child. Of course they do. This is a very traumatic, distressing, damaging process, but for a child whose life, safety, or mental or physical health is at risk, it isn't as bad as the alternative. For the vast majority of children, however, it is very much worse than the alternative – which is being left alone – but it is considered worth taking that risk with the many for the sake of the few. Professionals outside your family can't know definitely which are the abused children and which are not, so they have to cast the net widely: to put it crudely, risk some damage to a lot of children, in order to avoid greater damage to one or two. They can't necessarily tell the difference.

But you can. You know your child is not being abused, so you want to make darn sure he doesn't get scooped into the net and hurt in the process. By asking for help, you risk your child being caught up in that net. I am sorry to sound so pessimistic, but I know a number of families to whom this has happened.

One involved a twelve-year-old girl who was causing her parents considerable worry. She had special educational needs and was going through a rebellious phase, during which she briefly had a liaison with a boy a few years older than herself. Her parents reported this to the police, who were not interested because the girl herself was not pressing charges. When their daughter was found to be pregnant, they turned to social services for help. Within months they bitterly regretted it. She was taken into care. In addition, they could only get her back by never seeing their granddaughter again: their daughter was told that she would not be allowed home until she put her own newborn up for adoption. She wanted to keep her, and her parents longed to help her bring up the baby. But she was thirteen and had just given birth surrounded by strangers. She was homesick for her mummy and daddy, and her own bedroom and teddy bears. What would any child do? She gave her baby away so she could go back home. Her father believed they had been 'punished' because, being Catholics, they wouldn't pressurize their daughter into having an abortion.

I know a number of excellent social workers, and I believe society needs them for the unfortunate Victoria (Anna) Climbiés of this world, for the cases where there is serious abuse and a child is genuinely at risk. But unless this is true of your child, you don't want to give someone else control over your family. Social services are bound to view the family critically, because that is their job. For the vast majority of families this is pretty unhelpful.

There is another profession that also, in my experience, undermines the family, but without such good reason. When I had a problem page in the *Daily Telegraph* I received a letter from a father whose daughter had gone away to college. Upset by the death of her grandmother, she had accepted counselling. As a result, a year later she had broken off all contact with her parents and they no longer even knew where she lived. They were understandably devastated and had no idea what they had done wrong.

On the advice of a psychiatrist friend (and somewhat against my better judgement), I replied that the counselling might have been much needed, that it could be addressing issues he and his wife were not aware of, and that in the long run it would probably do good. I was inundated. Family after family wrote to me with similar stories. In each case the child was nearly adult, had usually left home to study, had accepted counselling for some fairly commonplace problem (exam pressure, or breaking up with a girlfriend), and the family had been torn apart. Occasionally the parents knew they had been accused of something, or suspected false memory syndrome, but mostly they had no clue. There were so many families telling almost identical tales that eventually I put them in touch with each other for support.

A few years later, when I knew more about psychotherapy, I criticized this kind of counselling in a brief broadcast. I subsequently received several more letters describing the same experience: a nearly grown-up child had embarked on counselling for some minor reason, and it had resulted in a major split with the family. The evening of my broadcast I attended a debate on psychotherapy at the Royal Geographical Society, hosted by the organization *Intelligence*,[2] and from the audience two more stood up and, yet again, recounted similar experiences. One was a man who had been accused of something by his granddaughter, who now refused to have anything to do with both her immediate and her extended family as a direct result of counselling. Another was a woman fighting back the tears, who summed up by saying, 'You think death is the worst thing that can happen to your child. It isn't; believe me, it isn't.'

The next day I went back on to the *Today* programme to defend my views against the psychotherapist Susie Orbach. John Humphrys was, as always, scrupulously impartial in his chairing of the item, but once we were off the air he too recounted the story of a friend of his whose previously happy family had been destroyed by a similar process.

It is important to establish that this tendency does not apply to all counselling. Counselling is a nonspecific term, which can include ringing the Samaritans or sitting in a friend's kitchen with a cup of tea. Cognitive behavioural therapy, for instance, which is sometimes loosely called counselling, has definable goals, usually a fixed term of treatment, and measurable benefits. It is not at all like psychotherapy, and I strongly recommend genuine CBT for those for whom it is medically necessary and properly prescribed.

Naturally, too, I know one or two people who seem to have been helped by psychotherapeutic counselling. I know many more who *think* they have been, though it's hard for their friends to see how. And admittedly those who have suffered the dreadful abuses I have described are a minority. But they are a very significant minority, not necessarily in their numbers but in the anguish they have endured. As the lady said, there are worse things than death. What pain could you inflict on a parent greater than the pain of turning his child against him? What could be more destructive than persuading someone that her parents, who love her more than life itself, have harmed her and should be shunned? Even if it were true that 10 or 20 – even if it were 80 – per cent of those who have psychotherapy feel some marginal benefit from it, their gain weighs next to nothing in the scales against such terrible loss.

How can something so idealistic do so much damage? Most of the psychotherapists I know are kind, well-meaning people, doing what they do with the best of intentions, sometimes putting in extra, unpaid hours or even working on a voluntary basis. But the same could be said of doctors in previous centuries who bled their patients instead of binding them up, and gave remedies that attacked the body instead of the disease. Sincerity is not enough, if the science is flawed. You can be charming and wrong. Is it possible that there is something in the psychotherapeutic philosophy that is profoundly anti-family, surreptitiously assaulting what it purports to support?

Consider the title of one of the most popular books from the psychotherapeutic profession: *Families and How to Survive Them*. The implication, however tongue in cheek, is that the family is a dangerous place that inflicts damage on its members. And, as with psychotherapy itself, there is an insidious half-truth in this: we all injure those we love most, more indeed than we wound strangers or acquaintances or even close friends. Consequently, we can all remember things that members of our family have done wrong. And most of us don't put up much resistance if someone tells us we have been badly treated. So if you suggest, when I'm feeling low and sorry for myself already, that it's not my fault but my parents' for failing to affirm me or understand me or love me enough, you will find me fairly malleable.

The truth is that families provide the most secure, loving environment most of us ever know, where hurts are healed, values shaped and lives forged, where the people who care most about us and are best equipped for the job are doing their utmost to nurture us. Ask someone who was brought up in a children's home whether he preferred his lot. To quote Frank Furedi again, we get over parental mistakes, just as we heal from a grazed knee. Children are remarkably robust. But the default position of psychotherapists seems to be that family life is deeply flawed and causes lifelong scarring which only they can put right. Over and over again I have found evidence of this attitude.

A few years ago Shaun and I went on a day of what is rather gawkily called 'marriage enrichment'. As with most such events, the very discipline of talking to one another about one another all day long was a positive and stimulating thing. But at one point there was an obvious giveaway that revealed the underlying assumption of the organization. We had to answer various questions about our childhood, including, 'What one thing did you most long for from your parents, that they didn't give you?' I racked my brains and wrote the honest answer. A pony. It was the only thing I longed for that they didn't give me. (Oh, and a parrot.) There aren't supposed to be any right or wrong answers in these things, but that was definitely the Wrong Answer. I was advised to rethink, along the lines of 'time', or 'affection', or something; even 'a bedtime cuddle' would probably have been acceptable. But it was certainly not done to suggest that my parents had supplied all my emotional needs.

One psychotherapeutic counsellor, after having fruitlessly and persistently asked me to criticize my own parents, said, 'We invariably find that, when people won't share the darker side of their childhood, this is because of some deep trauma such as abuse which has caused buried memories.' The idea of my own parents being guilty of abuse is so grotesque, I still don't know whether to laugh or sue.

Painful though these experiences may be, a confident and happy adult can shrug them off: I'm grown up and can view my childhood from a distance and I know my parents are terrific. But if I'd heard this kind of stuff at the age of eighteen or twenty, I wonder how gung-ho I would have been. Unfortunately it is when we are vulnerable that we're most likely to be subjected to it.

For the last fifteen years or so, expert medical opinion on Obsessive Compulsive Disorder has been that there is a genetic predisposition to the condition. Our family history certainly reinforces this theory. My sister's family was afflicted with it shortly after we were: my nephew has also suffered greatly, spent much of last year in hospital and is still very ill with it. In other words, OCD strikes much as cancer does: it isn't anybody's fault and there isn't much you can do to avoid it, though an early diagnosis is a great help in treating it. And yet, when our daughter became ill, one psychotherapist after another suggested in one way or another that we had 'done' something to cause it.

Within a week or two of her starting to see a psychotherapist, I began to sense that she was seeing her family in a new light, as a place of pain and problems. It was distressing, but I told myself that it must be a positive thing, that it was like lancing a boil, that if the feelings were there it was better she talked about them. With hindsight and much more experience, I now believe that the feelings were not there at all until they were put there by the therapist. Each week there would be a new theory about what had caused her illness: bullying we hadn't stopped (or even known about) when she was five, something we failed to do when she was eleven, and so on. It was a long time before she, and we, realized that all these 'causes' were red herrings.

Shaun and I then started to experience something eerily similar. One psychotherapist said, as if to encourage us, 'When parents sort out their own problems, we always find their children's problems disappear.' What was insidious about this was its horrible plausibility. In a different context, if our child had been shoplifting because she thought we were on the point of divorce, for instance, it might have been true. But this was not the case at all. She was not rebelling or being naughty, but suffering from a real, and very painful, illness. The clear implication was that we had inflicted it on her, that there must therefore be something wrong with us, and that we could only find a cure for her by admitting this and 'getting better' ourselves. When our daughter herself heard this, she was incensed. 'Do they really think it's solved that simply?' she demanded, of the disability that was ravaging her life.

Another psychotherapist asked me, 'Do you feel very guilty about your daughter's condition?' When I asked her whether she thought I *ought* to feel guilty, she replied, 'Well, your child is mentally ill; you must feel responsible.' No, I hadn't, actually. Not until you tried to put the idea in my head. But if I hadn't been fortunate enough to have researched it and talked to doctors who specialize in the condition, it's easy to see how such a comment might have destroyed my peace of mind for years to come.

One only has to imagine making such judgemental comments towards parents whose child has leukaemia to realize how offensive they are. OCD is a recognized illness with established treatment. And yet for eighteen months our daughter was denied proper help in order to be subjected to the superstition of the age, that her family must be to blame. We even encountered this from professionals who should have known better. When we asked the consultant psychiatrist why he had referred her to hospital, and whether her stay there had achieved what he wanted, his reply was, 'No, not really. We sent her there to see whether the problem was caused by her family. It obviously wasn't.'

The book I found most illuminating at the time was *Job*, from the Old Testament. For no human reason whatsoever, one day Job's life simply falls apart. His children are killed, his wealth destroyed, his health turns to boils and sores. His friends visit him, supposedly to help him by working out why it has happened to him. Time and again these miserable comforters reiterate that his suffering is of his own making: he must have done something wrong. Time and again he insists it isn't and he hasn't. His self-confidence infuriates those who are trying to make him feel guilty. But he is right and God eventually justifies him. He suffered because sometimes, quite frankly, life is a pile of doo-doo.

When our son's apparent autism was first diagnosed, he was referred to a psychotherapist (goodness knows why). He went for three trial sessions preparatory to being offered much longer treatment if he wanted. She saw him on his own, with the door shut and no monitoring either by another professional or by us. Given the current sensitivity to child abuse, I found this astonishing: Shaun, for instance, won't see an adult female parishioner without leaving the door to his study open and ensuring there are others in the house. More to the point, however, I considered it irresponsible for us to hand our ten-year-old over to someone we knew so little about, for such intensive sessions, without any check on what went on. Since he himself found them unhelpful and confusing and was relieved at the idea of discontinuing, I rang to tell her so.

She was most disconcerted. At first she said she was worried that the child was calling the shots. Fine, I said; I had phrased it like that because she herself had suggested the decision should be his. We didn't want him to continue any more than he did. When she asked for an explanation I expressed my misgivings about our being excluded from the process. Something must be profoundly wrong, she suggested, if we expected child abuse round every corner. You can't win. It wasn't worth trying to explain that, though I didn't think she was physically abusing him, she wouldn't recognise emotional abuse if it hit her over the head. So I explained that I thought it was our duty, as his parents, to solve his problems ourselves.

'Children need someone to talk to', she protested.

'Precisely. That's what we're for', I said.

It was then that her philosophy showed its true colours. 'They need someone outside the family,' she returned, *'because the parents are usually the problem.'*

No. The parents are not the problem. The parents are the solution. If psychotherapy considers the parents to be the problem, no wonder it is so destructive of family life.

From time to time I receive anonymous letters (with great relief, usually, because I know no reply is expected). I was sent one a while ago that I absentmindedly pinned up in the kitchen: it seemed unfeeling to throw it unanswered in the wastepaper basket. It is still there, written rather simply and very briefly, in capital letters: 'TO ANNE ATKINS. THANK YOU. FROM PARENTS WHOSE CHILD HAS BEEN BRAINWASHED AND POISONED AGAINST THEM BY A PSYCHOTHERAPIST.' The handwriting is unsophisticated, and once or twice someone in our kitchen has spotted it and smiled, thinking it a joke, but it isn't. It is deadly serious. It represents the unspeakable pain of just two of the many people whose lives have been ruined by professionals interfering in their families.[1]

Society

There is something very odd about the English.

One *Telegraph* reader wrote in to my agony column with the following query: an old friend from college had invited her and her husband to her wedding, due to take place on a Saturday. Their children were not invited. Aside from the practical difficulties (her nanny did not work on Saturdays, and she had no one else she could easily ask to help), she didn't want to spend the day away from her children because the weekends were the only time she and her husband had free to spend with them, due to their long working hours. But she thought her friend would be offended if she did not go, and being childless herself would not understand the reason. What should she do?

I said there was no question about it: she should feel free to turn the invitation down. Her friend would have plenty of other guests at her wedding, but her children have no other parents. A wedding reception is supposed to be a joyous occurrence, and yet she would have a dreary day of it, wishing her children were there. She had a perfectly good pragmatic reason for not being able to go, having no childcare. But over and above all other considerations, if the British middle classes are such a miserable lot that we want to celebrate matrimony without the most visible and happy result of this blessed union, then we deserve to have our best friends refuse our wretched invitations.

Dowager madams all over the country wrote me cross letters explaining why it is inappropriate to have children squawking through such a solemn occasion. Stiff-necked Colonel Blimps insisted that children wreck enough of our peace and quiet already, and we have to escape from them sometimes. One of the oddest arguments came from a mother who explained that wedding receptions are eye-wateringly expensive already, without catering for children too. (I mean, imagine. You invite a friend to a dinner party but not her husband, as it would cost too much to feed them both ...) The most worrying aspect of it all, however, was that we don't seem to *like* having children around.

Shaun and I were invited to a party. When we arrived there were children there. I explained to my host that I hadn't realized we could have brought ours, and he said, 'Oh, you'll have a much better evening without them.' In that case, why would we have had children in the first place? A couple of years ago, close friends invited us to supper to cheer us up because of our daughter's illness. The invitation was for a Saturday, so I explained that we usually spent Saturday evenings with the children. At this our friend said we could bring them if we really must, and somehow we agreed to the evening before realizing that they were obviously not wanted. We had accepted. We had to go. We could take the children on sufferance. We discussed it with them and they told us to go without them and not to worry: they would watch a film together or something. When we turned up, our friend applauded the decision, saying we needed an evening away from our children so we could relax and have a good time. I'm sorry to be embarrassing, but I found this comment so hurtful that I spent the first half of the evening in tears. (We *were* very low at the time.)

This attitude is common. The pub is the symbol of British leisure and relaxation. So what do we do? Ban children. It is illegal under British law to take children to this supremely British place of recreation unless the landlord has made special provision. We pretend it is for their good, but this is nonsense: we think it would spoil our fun. In any case, why do we want to spend our evenings in an atmosphere so unwholesome that it would be detrimental to our little ones? The truth is that there is, deeply ingrained in our culture, a profoundly anti-child attitude.

We perpetuate a generational apartheid. We seem to believe no one can enjoy the company of anyone who is not the exact same age. Teenagers are supposed to spend time with teenagers, middle-aged people with other middle-aged people. Consequently we miss out on half the fun of having children. A neighbour, whom we only know because our children went to school together, invited us to a dinner party. When he heard that Serena was at home, he invited her too. She mingled with the other guests over the champagne, but when the time came to sit down we realized with astonishment that no place had been laid for her. Instead, she was invited to take a pizza upstairs and watch the telly with his teenage sons. It is not unusual for us to be invited to supper with friends, only to find that their children are eating a separate meal somewhere else in the house.

Shortly after I received the letter about the wedding, an engaged couple in our church asked if they could have their reception in our garden because their house was too small. He was German, she Korean, so the guests were a mixture of both. As the time drew near, a number of the German parents very politely rang me to ask whether there was any provision for their children: could they bring them to the reception? Of course, I said. They could hardly lug them over from Germany and put them in cold storage for the afternoon. Clearly, however, children are not expected to attend German weddings any more than British ones. But the Koreans never asked. I assume it never occurred to them that it would be otherwise.

And when the event took place, the difference between the two cultures, the Northern European and the Asian, was striking. The Korean children had their best party frocks on and looked like little angels. More to the point, they behaved like them. They ate what was offered them, never raised their voices, did as they were bid, sometimes smiling shyly from behind their mothers' skirts and sometimes playing happily together, and were a real joy to have around. Of course they were. Presumably, being routinely included in their parents' activities, they learn to behave in a way that their parents will appreciate. Expected to give delight, they learn how to do so.

The German children, by contrast, ran around upstairs without permission, didn't like the food, made a great deal of noise, and knocked over a stone birdbath that could have killed one of them. No wonder their parents don't take them anywhere. Individually, I am sure they are lovely children and will doubtless grow up into charming people. Collectively they were a menace, as British children probably are too.

It doesn't have to be like this. If we regularly include children in our pleasure we will derive pleasure from them. I wouldn't dream of entertaining people for supper without my children being at the table, because I enjoy their company. For all I know, my guests may not appreciate it at all, but they don't have to come. I love my friends dearly, but my children even more; if my friends stay away because they don't like my rowdy dinner table, I will still have interesting people to talk to.

And it works both ways. When I was young, my parents expected my siblings and myself to sit with their guests as soon as we were old enough for our bedtimes to permit it. As I grew older, I expected them to sit with mine. The first time I invited friends to a formal party, at the age of sixteen or so, I would have felt lost if my parents hadn't been there to help. And this lasts. Even last summer, when we organized a celebration for our silver wedding, I was devastated when my parents initially thought they couldn't manage the date.

When Bink was six she asked if she could have a dinner party to celebrate her birthday. She gave us a menu (which specified 'two beefs', I seem to remember) and a list of guests, including a couple in our church whom we would never have thought of inviting, considerably older than us and from a very different background. If it hadn't been for Bink's sixth birthday party, we would never have got to know them or realized how much we would grow to treasure them as friends.

By contrast, for Serena's eighteenth I organized a surprise. Some six months before her birthday she had mentioned how much she would like to have a bouncy castle, an animal man, jelly and ice cream, and everyone in black tie. Well, I managed to ship in a bouncy castle twice the size of our house without her suspecting anything. We cooked for thirty people and the penny didn't drop. We had a man turn up with a van full of birds of prey without her noticing a thing. We even got her to dress up for a fake trip to the opera. Believe it or not, she thought nothing of finding the house full of friends in their glad rags singing 'Happy Birthday to you', though when they got to the line 'Happy Birthday, dear *Serena*', she did begin to wonder why they'd all turned up on an evening when she was going to Covent Garden. (As her boyfriend says, she is *very* blonde.) The evening was a spectacular success. And the one thing I got wrong? I invited mostly contemporaries of hers because of something she had said the previous Christmas, so I didn't think to ask the vet she has done all her work experience with.

The other day I asked Bink if she would like me to organize her next birthday party. 'Shall I mainly ask friends your age?' I said. 'No,' she replied. 'Ask *all* our friends.'

And though this will probably not be true for most readers, some of us may even find we can include our children in our work far more easily than we think at first. When Bink was about three months old, I accepted a weekend's work and left her behind in London. As soon as I arrived, I wondered why. A small baby would not have been at all disruptive during rehearsals, and for the hour or two I was on stage on the Saturday night I could surely have found someone to look after her. For weeks afterwards I had to fiddle around with bottles and formula milk to supplement her diet because I had disrupted her feeding, and I determined that I would never do this again.

So when Rosie was born, I didn't. A few days after her birth I was asked on to the *Richard and Judy* show, so she came with me to the studio and was the star attraction in the greenroom. (When I went on the programme again recently, Judy was most disappointed that Rosie didn't turn up.) At two weeks' old she accompanied me to a filming of *Question Time*; when I

offered to bring someone to look after her for the duration of the programme, several members of the crew volunteered. In her first few months
she went to numerous jobs with me, and during one of them Bink was
paid to be the child-minder, so all three of us stayed in the hotel together
and had a great time.

When Serena was nine I was asked to provide some Shakespeare in
the Globe Theatre, for the launch of a book on Shakespeare written by
my literary agent. So another actor and I put together some favourite two-
handers, including Orsino and Viola's scene from *Twelfth Night*, which starts,
"If Musicke be the food of Love, play on ..." Actually, it doesn't start with
this line but with the music itself. So we asked Serena to play the harp,
as a young page at court. This went down very well. Unfortunately, when
we got to the horrific murder scene between Macbeth and his lady, made
particularly harrowing by the relentless knocking at the gate, Serena completely forgot to provide the knocking because she had become so
engrossed in the action ...

I know not everyone's work is like this. Three-year-olds don't go down
very well in the boardroom of Goldman Sachs. And a number of people,
particularly men, find it harder to concentrate when their children are present. But I believe many of us could learn to be far more flexible than we
are. Shaun has at last (fifth time around) learnt that if he goes on pas-
toral visits with a baby he will be greeted with a far warmer welcome.

And certainly, when we are at leisure it seems bizarre not to include our
children. If we don't enjoy their company, what on earth are they for?

The other day I heard of the following experience from an academic at one
of our leading universities. His subject is medicine, so his undergraduates
are the cream of our youth and the doctors of tomorrow. When he took
up the post he and his wife decided to entertain his pupils on a regular
basis, inviting them all to supper in turn. The experience was so painful
they had to drop the idea. Sat at table, with people to talk to who were
not their immediate contemporaries, these bright and brilliant students were

completely at a loss. They didn't even know how to make conversation, let alone pass the food or look as if they were enjoying themselves. He concluded that they must have spent their teenage years in front of a screen with a microwave meal on their laps. And soon they will be writing your prescriptions, and mine. Heaven help us.

So eat with them, drink with them, go out with them, stay in with them. Whatever you do, enjoy them, and the chances are they will enjoy you.

· · · · · · · · · · · · Action Page · · · · · · · · · · ·

It's party time!

The moment has come to organize an intergenerational party. Pick any event worth celebrating over the next six months or so. It can be your child's first birthday party, your tenth wedding anniversary, the end of exams, New Year, your baby's baptism, anything. The idea is to mark it with a party for all ages. Again there is a complete flexibility as to how you do this. It could be a supper party for half a dozen or a drinks party for hundreds, round the kitchen table or in a huge marquee, dressed in your jeans or dressed to kill.

The only absolute requirement is that the party spans the generations. Suppose you have three children under five, and you opt for a dinner party to celebrate your thirty-fifth birthday. Draw up, with them, a list of four or five people you would like to invite, a menu of two or three courses, and a dress code of anything you like.

I can see you thinking that wasn't how you planned to have your last major fling before you turn forty. Painting the town red and visiting a strip club was more what you had in mind. You can do that if you like, but I think you'll find three under fives more of an encumbrance.

And you wouldn't have half as much fun.

Freedom

'I wish I had been allowed to learn rugby.'
Alexander

'Alex, look at you.'
Bink

'Alex could perfectly easily have been a hooker.'
Serena

'Yes, but he said he wanted to play rugby.'
Bink

The other day Bink went for a walk with Ben's little dog, rather nattily christened Dog. Dog started to make a mess on the pavement, so Bink told him off because he knows he is not supposed to do this. A couple passing by told her she shouldn't rebuke a dog because it is cruel: she should simply scoop his poop without comment. Dear, oh dear. Things have reached a pretty pass when we can't risk hurting a dog's feelings for fear of some confounded Convention of Canine Rights. We desire control of everyone and everything, and over children more than all the rest.

A whole generation of parents is now bringing up children who experience far less freedom than we had at their age. We can remember playing unsupervised all day long. We benefited greatly from our early independence. Most of us are not deliberate killjoys. We would presumably love our children to have the carefree days that we ourselves enjoyed. But we are frightened. We believe the world is not safe enough for our children to play in.

And yet life is no more dangerous than it was. In many ways it is safer. Our parents were not irresponsible people, indifferent to our welfare or subjecting us to unreasonable risk. After all, we're still here. Is it possible they knew something we don't? Perhaps we could restore some of that freedom. Wouldn't that be more fun? And better for our children? Ah, if only we could.

I believe we can. With a dash of courage, a ruthlessly rational approach and a determination not to be cowed by the raised eyebrows of other adults, we can give our children a freedom that has almost been forgotten.

Choice

'There are times when adults could be more laid back
without any damage being done to anybody.'
Alexander

It was a Friday evening, and Serena was five years old. I was painting the kitchen, while she sat in the adjoining dining room convivially pottering away at something of her own. She had various busy tools of craftsmanship, including paper, pens and scissors, and eventually came to show me her handiwork. It was spectacular. She had cut off all her hair, right down to the scalp, but only on the front half of her head. So she looked like Yul Brunner from the front, but still like Goldilocks from behind. We laughed and laughed, she and I, till the tears ran down our faces: it was one of those wonderfully companionable moments that you remember for years to come. I also made a point of telling her she looked stunning. Not, perhaps, quite as conventionally pretty as she had half an hour earlier (though I wouldn't have dreamt of saying so), but definitely stunning.

On Sunday she went to church. It was then that I began to realize quite how rude adults are towards children. Not a single person commented favourably on her radical hairstyle. Fair enough, I suppose: if you don't like somebody's new look the best thing is to say nothing. And if her critics had confined themselves to silence it would have been acceptable, but somehow children are excluded from the normal conventions of courtesy. 'What a shame,' was one of the more civil refrains Serena was subjected to.

But this was nothing compared to the response she received at school on Monday morning. Her teachers were horrified, mourned her beautiful golden curls, and repeatedly supposed that her mother must have been furious.

Good grief. If a child can't choose her own hairstyle, what on earth can she choose? I can't think of any decision a young child could make that would be less harmful in its consequences. It impinges on no one else's freedom. It does no damage to the child herself. It has no permanent adverse results whatsoever. If she doesn't like it she can grow it again. If she likes it but isn't quite so keen on the insulting comments from all the ill-mannered adults around her, she can weigh up the one against the other and decide whether to please herself or others. For a five-year-old to choose her own hairstyle offers a level of harmless independence and autonomy that would be hard to improve on, even if a team of academic psychologists were to research into the matter for a suitably absurd prolonged period at exorbitant public expense.

We miss numerous opportunities to give our children choices. Hair is a good example. I was talking to a friend about secondary education in her area, and she said there was a good local school with a high academic reputation that she quite liked. 'But you hear ghastly things about the girls. Dyeing their hair green and so on. I don't want Sophie doing that.' Again, I can't think of any gesture of independence Sophie could make that could be less disruptive of her educational process.

We can offer our children far more freedom of choice than we often do. If the issue does not have permanent consequences, we can surely let them decide for themselves. We perhaps shouldn't let them decorate themselves with tattoos, as they are likely to regret this before they are grandmothers; but the great thing about hair is that there is nothing much you can do to it (short of electrolysis) that God won't soon undo again. Similarly, I wouldn't advise letting them decide whether or not to do their homework, as neglecting it will (eventually) have permanent consequences; but there's no reason why they shouldn't be the ones to decide whether or not to have a bath tonight, since the worst that can happen is being a bit whiffy tomorrow (or, with pre-adolescents, just being grubby tomorrow). We may not leave it up to them to choose their next school as they might live to regret it, but they can often help choose the next family holiday.

An old schoolfriend of mine was staying with us for the weekend. While she was out on Saturday morning doing a spot of shopping, her five-year-old got out of bed. He had wet himself in the night and had sensibly removed his pyjamas, so I suggested he got dressed. 'I don't know what I'm supposed to wear,' he said. 'I'll have to wait and ask Mummy.' His clothes were all there in his suitcase and he was stark naked, so I overruled his doubts and confidently said he could choose something for himself. He did so, and came down to breakfast with a certain amount of pride. Alas, he was right and I was wrong. As soon as Mummy came home, she said he had put on his Sunday clothes and would have to change. Poor child. He clearly felt the humiliation, and was unlikely to offer his initiative again in a hurry. But surely it was more important for him to learn how to dress himself than to look smart the next day? Surely she would derive more pride from her son's independence in the long run, than she would from his appearance that brief Sunday morning?

Provided we give children a range of wholesome options, whatever they choose will be good. We might not give them a choice between meat and ice cream, but they could surely decide between meat and fish; perhaps not whether to practise the violin or watch telly, but presumably whether to learn the violin or the flute; not whether to wear properly fitting shoes or stiletto-heeled fashion statements, but undoubtedly whether to wear blue shoes or red. Any decision that will not compromise their future is a decision we should be glad to let them take.

So we can give them considerable freedom *of* choice. However, we should also give them freedom *from* choice. There are some matters we should not expect them to decide.

When I was eleven, my parents generously let me choose my secondary school. I went to look at the Perse, an independent girls' school in the heart of Cambridge, and saw a muddy yard on a rainy day. Then I visited the High School, a grammar school on the outskirts, and saw acres of rolling green and a weeping willow shaking its hair in the sunshine. What I did not see was that the High School had little Latin and less Greek. What I did not know was that within a year of making my decision I would want to read Classics at university. The High School would not even let me learn Latin, as a point of discipline, because I hated German and frequently shirked my German homework. I changed to the Perse for my sixth form, but it was too late. I still regret my decision to this day. The irony was that I was never even allowed to play under the willow, which turned out to be in a garden exclusively for staff.

Some choices are simply too important for children to be asked to make. When the time came for us to buy a house, I very much wanted one that we would all like. I said we must all choose it together. Serena wanted one with a tree outside her window, so she could climb down in the night. Ben wanted a swing. Alex was keen to have an electric socket so he could plug in his computer. Bink thought property was theft so we shouldn't get one at all. I wanted medieval, cob, thatched, with a stream and paddock and barns and no sound of traffic. And Shaun wanted an affordable one that wasn't falling apart. Eventually we found a house that fitted his criteria and mine. But it didn't please all the children. I think the veto was probably Bink's, still unpersuaded from the Marxian line. Five years on, when I was in tears because property prices had tripled and we still had nothing, they asked me why we hadn't bought the house I loved.

'You didn't all like it,' I sobbed.

'You shouldn't have taken any notice,' they chorused. 'We would have loved it now.' More fool me for expecting children to make a judgement on what house to buy.

It is not fair or sensible to give children responsibility for decisions with serious long-term consequences. They may have strong views on where the family is to live or whether we should change jobs or accept promotion, but they cannot possibly be expected to weigh up all the consequences. It is courteous and reasonable to ask their opinion, but only fair to explain that the parents' is the final say. And the same is true of important decisions concerning their own welfare. Where they attend school, what subjects they study, how long they spend on their homework, what time they go to bed in term-time, are all matters that we must decide for them when they are young. Then, the burden for wrong decisions can be carried by the adults, not the children.

It is important for them to know this, particularly if any mistakes made are serious ones. Children shouldn't have such accountability, even for their own wellbeing. How often have you heard an adult say he wishes he had been made to practise the piano when young? I have not only heard it, but often wished it too.

And yet there is definitely an aura of disapproval hanging around any parent who could possibly be described as 'pushy', making his child do something before the child is mature enough to motivate himself. As I say in the next chapter, I think many modern children need more free time and fewer achievements to their names. But this doesn't mean they should have no achievements at all.

The story is told of a seven-year-old boy who had long dreamt of learning to play Beethoven's violin concerto. One Wednesday afternoon his teacher finally gave in to his pleadings, and told him he could do so, provided he learnt the Mozart A Major first. Two or three days later he performed the whole Mozart concerto to his teacher from memory, after eight hours' diligent study. But his teacher was not pleased by his too slick performance, and told him to go away and not come back until he had given due consideration to every single note. Such was his disgrace that, when he got home, his mother confined him to his room with a solitary supper, while his father thrashed him with a belt.

I'm not necessarily advocating quite such an energetic approach (not nowadays, at any rate, unless you want to try a spot of porridge). But it worked. The boy went on to become the greatest violinist of recent times. More significantly, he tells the anecdote himself, with gratitude for the part his parents played in it.[1]

We can stop short of such dedication to our children's accomplishments without letting them down, you'll be relieved to hear. Nevertheless, caring about her academic achievements is not (yet) a criminal offence, and making him do a few minutes' piano practice is not child abuse. But we are sometimes made to feel it is. A friend once said to me, with some self-righteousness, 'I wouldn't dream of making Jeffrey play a musical instrument. I'm taking him to circus class, to learn unicycling, because it's what he wants to do.' Jeffrey was five. How can he possibly have known what he wanted to do? And who put the idea in his head, I wonder? How many five-year-olds do you know who wake up one morning and say, 'Dad, there doesn't happen to be a circus class in the vicinity, does there, because I've always dreamt of being an international unicyclist?' If his father simply meant it was what *he* wanted Jeffrey to do, why not be honest about it? But I suspect he really wanted Jeffrey to want to do anything that was whacky enough for his father to believe that Jeffrey himself genuinely wanted to do it rather than wanting to please his father who wanted him to want to do anything ...

Oh, for the confidence to stand up and be counted as a pushy parent! To say we are simply going to make our children do this or that: their homework, because it will help them get into a good senior school; or tennis, because we think it will give them pleasure in later life. Or even (for some bizarre reason) unicycling. Parents are supposed to make their children do things they don't feel like doing, because it teaches them discipline and gives them skills they may later appreciate.

If we are to give children freedom, we owe them freedom *from* some decisions, as well as freedom *of* others.

Intellectual freedom

'I don't think adults should expect respect from children as of right. They should have to earn it. If children respect all adults just because they're adults, then they won't question them, and that's dangerous. Not necessarily because the adults might abuse them physically, or anything like that, but because some teachers teach rubbish, for instance, and ought to be challenged.'

Bink

One of the most exciting milestones in child rearing is the moment when your child confronts you with a view that is not your own. It is wonderfully satisfying to realize we have endowed them with the freedom to think for themselves: to question, challenge, debate, discuss; to come to their own conclusions, make up their own minds, go against the spirit of the age, resist the tyranny of peer pressure; to swim against the tide.

I grew up in a university city, where it was commonplace to argue for the sheer enjoyment of the dispute, to try on a contrary viewpoint in order to get the feel of it, to disagree without animosity. It wasn't until I left university myself and entered the suburban world that I realized this is not the norm. Many people take a differing opinion as a personal affront, or follow a catchy soundbite rather than a logical argument, or even simply adopt a point of view because the newspapers do.

I also had the privilege of being brought up in a Christian family. Even a generation ago, society was already sufficiently secular for the Christian faith to be an anomaly, a viewpoint subjected to ridicule and demanding a vigorous defence. Arguing for a minority belief is a great training in intellectual autonomy. Now, in our even more post-Christian environment, children in Christian families should be imbibing intellectual independence with their mothers' milk.

If we want to encourage this liberty of the mind, a good place to start is with freedom from the tyranny of technology.

Television

Television is like alcohol. None is better than too much, but the judicious appreciation of a little is the best of all. The overwhelming majority of us have far too much.

Excessive television stultifies the mind for several reasons: it feeds us pre-digested opinions; the participation it demands is almost entirely passive; it is easy to go on watching long after we intended to instead of turning off and reflecting on what we have seen; and above all the stimulation it offers is primarily visual, not verbal, so it conveys images and impressions rather than thought and argument.

As if this weren't enough, scientists have now discovered what we have known all along (as scientists are always doing, bless them): that watching telly can actually damage very young children, and doesn't do the older ones many favours either. Exposing those under two or three to television can permanently affect their brain structures, impairing their ability to concentrate in later life; even after this age, every hour a child watches television each day increases the risk of attention deficit disorder by 10 per cent.[2]

If you don't think you can control the amount of television watched in your home, there is a very easy answer: the dustbin. Or, if you baulk at that, the local charity shop. There is life without television, and it's good. Some of the best periods of my life (as a very young child, as a teenager and as an undergraduate) were almost entirely television free. You'll save yourself years: think of all those docu-soaps you won't have to watch any more. And if there's any screenaholism in the family you'll be sparing your children a lifetime of *The Weakest Link*. Imagine. But think ahead: you'll find it easier to dump the set before they are old enough to protest, probably before they are born. Don't listen to interfering friends telling you that you'll be making them into oddities at school. For goodness' sake, if we can't do anything that isn't conforming to the lowest common denominator in society, half our freedoms are gone at a stroke.

(A less radical way to save yourself time is just to record everything. For maximum efficiency, only ever allow yourself one tape, and no labels. This happens organically in our house: there are never any labels, and there's certainly never a spare tape. Then, every time there is a programme advertised that you think you ought to watch, simply tape over the last thing that you thought you ought to watch, which you can now no longer remember the name of and certainly haven't found time to see. The miraculous thing is that you never really need to turn the television on at all: you just tape it, then you tape over it. Strictly speaking, I suppose you don't even need a set in order to operate the system – thus even saving yourself the licence fee – in which case the dustbin might come in handy after all; but you'd have to be quite self-disciplined to keep on taping programmes that you absolutely know you can't watch.)

I confess, though, it's better to use the television discriminately. To do this, it helps to implement a few simple rules.

1. *Never let your children watch television before they can read.* I'm amazed at how many two- and three-year-olds are plonked in front of a video machine. Actually I'm not amazed, because tiny children love TV (just as they love anything), and it's a very easy way of entertaining them, especially if you're trying to breast-feed a younger baby and help an older one with his homework and cook supper for the family and answer all your letters, or merely attempting to write your first concerto for didgeridoo to a deadline in the next room. But it's like giving gin to the natives. You aren't doing your children a kindness. Far better to teach them to love books. Throw away the children's videos, give her an old saucepan, a wooden spoon and a set of biscuit cutters, or a board book with pictures, or scrap paper and crayons, and as soon as you can, teach her to read. Television is for later, after she has learnt the joys of entertaining herself with books.

2. *Never allow television while the sun is up.* Yes, it is a totally arbitrary rule. But then so is not having a cocktail before the sun is over the yardarm, or whatever the rule is; it still helps us not to become alcoholics, doesn't it? If the sun has got his hat on, children should be outside screaming around the garden terrorizing the neighbours, not inside watching them. And if it's raining, they should be jumping in puddles under sou'westers and catching their death, or discovering all your faded and embarrassing love letters in the attic, or sitting around saying, 'I'm *bored*, Mum,' and driving you nuts. Television starts when the sun is down over the horizon and the darkness is drawing in. What do you mean, there is a brilliantly educational programme on at two o'clock in the afternoon? What is the video recorder for?

3. *Never, ever, ever allow your offspring to have televisions in their bedrooms.* Not at any age, not at any price, not ever. There should be one, and only one, television in the house. (Unless you have a nanny or *au pair*, in which case by all means give her a set and get yourself some peace

in the evenings.) I don't care how you justify it, or don't. You just never have more than one TV, that's all. Yes, you will occasionally disagree about which programme to watch. That's what families are for: learning how to compromise, give and take, argue your corner, and appreciate other people's choices. And there will sometimes be two good programmes on simultaneously: again, make the video machine earn its keep.

In our house the telly is in our bedroom, because when we were first married we lived in a bedsit and I learnt the joys of watching it in bed; now I can't watch it anywhere else. I know I said no televisions in bedrooms, but we're the parents, so it's different. It just is. Because I say so. (Also, living in a drafty vicarage as I do, I can't go to bed in the winter without having a bath to warm up first. So when *Pride and Prejudice* with Colin Firth was on at half past five some years ago, I had to have my bath and go to bed at teatime every Saturday afternoon. Sad? Pathetic.) When we want to watch, everyone in the family crowds into our bedroom and sprawls all over the bed, floor, each other, the popcorn, etc. And they can't watch anything that's on after our bedtime. Yes, it is hugely unpopular. We've been doing it for twenty years and they still moan about it on average once a week. Life is tough.

4. *Encourage group viewing.* Watching TV with your children is an obvious way of taking an interest in their interests, and it enables you to discuss their favourite programmes, which is the intelligent, sociable way to use television. I know it's hard. The one time I tried to watch *The X-Files* I ran from the room screaming and had nightmares for days; I never tried again, despite Serena's attempts to assure me that Gillian Anderson doesn't always have maggots falling out of her eyeballs.

5. *Plan your viewing.* If you live in a household that is more organized than ours, you can teach the children to look at the TV schedule at the beginning of the week, mark the programmes they are interested in, plan around them, and turn the television off as soon as they are finished. (If you're that organized you can get your tax return in on

time and write my next book for me.) In return, try to respect their choices and not serve a meal five minutes before the start of a programme about ancient Rome that was marked with a triple asterisk five days earlier. And never turn the set on 'just to see what's on.'

6. *It stands to reason you don't want satellite, cable or any of the other options.* There's enough rubbish on the basic terrestrial channels without having to plough through all the additional nonsense on the extra channels too. Not to mention the horrors of twenty-four-hour sport or news. Believe me, if it's any good, it will be mainstream. (Actually, I haven't got a clue about this, because I've never watched satellite or cable. And look at me. Enough said.)

7. *Buy plenty of radios.* Unlike a TV set, a radio in each bedroom is perfectly acceptable.

Computers

> 'I think one of my problems is having two parents
> who don't understand computers. At all. You think all
> activities that are done on computer are the same.
> It's like trying to play a tune to deaf people.'
> **Alexander**

It's harder to have such clear rules for computers because they are used for far more functions. They have more advantages, but also more drawbacks than television: they are useful for homework, but they can be more divisive and solitary, because generally, unless it's been set up for watching DVDs, several people don't sit around the computer enjoying it together. And they can waste even more time on even more pointless activities, such as Zap the Monster or Blast the Baddy computer games.

For what it's worth, the following more or less workable system seems to have evolved in our home. We have one main computer, tucked away at the top of the house. (Also, because it is a tool of my trade, I have a personal laptop from which I can transfer work to the master computer.) As we frequently remind everybody, the parents paid for this machine; it is not a household commodity like the kettle or the piano, to which you can just help yourself any hour of the day, but a personal possession which you have to ask permission to use. In theory, therefore, we have a rough idea what it is being used for – unless Alex is on it, in which case he could be hacking into half the major world banks for all we know, and only two things are certain: that he isn't working and that he'll be late for dinner. (Mind you, both are also true if he is not on the computer.) They say there's some comfort in certainty, though I haven't found it so myself.

We have a five-minute warning gong before a meal is served, originally to give people time to wash their hands and comb their hair and come and help lay the table and all those other civilized things that happened in the Middle Ages, but now to give whomever it might be enough time to log off and disconnect – unless Alex is on it, in which case a week wouldn't be enough and only two things are certain … etc.

The Internet line is the same as our main telephone line. There are pros and cons to this. The advantage is that it's so annoying to all your friends when the telephone is permanently engaged that they do the nagging for you. By the time your daughter's boyfriend hasn't been able to ring her up since Christmas because your son has been on line all that time, one or other of them will sort him out. Or the boyfriend will give up and buy her a mobile for her birthday. The downside is that no one can get through for weeks on end. Did I just call that the downside? On second thoughts, there are pros and pros to the one-telephone-line method.

Finally, don't have any computer games. Just don't have them. If they came free with the machine, wipe them off. If they were a Christmas present, lose them. What do they achieve, eh? Well, what?

And for as long as you can hold out, you could try not having a computer at all. Anything your children really need it for, they can probably do at school.

Telephone

An answerphone is a great invention. Don't answer the telephone during family mealtimes; you are – or jolly well should be – in the middle of a

conversation already. Don't answer it after you go to bed either; you are –
or should be – doing something far more interesting. In fact, you could do
what Shaun does and never answer it at all. It's very annoying for everyone else in the family, or would be, if any of them answered it instead. As
it is, it's even more annoying for me, because I end up answering it every
time. I don't know why. It annoys Bink when I do, as she's usually talking
at the time. In fact, the telephone is a pretty annoying contraption. Just ignore
it, and talk to your family instead. Unless a member of the family is away
somewhere, in which case the telephone is a marvellous invention.

What you do in this instance – in other words, when your children are
old enough to be the ones ringing home – is to contact British Telecom and
ask for 'Call Sign'. This enables you to have a different number on the same
line, which results in a different ring tone. You keep this number secret,
known only to yourselves and your children. So there you are, sitting at dinner, and hey presto! The telephone rings with the secret code so you know
it's one of the family and worth interrupting your meal for. The only snag
being that Alex and I are the only ones who can recognize the code, so I
still end up being the one to answer it. While if I'm away from home I can
ring and ring till Christmas, and if Alex isn't in no one will pick up ...

(But perhaps this tyranny of the telephone only occurs in vicarages
and headmasters' houses, so my phonophobia may be a mystery to many
readers. Indeed, I occasionally dream of private homes where the telephone
only rings a few times an hour.)

Books

'Book.'
Rosalie

'Rosie said her first word! She said "book" – she really did!'
Everybody

Lots of them. Lots and lots and lots. Cloth books, board books, bath books,
picture books, word books. Library books. Books on tape. Fiction. Fact.
How-to books.

Fill your house with books. Ask for them for Christmas instead of toys. Buy them second-hand if you can't afford them new. Take them out of the library if you can't afford them second-hand. Encourage your children to read masses of what they are interested in, and some of what they are not. Read books to them. Play tapes to them. Listen to them in the car. (Don't neglect really good music, though.)

And encourage them to read critically, just as they should approach everything critically: *why* won't J.K. Rowling ever win the intellectual acclaim of the Booker Prize? Fair enough, but *why* is the Booker pretentious bourgeois politically correct nonsense?

Mealtimes

This is in danger of becoming a bit of a theme, but always eat with your children. All right, not when they are three years old and have tea at five and go straight to bed two hours before you get in from work, but you know what I mean. Even then, though, you could do what we've done with Rosie, and train them to be Bohemian children who have a long sleep before you get in and then come down in their pyjamas when life begins at eight or nine at night.

I find it really distressing to go to someone's house for supper and hear, yet again, that the teenagers are upstairs having a snack on their own, or have eaten already, or will cook something for themselves later. It is one thing to do this rarely, in order to have a private gossip with a couple you haven't seen in ages. We have friends who occasionally have us over for a foursome and it is very relaxing: there are some things we wouldn't discuss freely in front of one another's children. But to do it regularly flies in the face of everything that families and mealtimes are supposed to be about.

How can they learn to express their views if they never have to sharpen their wits against those who are older? How can they develop opinions if they never listen to yours? How can you know what they believe about the world if you don't sit down with them every evening to hear them enthuse about the latest music, or film, or game of football? How can they keep you young if they aren't regularly keeping you informed?

Lastly, of course, encourage them to disagree with you. Not, perhaps, on matters of life and death: the use of heroin, seatbelts in the car, swimming after a drinking bout, promiscuity, or the ultimate truth of Christianity; in other words, anything that seriously affects their future. But on politics, ecology, music, science, feminism, or anything else that gets you going after a glass of wine but doesn't make much practical difference in the end, the younger they are when they take you to task, the more interesting your old age is going to be.

Risk and danger

> 'All children should be taken skiing.
> At least once a year. That means me.'
> **Serena**

When Benjamin was five years old he had a half-term week that didn't coincide with any of his siblings'. He had just learnt to ride a bicycle, so Birgit, our *au pair*, escorted him onto the green outside our house and told him he could cycle up and down to his heart's content, provided he didn't leave the green itself or cross the road back to our house on his own. She said she would look out of the window every ten minutes or so to ensure he was all right and so that he could wave at her if he wanted to come home. She also told him he could use the telephone box at the corner of the green if necessary, since he knew how to reverse the charges in an emergency.

He had been playing happily for about fifteen minutes when a contingent of horrified women rang our front door bell. Two had brought Benjamin home and one had gone for the police. By the time I came downstairs an astonished Birgit and an oblivious Ben were sitting in the kitchen together.

5. Freedom

'Who is Jamie Bulger?' Birgit asked me. I explained that England was still reeling from the shock of seeing two ten-year-olds caught on security camera abducting little toddler Jamie from under his distracted mother's nose.

'When I was five,' Birgit mused, 'I went to school on my own every day. I was given the money for the bus, which I caught by myself, and on the way home had to walk the last few kilometres alone through a dark wood. What is so different now?'

It is a good question. One answer is sensitivity to press coverage. If the harrowing murder of two-year-old Jamie hadn't recently been in the papers, it is unlikely that anyone would have thought anything of Ben contentedly pottering up and down. 'Do you know,' Birgit said, 'they weren't so shocked that he was playing on his own. What really scandalized them was that I hadn't heard of the Bulger case.'

When I was a child one of my favourite playgrounds was a stretch of countryside a few hundred yards from where I lived, called the Rifle Range. It was called the Rifle Range because that's exactly what it was: a practice area for the army. To be fair, I don't think shots were often fired, because the army only blocked access to it about once a year, though even then it was still possible for a child with initiative to circumvent the barriers. On Saturdays or after school I would roam at will, playing in the stream, befriending the horses or collecting acorns. Like most children of my generation, I was not required to tell my parents where I was in my free time, as long as I turned up for meals.

Years later, when I had a seven-year-old of my own, I took her on holiday to Norfolk. There was another girl of about her age visiting her granny, and the two of them disappeared through the churchyard and up the lane while we two adults had tea. 'Shouldn't we know where they are?' I said anxiously after twenty minutes or so.

'No,' said the grandmother confidently. 'They'll come back when they're ready.'

Why did I think my daughter needed so much more supervision than I'd had at her age? I never came to any harm, though I remember several alarming incidents: being followed on the common by a strange young man with wild eyes; being flashed at by a man in a mac on the way home from school on my bicycle; coming across a man tied up in a straitjacket wandering around the Rifle Range. He told me he was a soldier and was being disciplined by the army: for all I know he was an escaped lunatic. If I ever told my family, no one expressed any particular concern. But I know plenty of modern parents, particularly mothers, who would become nearly hysterical if their pre-teen daughters encountered such trivial excitements.

We now form an irrational *impression* of danger. One sweet, pretty little girl is horribly murdered, we read about it in the paper, feel as if we knew her, and react as nature programs us to do if someone in our immediate circle were to meet such a death: in other words, we conclude that our own children are in danger and we mustn't expose them to the same risk. What our emotions don't take into account is the fact that this child was one amongst millions of others who have remained safe and well.

Our reaction would be appropriate if the child genuinely were of our own acquaintance, since it would much more accurately reflect the risk. For instance, in the course of my life I have had three friends killed and several badly injured in car accidents. Most readers will also almost certainly know, or know of, someone who has been hurt or killed by a car. Cars are dangerous. But I neither know, nor directly know of, any child who has been abducted, kidnapped or murdered by a stranger, and if you do, you are unusual. Such occurrences are rare indeed. Strangers, by and large, are not dangerous at all. They have a strong instinct to protect small children, even those they are not connected to, just as we do.

It is not the risk itself, but the perception of risk that threatens children's freedom. It is well known that our fear of danger often bears almost no relation to the danger itself. Take the respective risks of transport by rail and by road. Road deaths are so common that ten people are killed on the roads every day in Great Britain, without any news coverage at all. Whereas rail injuries are so rare that every time there is a train crash it makes the headlines as a shocking occurrence, even if no one is seriously hurt. In the wake of such adverse publicity, rail companies are constantly undertaking to improve security still further (sometimes to an impossible

100 per cent'), disrupting services to pour even more money into rail safety. This is despite the fact that rail travel is so safe already that it takes ten million pounds of expenditure to save one more life, whereas the outlay of a mere hundred thousand will save another life on the roads. The topsy-turvy result of this is that rail becomes more expensive and less likely to get you to your meeting on time, so fewer people use it. They get into their cars instead, where they are thirty times more likely to be killed than if they were in the train.[3] Add to all this the fact that it benefits both rail and road travellers for more people to go by train and fewer by car (the more passengers, the cheaper and more frequent the train service will be; whereas the more drivers there are, the more traffic jams), and we see how daft it all is. It would be in everyone's interests (except a few motor millionaires) for some courageous politician to blow the whistle: 'Forget rail safety. Just make the trains cheaper, more frequent, more punctual and more comfortable, and lives will be saved anyway'. Can you imagine the outcry?

We are just as illogical over children's safety. Consider the tragedy that took place in the little village of Dunblane. One terrible day some years ago, Thomas Hamilton walked into a Scottish primary school and shot dead fifteen children and their teacher before turning the gun on himself. The act was so insane, so wicked, that parents up and down the country sobbed at the six o'clock news. But it is one thing to be moved to tears by sentiment, quite another to be moved to legislation by sentimentality. As a result of campaigning after Dunblane, the possession of handguns became a criminal offence in Britain. But the law should be governed by reason, and reason fuelled by facts. There was never any evidence that changing the law regarding handguns would increase safety, and indeed, since then, shootings from handguns have increased.[4] Whereas reducing the speed limit by a mere 10 miles per hour in residential areas can reduce accidents to children by a massive 70 per cent.[5]

In both instances we are going to a great deal of expense, bother and annoyance in the name of safety, without actually making our lives any safer at all. With a more logical, less alarmist approach we could not only enhance the quality of our lives, but also be safer.

Now of course most parents are far too busy to rampage about the countryside campaigning about public safety, so we're probably not going to do much to change government policy on rail safety or the merits of speed limits versus the banning of handguns. But we can have a huge impact on our own children's lives, by resisting the irrational fears of the society around us.

As soon as the GP confirmed that Serena was indeed on the way (though he didn't call her Serena, but Ethelbert: Ethel for a girl and Bert for a boy), we said we wanted her born at home. A few years earlier I had been buttonholed on the King's Cross to Cambridge line by a wildly enthusiastic father fresh from his child's home birth, and he drummed into me for the entire hour that the journey used to take in those days, that we mustn't take no for an answer and that everyone had a right to have her baby born at home.

Well, the horror stories abounded. Everybody's mother and aunt and sister-in-law said we were taking a terrible risk. The kind doctor confessed that one of his colleagues had a child brain-damaged because it was born at home. Eventually the other partners at the surgery insisted we be struck off and reproached him for continuing to see us. It was nerve-racking stuff, and we would have been pretty reckless not to have had second thoughts.

But I remembered the father with the mad enthusiasm, and some distant memory whirred into life, prompting me to contact an organization[6] that not only told us how to cut through all the red tape, but how to research the risks properly. And what do you know? It is, statistically, considerably safer to have your baby born at home.[7]

Of course, like all statistics, these must be intelligently interpreted: the ones we read at the time included, among the hospital births, mothers who had planned to be at home but had to transfer to hospital because something unforeseen went wrong (and who are therefore obviously high risk); but they also included amongst the home births children who were born at home by accident because the mother was too disorganized to go into hospital (similarly high risk). Other statistics may be slightly skewed in favour of home births because women who opt for them tend to be healthy in the first place. But the point is that there is probably not much in it, from a safety point of view. Certainly the popular image of home births being far more dangerous is wildly inaccurate and probably based on the folk memory of most babies being born at home at a time when all births were more hazardous. Modern medicine has made birth safer, wherever it is.

It was wonderfully liberating. We could do what we wanted. Yes, it might go wrong. But any birth might go wrong. If it did, we need not carry a burden of lifelong guilt that we had made an irresponsible decision.

(We also discovered, as a bonus, that post-natal depression is almost unheard of amongst women who give birth at home. Having now had all ours born at home, I find it hard to imagine what persuades most mothers to endure the hideous bossiness of hospital unless there are compelling medical reasons. Well, no, that's not quite true. Our last midwife told us of a mother of five who went in half an hour before her youngest was born and discharged herself twenty minutes afterwards, on the grounds that she'd rather dirty someone else's sheets. Fair enough.)

There are plenty of activities that carry a risk. But they may not carry any more risk than abstaining from them, and may even involve less.

Having been raised in Cambridge, where all the inhabitants, rich and poor, young and old, student and don alike, travel by bicycle, I have brought up all my children to do the same. Everywhere, in all weathers and all clothes and all conditions, and more to the point in the cyclists' death trap of London streets. Naturally I have taken reasonable precautions, bicycling with them when they were young and meticulously teaching them that every bus contains a suicidal old lady determined to step into their path, and every parked car hides a concealed driver with his head down who wants nothing more than to sit up suddenly and open his car door into their faces, and that everyone, but everyone, is blind to cyclists except the policeman three hundred yards away who spots you going over the red light of a deserted pedestrian crossing. Since I don't know a single London cyclist who hasn't been hit by a car I assumed that, despite all this careful training, I must be preparing at least one of them for an early grave. But riding a bicycle is fast, free, healthy and doesn't kill other people. So, true to my instinct and the philosophy of this book, I persevered with stubborn disregard.

Then one joyous day a few years ago, I heard an item on the radio. Those who learn to ride bicycles as children, it said, have a longer life expectancy. Even taking into account those who are run over and killed on their bicycles, the health benefits are such that these are more than cancelled out by all the Lycra-clad lunatics who don't suffer from road rage, obesity, sedentariness, being struck by lightning while getting into a Mercedes and so forth. Rah rah. I don't need evidence to justify my eccentric prejudices, but it's nice to have it nonetheless. Another goal for maternal instinct. And freedom.

We know that it is our responsibility, as parents, to keep our children safe: the urge to do so is so strong it is sometimes almost overwhelming. But if we don't bother to think through what genuinely poses a threat to our children, we are likely to expose them to danger when we should be protecting them and, far more frequently, to lock them up when they could run free.

You might not think it to look at the average statistician, but statistics can be extraordinarily liberating. For instance, many parents might be nervous of allowing an eight-year-old girl to nip to the shops. If you asked them whether they would feel the same of a twenty-five-year-old man, however, they would look at you as if you were mad. And yet he is ten times more likely to be attacked than she is.[8] Just as, the day you marry, you move in with the person most likely to murder you in your bed, so the day you give birth, you put your baby into the arms of the person most likely to kill her: there is far more chance of you harming your child than of the stranger in the street doing so.[9]

I know, I know. This is getting to be a bit like the Irishman who always took a bomb in his hand luggage for safety; when asked why, he pointed out that, whereas the chance of there being one bomb on an aeroplane is around one in ten thousand, the chance of there being two is one in a hundred million.

Nevertheless, when we look at the figures we realize that the likelihood of anyone's abducting and harming your child or mine is so small as to be negligible. We think we can't let them play in the fields or the woods or the park unsupervised. But it is far more dangerous to bundle them into the car.[10]

With any children's activity or event that makes us nervous, we need to ask ourselves three questions. How high is the risk? How serious is the risk? And how much will they miss if they can't do it? Take travelling in a car without proper restraints, for instance. Is your child likely to come to harm? Well, several dozen children are killed every year because they are not in proper car seats, so although it's very unlikely that your child will be one of them, there is a slight but significant risk. Second, would he come to serious harm? Very much so: he could be killed or seriously maimed. And last, does it curtail his freedom to be strapped in when he travels by car? No, not in the slightest. So it's inexcusable (and illegal) not to put our children into proper child seats.

But what about going down to the park on her own and playing on the swings? She is not going to be abducted, so we won't even waste time on that. She might get run over if there is a road to cross, so you need to make provision for her to cross it safely. Which leaves us with the threat of her falling off the play equipment, a risk for which more and more play-grounds are being modified or neutered or even closed down altogether. How likely is it to happen? Almost inevitable, I'd say, given the average child. And how much will it matter? Hardly at all. She might get a grazed knee, a sprained wrist, or, if she's very unlucky, a broken tooth. This last would be a shame, especially if it involved expensive orthodontic work one day, but it's hardly the end of the world. Two of mine have knocked out their front teeth, and you wouldn't know it now. On the other hand, what will she miss if we don't let her go? Independence, exercise, a chance to meet friends, a healthy afternoon in the fresh air, a life of freedom.

If you must, tell her not to accept suspicious-looking packages from strangers on the way, especially if they have sizzling fuses and the letters B-O-M-B on them. Nor to get into a limousine with blacked-out windows and a man with a shotgun and shades in the front seat. Particularly if there is an elderly man in the back who is talking like Marlon Brando. She'll probably forget as soon as you've told her, so it won't matter much. But let her go for goodness' sake.

Some years ago we were on holiday in Ireland, in a rural area almost devoid of traffic. The children were aged eleven, nine, eight and six. The first morning there we gave them some sandwiches and a bottle of lemonade in a back pack, told them not to swim, not to split up and to come home when they were ready. Some hours later Bink and Ben drifted in: Alex had stopped to look at a butterfly (which, in Alex's case, could take hours), so Serena had gone back for him. An hour or two later Serena returned, having searched for him in vain.

Alex was eight years old, in an unknown country and an unknown area. It is always nerve-racking to lose a young child, but being rational we knew that he was not in great danger. Or rather, I thought I knew this until I stupidly asked in the post office, as worried parents do, whether the region was a dangerous place for a child to get lost.

'I'd say so', the postmaster replied, sucking air ominously through his teeth. 'A little girl got lost somewhere in Ireland, ooh, twenty years ago or more, and it's said that she was never seen again ...'

Anyway, the long and short of it was that Alex kept his head, and spent several hours working his way down the road, meticulously inspecting every lane and track until he could eliminate it as not being the one that led to our cottage. By this scrupulous method he would eventually have tracked us down if we hadn't found him first, wandering along, twiddling his hair in the early evening sunshine. He saw us, started to run, and for the first time allowed the tears to fall in blessed relief as he admitted to himself how frightened he had been. A generation or two ago every child had experiences like this, and from them learnt resilience and initiative, how to overcome fear and handle an acceptable level of danger. And since then he has made rather a thing of getting lost, turning up at odd moments in almost every railway station from Newport to Newport Pagnell, but he seldom lets it get him down.

I remember, at the age of five, approaching a policeman by the seaside because I had forgotten the way home (and I also remember how difficult it was to shake him off again once I realized where I was; he insisted on taking me right up to the front door). My cousin can recall, on the same stretch of beach, swimming out too far one morning at the age of eight or so and being convinced he was going to die as he battled back against the tide for what seemed a good half hour. On another occasion, when I was about four, my playmate and I spent the morning secretly sliding on a swimming pool frozen over with a quarter of an inch of ice. When my father found out his heart skipped a beat, and he had the bottom of the pool gate boarded up so we couldn't wriggle under it any more. After that we climbed over the top instead.

Show me the modern children who can relate similar episodes, poor things. Unless they are old-fashioned enough to play rugby or go kayaking, the biggest thrills they are allowed to experience are the artificial horrors of a white-knuckle ride or a scary movie or a violent computer game. No wonder they take to nicking cars and driving them into things.

I have a theory that, just as exposing them to some germs makes them healthier, so allowing them some danger actually makes them safer. It seems to me that all of us, and particularly young people, have an innate need to experience a certain amount of risk. We have a hunger for the adrenaline it gives us, and find the excitement exhilarating. There is an obvious evolutionary advantage to this. In order to be safe in later life, we need to learn to negotiate danger, to weigh risks and know how to handle them early on.

But this means that if we keep young people too safe, that hunger will go unsatisfied, and they will have a yearning for something, anything, that carries a certain amount of danger. Now, some risky activities are good for us. Provided rock-climbing or steeple-chasing doesn't disable or kill us, we will usually be glad we have done this kind of activity: it gets us out into the open air, develops team work and stamina, and generally turns us into good chaps. But if we deny children these activities they may find other dangers that are not nearly so wholesome: promiscuous sex, drug-taking, drunk-driving. These things can harm or even kill them without doing them any good at all. (Yes, all right: any activity that kills us isn't doing us a great deal of good. What I mean is that, unlike mountaineering or windsurfing, these things aren't much good for us even when they *aren't* killing us.)

A few years after the discovery of AIDS a survey was taken of teenagers across the European Union. It revealed a fascinating trend. One finding was that their second biggest fear (after a third world war breaking out) was of catching HIV or AIDS. The next was that almost all of them knew how HIV was transmitted and how to avoid catching it. And the third discovery was that, despite this, the majority of them had had unprotected sex. They deliberately engaged in an activity that they knew caused the very thing they were frightened of.

Some years ago when there were renewed calls to abolish fox-hunting, I was commissioned to go on a hunt in order to write it up. I managed to persuade Serena, who was fourteen and very right-on about the issue, to come too. She disapproved, naturally, as any fourteen-year-old would who has never been hunting, but couldn't quite resist the idea of a day galloping about the Somerset moors. It was a hair-raising day, and once or twice I wondered how I would tell Shaun the news when Serena broke her neck. But by the time I sank into a hot bath at the end of the day, shaking so much with cold and exhaustion that I was spilling a stiff dram into the bath with one hand and tea with the other, I firmly believed that if all the teenagers in the country went hunting once a month there wouldn't be any delinquency left at all. Why would you need to go joy-riding if you'd just been thrown over a five-bar gate into a ditch and nearly trampled to death?

Serena (later joined by Bink) went to a secondary school a couple of miles from home, so when she started I decided to bicycle with her until she got the hang of the route and the traffic. A week or two after term started I met another mother, whose daughter had also just begun there, who lived in the next street from our house. I offered to accompany her daughter too, until the two girls were sufficiently independent. She politely refused, telling me she had no intention of letting her daughter out of her sight. 'I'm planning to take her and pick her up every day,' she said.

'Until when?' I enquired.

'Until she leaves school at eighteen.'

I wouldn't be surprised if that deprived child is now vine-jumping in the jungle, or more probably having unprotected sex with her boyfriend and popping Ecstasy pills.

Recently the Roman Catholic Archbishop of Westminster gave a talk on being fulfilled and human. Having outlined three fairly obvious traits of modern society (that we are emotive, consumerist and individualistic), his fourth criticism was that we never want to take risks any more. We expect life to be 100 per cent safe. It seems to me that this fourth characteristic, just as much as the first three, is a symptom of a culture that has lost faith in God. If we have nothing to look forward to beyond this life, the prospect of leaving it is terrible. We will do anything to avoid it. And the thought of losing our children to an unknown future is too dreadful to bear.

But life is not safe. If we try to make it so, we diminish it to something less than it is, and less worth having. We end up putting our children in a cage, which makes them no safer and only serves to make us feel better as we look at them in their gilded captivity.

Before I had children I read a book by a missionary who said that he never aimed to keep his children completely safe. He then recounted various incidents of them falling off roofs and having alarming accidents on the mission field. I was shocked, and couldn't imagine how a parent could be so casual about his children's lives. Twenty-one years and five children later, I agree with him. One day our children will die. We hope and pray that it will be after us, and for most of us it will be. But it will still happen. If we bring them up as if they could be safe from death, we are bringing them up with a lie. Making ourselves face losing them, and then letting them take that risk, teaches them one of the most important truths of all: that, with God's protection, death does not have to be such a terrible place to go.

When our daughter took two dozen (rather old and ineffective) sleeping tablets in an attempt to get proper treatment for her illness, we were subjected to intense emotional manipulation. Various professionals, including a close friend, told us that any teenager who does this once will do it again, and she needed to be secure in hospital. How would we live with ourselves if we didn't take the proper precautions? Where we succeeded many years earlier – resisting the pressure put on us, in order to have her born at home – we failed this time and gave in. I believe it to be the biggest mistake we've ever made, and it took nearly two years to undo the damage again.

It is a dreadful thing to threaten a parent by saying that, if you don't toe the line, your child might die. The only answer is, 'Yes, she might. We have weighed the risk carefully, and consider it worth taking.'

If I had to draw up a list of modern dangers to children that parents should beware, it would go something like this:

1. Laziness
2. Lack of initiative
3. Loss of spirit of adventure
4. Late lie-ins
5. Leaflets that you get free at the doctor's from the NSPCC, telling you whether or not your mum giving you a bedtime kiss is child abuse (No kidding.)

And remember, most accidents take place in the home. So, obviously, it's safer outside.

Go on. Let them go.

Maturity

A few years ago the daughter of friends of ours embarked on her gap year. Her mother told me that she had expected to find it heart-rending, the prospect of her eldest daughter leaving home for months on end. When it came to the crunch though, she welcomed it: her daughter had come of age, it was time to spread her wings, and her mother was happy to wave her goodbye. Her explanation at the time was that this was because she had always been a full-time mother who didn't go out to work, so she had spent plenty of time with her children as they were growing up. She had no regrets about the wasted years when the moment came for the eldest to go.

So of course, like mothers the world over, I was flooded with waves of guilt. I couldn't imagine ever being content to see any of my children disappear over the horizon. I was filled with horror at the thought of the house being quiet, clean, tidy and civilized one day, and I assumed this was because I'd neglected them years ago and I would pay the price for the rest of my life, with searing loneliness, an inability ever to move on, and permanent regrets that I hadn't done elementary crochet and advanced finger painting with them when they were in nappies.

My friend's children are slightly older than ours, and I now know exactly what she means. Serena has had her gap year, and I was the one who encouraged her into the Malaysian jungle out of reach even of the eponymous email. In fact, I was rather disappointed that she couldn't become properly cut off for months on end, as we did at that age. Now she is away at university, and though I was more delighted than I can say the other day when her lectures were cancelled and she unexpectedly took a train home for the afternoon (presumably to catch up with her dog), I don't miss her with that agonizing hour-by-hour wondering and picturing and imagining that I went through when the boys went to boarding school before they were teenagers.

There is something right about it. There comes a moment when you don't worry any more. It's partly to do with age, more with responsibility, but most of all with her having got herself to where she wants to be. She has set herself goals, and achieved them against the odds. She knows what she wants to do, and how to do it. The other day she rang me for advice, and despite the seriousness of the topic, after I put the telephone down (naturally having rung her back, because mobile telephones cost a fortune and it has to be our fortune not hers), I realized what the feeling was. It was freedom. Mine, actually, not hers. I had given her my opinion, and that was that. Even a year ago I would have felt the weight of responsibility for her decision pulling on my shoulders: had I impressed on her forcefully enough that she should do this or the other? Not any more. I feel for her and care every bit as much about her and love her as much as ever, but I don't carry her any more. That moment, the one that modern parents try to achieve far too early, has come. We are equals now, and that means we're friends. As far as I'm concerned anyway.

In my observation, the age at which this starts to happen is around twenty-one. It certainly isn't eighteen. Eighteen may be an appropriate age to start voting (indeed, some eight-year-olds would vote more sensibly than many adults), but as an age to mark the onset of adulthood it is daft. I certainly wasn't grown up at eighteen, and I don't know anyone who was. (Half our eighteen-year-olds still need several years of university fees, for goodness' sake.)

I wasn't fully grown up at twenty-one either, but I had accepted a proposal of marriage, travelled alone across half the world, and could almost mend a puncture on my bike. (That is to say, I knew how to persuade a bloke to mend it for me. Anyone but Shaun: I've never learnt that particular skill.) Twenty-one is a good age at which to celebrate the onset of adulthood. In good old-fashioned murder mysteries the heroine often doesn't come into her vast inheritance till twenty-five, and by this age I believe children should aim to be financially independent (though it's a vain hope for us: Serena won't even have finished studying).

But the day he is truly independent, the day she forms an attachment more important than her loyalty to you, the day they should and must leave home – if they haven't already, because she has work elsewhere or he can no longer stand the way you leave your mustard on your plate and don't recycle the wine bottles – is on their wedding day.

On that day, we really have to let them go.

············ Action Page ············

Answer the following multiple-choice questions:

1. How many children is the correct number to have?
   a. As many as you like.
   b. Four.
   c. As many as possible.
   (NB: the correct answer is 'Yes'.)

2. Your child wants to go bungee-jumping. Is this activity:
   a. Safe.
   b. Fun.
   c. Necessary.
   (NB: if your answer to any of these is 'Yes', you need psychiatric help.)

3. You need psychiatric help. Should you:
   a. Take a cold shower.
   b. Take up hunting.
   c. Tell Sigmund Freud to take a running jump.
   (NB: if your answer is not 'Yes' to any of these – Return to Go, do not collect £200 …)

4. Is Freud:
   a. Not a psychiatrist, dummy.
   b. Wrong.
   c. Dead.

Pain, Loss
and Deprivation

'There's only one thing I can't stand, and that is stress.'
Alexander

I am an incorrigible optimist.

When Prince Charles married Lady Diana Spencer, I prayed for a happy marriage … along with half the nation. When the tabloids started publishing photographs of them looking miserable and accounts of them cheating on each other, I told myself the papers will say anything and went on praying … and I was probably not alone. When they initiated divorce proceedings, I told myself what an encouragement their reconciliation would be to other couples with problems and prayed rather harder … no doubt as a member of a tiny and manically cheerful royalist rump. After the *decree nisi*, I insisted that there was still time for a reunion … almost certainly the only person left. It was not until she died in a French hospital that I finally admitted defeat. After that, I conceded that it really was not very likely they would get back together again.

Optimism is one of the advantages of being a writer. After all, even personal misfortune is good copy. A few years ago Shaun and I went to Istanbul for a weekend for a friend's birthday party. The guests all set off for Turkey and checked into various hotels. We had each selected accommodation according to our budgets, some going for ultramodern five stars with all mod cons, others for Imperial-style establishments with vast old-fashioned ballrooms; the Atkins' finances had stretched to the nastiest, most cockroach-ridden dive in the entire capital. We arrived on Thursday night (after everyone had dutifully voted in the General Election) and spent Friday sightseeing, bumping into one another, and having the skin scraped off our backs in the baths by – I swear – exactly the same fat, naked attendant who had poured scaldingly hot water over me two decades earlier when I hitchhiked through Istanbul on my way to Nepal.

So far so good.

We went somewhere wild for dinner, danced on the tables, drank the local poison, and eventually, at one a.m., happy and exhausted, all split up again to collapse gratefully in our various luxurious bedrooms. The only snag being that when Shaun and I managed to track down the alleyway where we thought we had left our boarding house, we found our cases outside in the street, a manager who couldn't speak any English, and a distinct impression that we were not going to see our passports again. I was in my element. If I'd wanted nothing interesting to happen to me, I would have stayed in London. And if nothing goes wrong, what is there to write about? The only fly in the ointment was that Shaun seemed to find it rather distressing.

I am the same wherever we go. Last summer when, as a family, we were riding an unguided trail in Donegal and we got lost, cast a shoe, dropped the map, ran out of food miles from anywhere, and our horses sank in bog up to their shoulders, instead of bursting into tears I was thinking how ripping it would all sound in the article I would write when I got back to my desk. No doubt it is a most annoying trait, but it keeps me cheerful through the most unpropitious circumstances.

And I have found it a most encouraging attitude to take in bringing up children. I reiterate my writer's motto: Disasters are Great Copy. It is as true of creating the characters of our children as it is of the people in a story. Everything in a writer's life can be used in the shaping of a better book. And everything in the life of a child can be a positive factor in shaping a stronger future. Some of the most successful people have had the worst childhoods, and it is often the very awfulness of their early experiences that has spurred them on to momentous things. I recently read of a girl whose mother died when she was five. Though of course she was heartbroken and missed her mother dreadfully, she later saw it as the event that made her life. Her teachers were especially kind to her, took particular care of her, and nurtured her in a way that enabled her to achieve great things when she was older.

For most of his life I have watched one of our children overcome the challenges the Almighty chose to give him, and which society unthinkingly compounds. Inevitably I have wondered whether the inexplicable hurdles he has faced have anything to do with the fact that our lovely midwife, who successfully delivered two of our others with skill and expertise, on her own admission made an error of judgement in her instructions to me over the timing of his birth. It begs the question, if I could ask God to take us back in time so we could get it right … Well, it doesn't beg the question at all: any parent would give her eye teeth to take away her child's difficulties.

And yet, and yet …

Because of his struggles he has grown unbelievably strong. He is now the most emotionally robust person of his age I know. He has coped with his sister's illness in some ways better than anyone. He has been misjudged so often that he is now independent of the opinions of others. He has tried to fit into society's mould for so long that he has realized the futility of the task and thrown the mould away. Though I have frequently had worries about his immediate future, which often seems clouded in mystery, I don't worry about his long-term welfare at all. He has the unmistakable stamp of a survivor. He knows how to care for others even if he is occasionally slapdash about looking after himself. He may forget to go to bed but he will never forget to love his wife and children. I know it is partly thanks to the challenges he has overcome that he has become such an extraordinary person. I would never have had the courage his Creator had, to put the grain of grit into his shell that has caused him so much pain. But the pearl he has produced with it is without price.

And I have no doubt whatsoever that, when she is finally out the other side, the same will be true of our daughter and the illness she has endured.

God bowled her a ball that was fast and hard, and for a moment it almost looked as if it might hit the wicket; but even now he is watching her gather up her strength, as he must have always known she would, to hit it back again, for six.

Not only does every cloud have a silver lining, but if we didn't have clouds, our gardens would dry up. And a childhood in which nothing went wrong would be a woefully inadequate preparation for the rest of life. Think of it as inoculation. When Jenner realized that a relatively mild ailment, cowpox, could immunize us against a far more serious one, small-pox, he discovered a principle that applies to more than infectious diseases: a small problem, overcome in childhood, strengthens us to withstand far greater challenges later.

Bereavement

His children had no pets at all. Not even a goldfish. Certainly not a dog or cat. I assumed this was because they didn't like animals; but one day, while making a big fuss of our new puppy, my friend told me his own children had always longed for a dog themselves.

'But I couldn't do it to them,' he explained. 'It might die, and that would be devastating.'

I was astonished, particularly as I admired him greatly as a father: sensitive, affectionate, and always stopping work by teatime. But of all the reasons I have heard for not allowing children to keep pets, this has to be the worst. Children need minor bereavements, to give them practice for the major bereavements they will experience in adulthood.

Modern life is unusually sanitized, and contemporary children have little acquaintance with death. I'm not advocating the reintroduction of infant mortality so we all learn how to lose a sibling or two. But death and the hard disk crashing are the only certainties here on earth, and we have to prepare our children somehow.

I experienced two bereavements as a child. The first was the death of my brother's dog. I know one shouldn't speak ill of the dead, but Prince was about as revolting a specimen of canine life as it was possible to be.

He had been hit by a car as a puppy while making an injudicious dash across the road, and as a result he walked with a limp, loathed exercise and was grossly fat. This last was exacerbated by the fact that we lived in a school and all the pupils fed him their tuck. He rewarded this generosity by offering to amputate their fingers for them, and a week into the first term of my father's headship Matron ran clean out of sticking plaster, thanks to Prince. He also had an extremely hospitable porous-border policy regarding the vast population of crawling asylum seekers living under his fur. But when he died I cried my heart out. With a fortitude and stoicism remarkable in one so young, I bravely continued with school, despite the fact that all the clocks had stopped. And what do you know? I recovered.

Sobbing buckets at the death of an animal is an essential element of our emotional education. It is short-sighted to protect children from it. It is also unnecessary. Though they often seem more upset than the adults, it is usually for a much shorter time. Just as when a child's bone breaks or his skin is grazed it seems to heal more quickly than a grown-up's, so they often bounce back more easily from events that we consider traumatic.

When ours were all small we acquired an ex-guide dog called Clint. He was quite a character, was Clint. Shaun had said for some time that he would like a dog to exercise, though he hadn't bargained on the embarrassment of having to call 'Clint' across the park. He needn't have worried. Clint was uncannily like Prince in the extra-curricular section of his CV. The first and last time we tried to take him for a walk he read our minds like a psychic as dogs so often do, and sat down at the gate to await our return. Nothing could budge him. His only interest in life was food. On his first day as a guide dog he ate all the canapés at a wedding while the guests were still in church; his previously proud owner was so embarrassed that he bunked off his own sister's reception. And at Clint's first communion he accompanied his master up to the rail and made short work of the wafers when the vicar's back was turned.

When the day came for him to ascend to the great Dinner in the Sky I took the children with me. The vet was shocked, but not nearly as shocked as when I said we all wanted to accompany him. I didn't mean into heaven, but into the little operating room where he was to have the injection.

It was one of those occasions, which we parents must sometimes man-fully endure, when one simply has to brave the disapproval. The receptionist said she thought my children might find it upsetting. The vet even hinted that it might distress the dog. They both clearly took a dim view of my position on the Richter Scale of Compassion. But I was paying (rather a lot) for the procedure, he was our dog and they are my children, and who is the expert around here anyway? So we all trooped in, the vet lifted Clint onto a table, and as his great overfed body slowed down and his doggie-bone-dazed eyes began to close, Serena stroked and talked to one end, Bink patted the other, Alex asked interminable questions and Ben closely inspected the poster of the anatomy of a gerbil on the wall. I can't think of a more beautiful way for a dog to say goodbye to all the bowls of Pedigree Chum (and communion wafers) he would never see again this side of the Jordan.

And after they got home, for the rest of that day, the children played a fascinating game of getting-the-dog-put-down. In fact, I think they played getting-almost-everyone-put-down: guppies, horses, policemen, goodness knows what. They didn't seem the slightest bit upset. Maybe they were, deep down, and this was how they were handling it; but I suspect they weren't. So either we had brought into being four monsters who were as hard-bitten as Cruella de Ville, or this was nature's and a child's way of coming to terms with the harsh facts of life in a far more natural, effective and healthy way than years of bereavement counselling and happy pills at the taxpayer's expense.

The other loss I experienced, when I was thirteen, was that of my grandmother. This may sound shocking, but her death didn't upset me as much as Prince's. I have no idea why. I was very fond of her, and still am. I revered and respected her greatly, and was even more admiring of the strong, talented, unusual woman I knew she had been long before I was born than of the frail, crippled octogenarian who lived with us. But I didn't cry at all when she died. In fact I was puzzled and rather embarrassed. My parents had sent me to spend half term with a friend, presumably because they had known Granny was dying, and my friend's mother had to break the news to me and wait politely for me to show some emotion. I had none to show. I had said goodbye, I knew I wouldn't see her again even though no one had told me, and I was somewhat mystified and even miffed that I had been sent away so tactfully. It wasn't the fashion then for children to attend funerals either, so that was that. It's a shame. I wanted to tell my parents that all their precautions were unnecessary. I would have liked to have been there when she died, but it wasn't the thing. Silly really: my father must have been infinitely more upset than I was, so it would have been more logical to send him away.

Most of us can take the death of a grandparent in our stride. We are designed to. We know they'll be dead before we are grown up, or before we're middle-aged, anyway. What is going to knock us off balance is the death of our parents. Our grandparents' death is the obvious childhood dry run: as with so many things, we see our parents handle it, then we know that we will get through it ourselves, somehow, when it happens to us years later.

(Though we should, of course, allow for the possibility of its happening sooner than we think. Parents must make provision for children in the unlikely event of their premature death. Though we have many wonderful friends, we had to think long and hard about this. We obviously wanted guardians who would continue to bring up our children in the same Christian faith. And as we had four quite noisy and energetic children we thought it wouldn't be fair to approach anyone whose family would be swamped by ours. Martin and Nicky Bailey, a clergyman and a doctor, have five children whom they have brought up flawlessly as far as I can see. They never raise their voices to them, they explain everything meticulously and courteously, and when Serena went out for a meal with them recently she recounted the event in amazement to us later, describing the quiet and wonderful manners all the children showed towards each other. Martin and Nicky generously agreed to being specified as guardians in our will when our children were small, and we explained to the children the arrangement we had made in case we should both die. The enthusiasm with which they greeted this piece of news was rather a blow. We could almost see them calculating whether they would more easily get away with pushing us under a Number 22 or putting arsenic in our tea.)

Happily, we are not likely to die yet. But we should not prevent our children preparing for adulthood by shielding them from all sorrow.

Children are survivors. I know we can all remember one upsetting thing that happened when we were five, but think of all the hundreds and thousands of upsetting things we can't remember. Well, obviously, we can't think of them because we've forgotten them, but that's the point. We get over them. And getting over them is what helps us to grow up and get over bigger upsets later. Just as we shouldn't protect children from every germ or they will grow up catching everything, just as we shouldn't keep them from minor risks in case they rush headlong into worse danger, so we shouldn't shield them from every upset lest they grow up emotionally stunted. We will suffer loss, if not as children then as adults. And if not as children, it will surely be harder when we are adults.

Material want

'You need to bear in mind that, if you don't have any money, your children will learn from a very young age how important money is.'
Serena

Being headmaster of a prestigious choir school connected to an ancient university, my father had some pupils whose parents, or indeed sometimes whose whole families for generations, were distinguished household names. Usually this was because of some intellectual or musical achievement, but in one case it was because they were a well-known banking family. Their accolade was being rich. Their son had everything. He was even engaged to me, briefly, when we were both six, and you can't ask for much more than that, can you? He did have much more than that, however. He had *his own Dalek*. A real, full-size one. I'm not sure that it actually threatened to exterminate him (presumably his dad, or rather his nanny, had to hide inside it for it to do that), but even so it was pretty impressive.

My father used to invite every pupil in his final term to his study for a chat, no doubt to discuss in extensive detail the meaning of life and how to hitchhike around the galaxy, but also so that he could write some kind of report to tell the boy's next head a bit about his new charge. As was his wont, therefore, he asked this particular boy what his interests were.

'What do you mean, sir?' he replied.

'What are your hobbies? What do you do for fun, in your spare time?'

He has never forgotten the reply from this poor little rich boy. It was the saddest he had heard in all his years of teaching. He had no leisure pursuits, no hobbies, and nothing he did for fun. The answer was quite simply, 'Nothing, sir. I don't have any interests.'

He lacked for nothing, this boy. Presumably he had never known what it was to be without, to desire something, to ache for it and puzzle how to get it and work for it and eventually achieve it. Everything he wanted, he had. And if ever he wanted something new, he had that too as soon as think of it. So what was the point in anything? There was nothing to strive for, nothing to accomplish, nothing to want and nothing to get. No wonder he ended up interested in nothing. (And, though this may not be in any way connected, I read in the papers a few years ago that, despite a beautiful wife and lovely children, he had come to an end even sadder than his beginning.)

An obvious characteristic of parenting is the way we want our children to have those things we longed for and lacked. As I've said, I passionately wished I could have learnt Latin and Greek at school. And guess what? My children have all had *amo amas amat* and λμω λμειζ λμει drummed into them since the cradle. I also deeply regretted that my parents didn't push me to become more proficient at music; surprise, surprise, all ours started learning a musical instrument before they could read or write. This doesn't matter much with harmless activities like Ancient Greek or playing the euphonium; in some cases it can even be a positive step, if you wish your parents had listened to you more attentively, or made the effort to attend your lacrosse matches. But we have to beware. The child-centred learning revolution of the 1960s presumably came about because grown-ups could remember being endlessly bored by mental arithmetic on dreary Wednesday afternoons. But instead of pointing out to themselves that they had got through it without any permanent, long-term damage and perhaps it is quite handy to be able to work out thirteen and a half hundredweight of Seville oranges at sixteen shillings and fourpence ha'penny per furlong, we scrapped the whole lot and now look at the mess we're in. No self-discipline and we've lost the Empire.

The current orgy of materialism inflicted on our children is a form of parental self-indulgence. We wish we'd had this, that or the other, so we get it for our children, thus robbing them of the privilege of longing for it themselves. I'm amazed when I hear a parent say he hated hand-me-downs or second-hand uniforms and so is determined his child won't suffer the same humiliation – partly because I can't quite believe anyone can be that weedy, but more to the present point because of the folly of assuming he didn't benefit from wanting something better, and that his child won't too. That early mortification is doubtless the reason why he's now running the biggest stockbroker firm in the City; if he'd had an easier ride he'd probably be a bearded teacher in sandals teaching Welsh literature in a provincial university.

Every year, when the newspapers start running Yuletide stories round about August, one hears afresh of the disgusting amount of money thrown at defenceless children at Christmas time. As we all know, when we were young we considered ourselves fortunate to get an orange in a stocking every leap year, shared out between all the cousins. But nowadays any child who hasn't received a Playstation of his own (whatever that is), not to mention all the gizmos, computers and mobile telephones he already has, is below the official poverty line and will probably be taken into care. What beats me is where it all goes, given the size of the average house. We live in a rambling Victorian vicarage, and if the information that the press gives us on the average child's Christmas is accurate, we have always been Scrooge-like to the point of child abuse. But we are still hard pushed to find space for all the toys we've acquired over the years, some barely used and one or two still in their wrappers. There's a child's loom somewhere we've never got the hang of, and a paper-making kit some kind relation gave us, which I got out one guilty afternoon and spent hours trying to put to good use, while the children were off outside doing something much more interesting like jumping in puddles or making a go-cart out of a few twigs and half a dozen insides of loo rolls.

Give them a break. They don't need all this stuff. There is a balance to be found, naturally, but before buying the telephone, trainers or latest gadget it's as well to ask ourselves a few pertinent questions: Is it necessary? Is it educational? Is it worth it? Will she be better off without it? (And finally, if the answer to all these is no: Will *you* enjoy playing with it?)

We all love seeing our children in gorgeous clothes surrounded by lovely things, and it's one of the luxuries of being a parent. But be in no doubt: money is a good servant but a terrible master, and if we enslave our children to it by giving them everything they want, they are the ones who will pay in the end.

Tension and strife

'Every child should be allowed to keep pets. Preferably a proper house pet like a dog or a Vietnemese pot-bellied pig; but if this isn't possible, then at least a hamster or even a fish. Why? It's obvious, surely.'
**Serena (Erstwhile owner of fish, hamsters,
guinea pigs, rabbits, snakes, rats, cats, hens, cocks, bees,
ducks, quails, rabbits again, and currently a Great Dane)**

'No child should ever be made to live with another child's pets.
Especially not a Great Dane.'
Bink

My best friend at junior school never argued with her brothers. What, never? That's what she told me, anyway, and I never witnessed anything to justify doubting her word. I *did* doubt her word, but only because I thought it so unbelievable, not because I was ever presented with any evidence. 'Even in the car?' I can remember saying to her, incredulous. I suppose we were about seven or eight at the time. And I simply couldn't imagine a car journey without the awful noisy build-up between us that always culminated in my father asking, as if anyone would ever want to do such a thing, why we didn't look at the lovely scenery instead. I mean, honestly. If any reader can find me a seven-year-old who genuinely prefers admiring a stubbly field with a cow in it to arguing with her brothers and sisters and asking 'are we there yet', I'll send you a fiver.

I thought my friend very fortunate. And still, all these decades on, I am pretty impressed with the achievement. If you can bring up several children who never disagree with each other, I think it's amazing. Indeed, if you can enable anyone to live in the same house as anyone else for years on end without them ever getting on each other's nerves, I salute you. More to the point, if you are one of those couples I've read about in fairy tales who never have a cross word for each other – well, what can I say? Anything is possible. One day we will have tamed Mars and inhabited other galaxies. I believe you, really I do; I just can't imagine it.

What I don't believe is that the rest of us, mere human beings, are in a hopeless case. Take quarrels between siblings. A friend of mine has two sisters. One of them he doted on as a child, perhaps because she was considerably older than he; with the other he scrapped all the time, possibly because they were of similar ages and temperaments. But now that they are adults it is the younger one he rings every week or two and whose children his children play with, whereas he sometimes goes a year or more without talking to the older one. I also know a married couple who came from very different families. He never argued with his brothers and sisters, who rather hero-worshipped him, whereas she had grown up bickering with her sisters ever since she could remember. Five years into marriage, however, he had almost lost touch with his siblings while she was still seeing hers regularly. We usually quarrel most with those we love the most.

I'm not advocating arguments in the family, any more than I advise you to bump off the family budgerigar so that your children have the benefit of surviving bereavement. I'm just saying they may not be such a bad thing in the great scheme of things: sibling rivalry, competition, even animosity, may be an important part of your children's emotional upbringing. How are they going to practise for marriage, if they never disagree with their brothers and sisters? How will they resolve more serious conflict later, if they have never pinched one another under the table and then said 'sorry' afterwards? How will they negotiate a pay rise if they've never negotiated a turn on the swing?

One of our sons keeps his possessions meticulously tidy, actually filing bank statements in a folder and keeping all the letters he has ever received in a shoebox under his desk. (Or he did, until an unimaginative *au pair* recently threw them away in a fit of tidying. All his childhood letters in chronological order. What a plonker.) The other makes Pigpen from *Peanuts* look neat, and considers it a stain on his honour if he can see the floor. One of the cruel and ironic twists of fate of which life is so fond is that they share a bedroom. And yet I have been watching, amazed and profoundly gratified, as they have spent the last few days reorganizing the room together and deciding how to entertain their friends in it. Children learn skills for a lasting marriage by practising on their brothers and sisters.

And by watching their parents. My grandfather-in-law, a Presbyterian minister and one of life's veritable sages, used to say he wouldn't marry an engaged couple who'd never had an argument. He considered it essential for their future survival that they should have learnt how to resolve conflict. In the same way, children who have witnessed their parents kiss and make up know that there is still a lifelong love affair the other side of the first row.

Boredom and underachievement

Whoever abolished boredom for children?

You remember what it was like. One Saturday afternoon you found yourself kicking stones around the garden, with nobody to play with and nothing to do, and no desire to read any of the books in the house. It was the most achingly awful, heavy, dull feeling and you didn't know how to get rid of it. So you rooted out your mother from whatever she was doing, and you said, 'I'm *bored*.'

'Right,' she replied brightly, 'you can start by doing the washing-up, then you can lay the table for supper, then do your recorder practice, then I'll teach you blanket stitch, and finally I'll get a typewriter down from the attic and you can teach yourself touch-typing so one day you can be a secretary and when you're grown up you'll never be out of work.'

And you took a solemn vow that, if you lived to be a hundred, you would never again suggest to your mother that you had time on your hands.

And the next time? There probably wasn't a next time, because as soon as you felt that familiar feeling again you looked around for something to do so you wouldn't have to learn shorthand and typing and lay the table. You built a dam across a stream, climbed a tree, found a friend, wrote a poem, visited your granny, fed mud and worms to your baby sister, scrawled graffiti on the local cathedral – you did something, anything, but you found an activity to do. And out of that awful boredom you discovered your love of drawing, or people, or cooking, or a certain writer, or cats, or stamps from the Philippines with birds on that only have the left wing showing. Or simply that you could occupy your own time and didn't need someone else to do it for you.

Now look at the children around you. Morning, noon and night their time is spoken for. They are expected to do homework before they are old enough to study alone. They have baby gym before they can walk and swimming before they can crawl. They are learning French before they've mastered English and have flash cards waved at them before they can speak, let alone read. They do ballet on Monday, trumpet on Tuesday, tennis on Wednesday, Scouts on Thursday, German conversation on Friday, and riding at the weekend. There is nothing wrong with any of these activities. Each one is excellent in itself. But when do the poor things have time to get bored? If they should find a spare moment anywhere in their schedule, they will be given a video or a computer or an organized trip to the park.

Do we think Shakespeare was entertained in this way? Would Einstein have had any time for relativity if he had been occupied every hour of the day? Would Jane Austen have started writing to amuse herself and her family if she'd had a cupboard full of videos?

Of course children benefit from opportunities. But provided they know where to find paper, pencil and crayons, are introduced to music, have a patch of outdoors to play in, and are given unlimited access to books –

and cardboard, loo rolls, string, Sellotape, Tippex, glue, and all the other things they can use to wreck the furniture – and provided they go to school or receive some other form of education for the lion's share of the day, then what children need for some of the time is to be *left alone*.

If they occasionally tell you they are bored, you have not failed as a parent. You are not obliged to entertain them. You are not the all-singing, all-dancing act. You are the people who provide them with emotional security, food, clothing, housing, a decent education and a moral map to show them right from wrong, not an around-the-clock children's party.

To assume children need occupying all the time is not only stultifying but profoundly insulting. They are already fully engaged, simply growing up. When Rosie was born, Alex (who considers some of the world's most flashy and successful people to be cerebrally challenged, and feels profoundly sorry for Bill Gates on account of his low IQ) was deeply impressed with her intelligence. She was a few days old, you understand. I rather rudely said she wasn't doing very well at advanced calculus, and he pointed out that she was working out what a ceiling is, which is much more difficult. Since then I have noticed how very busy she is. She is never idle. Her current ambition is to walk, and we have had to abandon the high chair we were using because she wouldn't even eat, she was so determined to stand up, turn around, hold on to the knobs on the back of her chair and spend the meal balancing first on one foot, then on the other. If I spent half the time and effort at my desk honing my writing skills, or indeed learning the bagpipes or practising real tennis or anything else, as Rosie does hauling herself to her flat little feet, hanging on to a piece of furniture and pointing her little tippy-toes, I would be a genius. And we think babies need flash cards. When would they ever have time to waste on our stupid flash cards?

Children have plenty to do. And just as they need time to teach themselves to walk and talk, so they need leisure to assess how we relate to one another, what our moral values are, how we are supposed to behave towards those in authority over us or those more vulnerable than we are, what to do when life seems unkind and dangerous, and much else besides. It may look to us as if they are just playing cops and robbers, cowboys and Indians, doctors and nurses, or mummies and daddies, but how do we know they aren't sorting out the morality of the judicial system, the rights and wrongs of imperialist policy towards indigenous peoples, medical ethics, and how to solve relational issues?

Far better to allow them the odd day or two of boredom than to inflict on them the modern alternative. When Serena was nine I was sitting with her in the doctor's waiting room, when she idly picked up a leaflet, as one does, on 'Coping with Stress'. It contained a mini-questionnaire to help you ascertain how overstrung you are, giving a spectrum of choices, from 'Not too bad', via 'In urgent need of psychiatric intervention', to 'On the point of throwing yourself off the Empire State Building NOW!!!' Serena, in all seriousness, ticked the second highest stress level for herself. Aged nine.

That was when I realized that my children were in danger of being burnt out before they got halfway through secondary school. They were coming home with homework from the age of five, and by the time Serena picked up the leaflet at the surgery she hardly had any free time. When was she supposed to *reflect* on all the things she was being told at school? We seem to want them to achieve more but think less, to have increasing amounts of information but a neglected intelligence, to be crammed with more and more facts but given less and less education, to be impressive rather than to be wise. It is a retrograde step.

When I was at school there was one girl who always swept the board when it came to tests, exams and reports. I shall call her Jane Turner. She came top of everything. After a year or two we hardly bothered to listen when results were read out, because if there was a prize to be had, she had it. When I left the school to do my A-levels elsewhere, Jane Turner was still the star pupil. When I got to university, however, the only other girls from my previous school were two who had never shone at anything. They hadn't been quite such dead losses as I had, always way out at the bottom, but they had been pretty mediocre. Certainly there was no Jane Turner there. Then about five years ago I bumped into her again. Her name was immediately on my lips, because I had heard it so often read out in some merit list or other, and before I'd even thought about what I was saying I told her I always remembered her being best at everything, and asked what she was excelling at now. To her eternal credit, she said, 'That was it. That was the extent of my achievement. I've never done anything notable since.'

People who have changed the world have not, generally, been the ones who have been able to show off a frightening number of different accomplishments at a young age. The world-famous botanist turns out to have been the dunce in the corner who failed all his exams but was always pulling earthworms out of his pocket and studying them under the desk. The millionaire entrepreneur is the one who left school at sixteen and started his own business. While the blissfully married mother of six who, arguably, has achieved more than anyone, was probably the one who bumbled along in the middle of everything, unnoticed by everyone.

When I left school at eighteen the headmistress read out all the leavers and their destinations, starting with the Oxbridge girls, then those going to the redbrick universities, then the polytechnics and colleges, and finally the hopeless cases who weren't going anywhere she had heard of. The one who was read out last of all in our year was going into cooking with her mother. Ten or fifteen years later, when most of the names had sunk without trace, hers was emblazoned on the spines on the cookery shelves in the bookshops.

It may be great for our egos when our children achieve, and when it happens we should glow with pride; but make no mistake, such success is about as important as a footprint in the sand before the tide comes in. It may make us feel we are doing the business when we ferry them about to activities from dawn to dusk, but it isn't necessarily the best thing for their development.

Provided we are giving our children the basics of a good education and a smattering of extracurricular opportunities, a little idleness and underachievement may be no bad thing at all.

Failure

We have a wonderful and much loved friend, adored by all our children, who is, by all accounts, pretty hot stuff in the City. Everything he touches turns to gold, and the horses he backs romp home every time.

I know nothing whatsoever about money, but I believe all glowing accounts of him, for a simple reason: he has the confidence of someone who succeeds. Some years ago, our friend decided to learn the guitar. After the cigars and port have been cleared away, give him half a chance and he will take the instrument out of its case, blow the dust off it, eschew tedious details like tuning it up, and give you his three chords with as much gusto as you ever heard in your life. He is, quite simply, the worst guitarist I have come across, in a varied career mottled with bad guitarists. In fact, his guitar-playing is only surpassed by his singing. Last Christmas Benjamin thundered out an appropriate piano accompaniment to his vocal rendition of 'The House of the Rising Sun'. Appropriate not only because he is Ben's godfather (though I'd better not give any more clues in case he should recognize himself), but also because they were perfectly matched in terms of musical accomplishment. They finished a page and a half apart and in different keys. It received a standing ovation. We have talked of it ever since. Friends who missed it are planning on queuing early next year.

It genuinely gave great pleasure. Why? Because he is so comfortable with himself that he is happy to do something imperfectly, not to impress anyone else but just for the sheer fun of it. Another friend of mine has a motto: if something is worth doing, it is worth doing badly.

All of our children play musical instruments. (Apart from Rosie; but give her a chance.) None performs to a high standard. Sometimes, when they were younger, I would hear other people's children playing the violin or the piano with superb technique, stunning musicianship and tremendous application, and be tempted to wish that my children could play half as well. But then I realized what a mistake this was. I have a number of friends who have graduated from music college and then, for one reason or another, put their instruments aside and hardly touched them again. Whereas, amateur though we are, we still play music together.

On our first holiday in Ireland Shaun and I visited a pub one night and happened to tell the children on our return that there had been live music there. The next morning Bink, aged nine, stomped into the pub, sought out the landlord and asked if she could provide the music the following night. He readily agreed. The whole of that day and the next was spent so industriously in rehearsal, that if you happened to wander down the lane in the valley far below, you could hear the arguments echoing all around the mountainside; quarrelsome squawks sparking out of our little cottage like the spells shooting out of the chimney and windows in Walt Disney's *Sleeping Beauty*. But they managed to put together enough jigs, reels and dances to perform for a whole evening, remunerated with unlimited Coca-Cola, crisps and chocolate bars on the house. In fact a British couple, who chanced to live about a mile away from us in London, heard the music from across the road and came in to hear the authentic Irish ceilidh.

Since they don't have to earn a living at it (though they have been given the occasional fee, since that night in Ireland, for playing at weddings or parties), they don't need to perform as professionals. They simply need to play well enough to enjoy it. If it doesn't cause too much suffering to others it's a bonus. In the last couple of years we've also taken up singing: Shaun, who had never read a note of music before, is learning to read the tenor part, with the occasional prod in the ribs from Alex. Even really simple four-part harmony is quite easy on the ear, at a family gathering or party. Especially for those older members of the family who are deaf.

I passionately believe all children should learn music, as young as possible. I've never yet met a child who doesn't love singing; nor one who isn't musical enough to play an instrument. And yet we seem to think music is only for the especially talented. If a friend of yours were teaching her child the alphabet, you wouldn't dream of saying, 'Goodness me, is she very literate?' If you know a child who is learning his five-times table, would you ask his parents whether he happened to be particularly mathematical? We recognize that every child should learn how to read and add up, whether he has an aptitude for it or not. So why do we say, of a child who is learning to read music or play the cello, 'Do you think she's very musical?' Does she have to be, to earn the right to learn?

There is a pernicious culture of excellence abroad, undermining our standards of mediocrity. I blame the television. There was a time when a bunch of lads would kick a football around the village green. Now, if they can't play like Beckham, they think it must be better to stay at home and watch someone do it properly on the telly. Nonsense. Far better to go outside oneself and mess it up. And better to be a second-rate musician deriving pleasure from it all life long, than a genius who never plays.

I don't want my children to ski to an international standard or play tennis at Wimbledon. I want them to have enough fun to do it. And I want them to have the confidence to do it badly, and not mind at all.

In addition, I want them to feel free to try things and fail at them. I know parents who can't bear their children to be unsuccessful at anything. One was telling me that her son was choosing his A-levels. 'He wants to do maths,' she said, 'but he's no good at it, so we've got to dissuade him somehow.' I know we are a society driven by results, but this struck me as a dreadful shame, so I asked her whether it mattered if he did it badly. 'I think it would knock his confidence,' she said. This told me far more about her than about her son. It's true that a poor A-level might blight his chances at certain universities, but it shouldn't be a blow to his confidence, if he knows he is no good at it but decides to go ahead anyway. On the contrary, it should be a terrific tribute to his self-esteem, if he felt able to do something simply because he was interested in it, knowing he wouldn't impress anyone else. His mother's confidence, of course, might be a different matter.

We must allow our children to fail. If they never know small failures when they are young, how will they cope with larger ones when they are older? When I was at drama school our teacher told us that one of the worst things that can happen to an actor is too much success too young. The same is true of us all. Life is never smooth from cradle to grave, so sooner or later we will have to learn to cope with some of its rough patches. Like every lesson, this is learnt more easily when we are young.

At our children's school was a boy who was good at everything. He was captain of several sports, leader of the school orchestra, head of school, and in his final term was given nearly every prize on offer by a headmaster who should have known better. His was not a fate I would wish on anyone: he was leaving junior school as the all-round superhero of the hour, and going on to a senior school of over a thousand boys where he would be nobody. His tale is not uncommon. A friend of mine tells me she used to succeed in everything she ever turned her hand to. That is, until she was in her mid-twenties. If only she had failed her piano Grade II at the age of eight, her driving test at seventeen, or her Cambridge entrance exam first time around, she might have had more preparation for the sadness of finding she couldn't conceive.

Several of the people I most admire did not get into their first choice of university the first time around, spending an extra year or even two before succeeding where they initially failed. I consider this every bit as impressive as getting the desired result the first time; and just as character forming as learning to be content with one's second choice.

In his refreshing, invigorating and sadly out-of-print book *The Myth of Neurosis*, Dr Garth Wood explains how human beings derive some of our deepest and most satisfying fulfilment from overcoming difficulties. If we want our children to be happy and successful, we should not encourage them to avoid problems. Instead, we should welcome the chance for them to embrace challenges head on, fail, pick themselves up, and try again. Bink thinks it soppy beyond belief, but I love Rudyard Kipling's poem *If*. Whenever I have made a real pig's ear of something, I quote whatever part of it happens to be relevant to my latest bosh-up, and tell myself the experience will help me to become a man ...

I have often wished I could do away with my children's difficulties, but I have never wished away the positive lessons their difficulties have bestowed on them. As with any learning curve, part of the secret is making it steep enough to be challenging without making it so steep it is off-putting. We would not want for any child discouragements too great for him to bear, family breakdown, severe handicap or loss of a parent, for instance. But when these happen, do not despair. Apply the principles in the first section of this book. Give them as much love and encouragement as you can muster, and help them to overcome it.

Most of us overprotect our children. We don't want them to suffer, we don't want them to fail, we don't want anything to hurt them and we don't even want them to be bored for an hour or two. And it is endearing that we are so concerned. But real life has pain and suffering and failure ... though I admit I can't quite remember what boredom felt like.

No childhood is perfect, and thank goodness it isn't. Because a perfect childhood would be a highly deficient one. What kind of preparation would that be for the rest of life?

You know those cheesy fitness instructors who tell you to 'feel the pain'? What is a horrendous idea in physical exercise is not a bad motto for childrearing. There will be pain, for your children. Feel it. Help them go through it. It will enable them to emerge stronger the other side.

Action Page

If your child has a genuine and significant disability, not something trendy like mild dyslexia or the attention span of a goldfish (I'm not knocking these, really I'm not. I have both. And please don't write to me defending the goldfish: I know it is a highly intellectual animal really), then you are exempt from this Action Page because you've done it all already. Otherwise:

1. Take a look at this list of essential ingredients for a real childhood, and ask yourself whether your child has:
   a. A pet. Preferably a proper one. A hamster is better than nothing, but better still a dog or a cat or a llama.
   b. A musical instrument. Ditto. I don't mean ditto as in a hamster is better than nothing – trying playing a hamster, and someone will rightly and properly ring the RSPCA – I mean ditto as in a proper instrument, not a mouth organ, jew's-harp or ocarina. Or descant recorder, actually. (OK, fair enough: like the hamster, it's better than nothing. And, yes, if it's played properly it can be sublime. After all, recorders have been played in the courts of kings: if they always sound so awful, why didn't the musicians get their heads cut off? Come to think of it, that's a good question: why didn't they?)
   c. Some activity that he or she is absolutely no good at, whatsoever, but does for the sheer fun of it. (Unless it's the recorder. Whatever else parents should put up with for our offspring, listening to a badly played recorder is a sacrifice too far.)

2. Take steps to supply any missing items. (Except . . . no, I won't say it. Enough. I will never mention recorders again.)

Morals, Manners and Etiquette

'Children should be seen and not heard is a very silly rule.'
Bink

'Sounds like a good rule to me.'
Serena

The current theory is that children grow up into teenagers and rebel against their parents' values. This is tosh.

Let me modify that. I concede that children do usually grow up into teenagers.

Caught or taught?

A few months ago I was taking part in a discussion on *Woman's Hour* with a well-known television presenter. We were discussing teenage rebellion, and he said his son was going through it with a vengence. Wine, women and song, with a few extra pints of beer thrown in, were the theme of his current refrain.

And what did his father do when he was that age?

'Much the same, I suppose,' he admitted.

It's not much of a rebellion then, is it? On a mutiny scale of nought to ten, I'd say his son ranks a pretty soppy minus two. What greater tribute could he pay the paternal example than to put his own feet straight into his father's footsteps?

Children catch our values as surely as they catch a cold from us. Two friends of mine were at music college together. Later they both got married and, coincidentally, had sons at the same time. Both maintained their musical careers, and both valued happy family life. However, they had subtly different priorities. The distinction was so slight an observer might not have noticed it, but it became evident when both families went away for the weekend together. One of the fifteen-year-olds was extremely disciplined in his music practice, spending several hours on his scales before he came down to help around the house, by which time most of the work was done. The other had brought his instrument with him, but first washed up in the kitchen and helped with the cooking, by which time there wasn't much leisure to play music. Similar though their upbringing had been, the two boys had picked up dramatically different subliminal messages: deep down, their mothers wanted distinctly dissimilar things. Both would have given verbal consent to the same ideals, that they would like their sons to be good musicians and pleasant people. But the first mother, if she could have had only one gift from her son's fairy godmother at his christening, would have opted for musical success; the second would have chosen good relationships. And each received exactly what she wanted in her son. I would lay a bet, if such things could be measured, that in ten years' time the first will be the better musician and the second the happier family man.

Who knows how they imparted their priorities to their offspring? Our own behaviour sets the tone in so many tiny and imperceptible ways that we could never itemize them all. But in a way it is quite a relief. When it comes to giving moral values to our children, we are right back to where we were in Chapter One. It is not so much what we do or say, but who we are, that has an impact on our children. Sometimes when I am trying to prompt one of my children to do her homework or another to work at his music practice, I am struck by a blinding Damascan light and realize where I am going wrong: if I left them alone and went into my study to meet my own deadlines, it would have a more compelling effect on their self-discipline than anything I could say. (The revelation never lasts long, however, and soon I am neglecting my work to 'encourage' them again.)

A positive role model lasts for life. A couple of years ago, when we were coping with our daughter's illness at its worst, when the demands on our time and patience were relentless and everyday life was harder than I would have believed possible, there was one thing that kept me going. When friends asked me, in various different (usually cryptic) ways, how we managed to keep going and why we didn't just give up on her, my mind always went back to my parents. 'They would have done more than this for me,' I thought. So I could do it too.

There are two methods of imparting mores to our children. We can give them information, and we can set them an example. It is not that the giving of information doesn't matter or isn't important. It can be a very effective way of teaching something. But the more profound the attitude we are trying to engender, the more it is communicated by living it; the more superficial the behaviour, the more it can be passed on simply by prescribing it.

Etiquette, for instance, is a trivial quality, easy to pick up and easy to teach. I read an article last year about a down-on-her-uppers Scots aristocrat who teaches etiquette to American gold-diggers during a weekend houseparty in the howling Highlands, and good on her. Hold your knife like this, drink your dry sherry like that, and you'll have a silicon billionaire within your clutches in a fortnight. Or even, should you want such a liability, an English lord. It is not necessary to have been brought up with the correct etiquette in order to use it: you can pick it up as easily as IT skills – or, if you're as dippy at computers as I am, much more easily.

Genuine manners are more deeply ingrained. Your children *can* learn consideration towards others later in life, just as they can learn French: by applying the rules, learning the vocabulary, working hard and making the effort. But obviously their manners will come more easily to them and be more graceful if the language has been spoken all around them, all their lives. Boys who have seen their father treat their mother with courtesy since they were in the cradle are likely to show respect towards their girlfriends.

. But morality is like music. Great musicians have usually been surrounded by music in the womb. It is in the air they breathe from the moment they are born. Amadeus caught it, like an infectious genius, from Leopold; Johann Christian from Johann Sebastian. In the same way, the lodestar of parental moral example has a terrifically strong magnetic pull: often without realizing it, our children will imitate us in all sorts of ways of which they, and we, are not aware.

It is one of the greatest compliments they pay us.

Morals

Consider some of the issues that parents worry about. We are always hearing it said, in discussions about sexual health or unwanted pregnancy among young people, that we cannot teach them, 'Just say no.' It doesn't work. They are bound to say 'yes', goes the current wisdom, so we should put all our energies into telling them to use a condom. But this is simply not true. Parents who said 'no' themselves before marriage are frequently successful in passing on to their own children the benefits of abstinence, particularly if they have positive and attractive reasons for their own behaviour and are able to talk openly with their children about it. I know plenty of young people who have decided to wait until marriage because they have been convinced by their own parents' reasons for having done so.

Does this mean that, if we had a wild and promiscuous youth, our children are necessarily programmed to do the same? Not necessarily: it is also possible for them to learn from our mistakes, if they genuinely believe we would do it differently if we were to start again tomorrow (though it is much easier for them to learn from the behaviour we get right than from what we get wrong). But what no teenager will be persuaded by is the hypocrisy of a parent who sowed his own wild oats with no remorse at all, and now thinks his daughter should be as chaste as the driven snow.

7. Morals, manners and etiquette

This is such an extreme example that we would all hold our hands up and protest that we would never do it. But we do, we do. When she was in the lower sixth, Serena used to write a weekly column in the *Express* in which she gave a teenager's view of the world. One week the government was inventing yet another trendy initiative to persuade youngsters to be less promiscuous. A bit rich, was Serena's reaction, considering the behaviour of plenty of adults, including a prominent member of the same government who, at the time she was writing, had both a wife and a mistress. We are constantly hearing forty-something journalists on chat shows discussing what we ought to do about the shockingly high rate of teenage pregnancy, without ever making the connection that the strongest influence on today's youngsters is the example set by yesterday's.

Or take the question of drugs. Again, we are frequently being told that 'all young people do drugs'. Again, this is just not true. The majority of teenagers don't. Most bright teenagers can work out that if someone bothers to classify something as illegal there may be good reason, that if they get sacked from school for criminal activity it won't enhance their CVs, and so on. The fact that something is against the law is a good enough reason for not doing it. Teenagers can understand, respect and obey such a prohibition. But it is not reasonable at all if they know that the parents who are being self-righteous about a twist of cannabis are the same parents who cruise down the motorway at eighty miles an hour – which, let's face it, is far more dangerous, antisocial and potentially devastating in its consequences. If the law is not compelling enough to dictate our behaviour, why on earth should it dictate theirs?

If we want our children not to steal, we have to be scrupulous in our dealings with the taxman. They will find it hard to respect their teachers if they constantly hear us criticizing our employers. If we would like them to treat us well, they need to see us treating their grandparents well. And if we don't like them craving the latest brand of designer trainers, it would be as well for us not to covet the latest car. In our children, we are likely to see our own hidden values embodied.

We often think we react against our parents' example. I have a friend who claims she is resolutely strait-laced because her mother was so embarrassingly unconventional; another goes out of his way to be affirming because he feels his father didn't give him enough confidence. These examples, however, do not contradict the inherited fundamental principles of morality. My friends are not rejecting their parents' ideas of right and wrong; often they are actually reinforcing them. Take the father who refuses to let his son go away to boarding school because he hated being away from home as a child. He, like his father before him, is simply trying to find the most appropriate education for his son. He is not rejecting the underlying ideology on which he was raised (that the right educational environment matters) so much as reinterpreting the modern outworking of it.

But what about the proverbial 'black sheep'? The layabout son of a hardworking father, the promiscuous daughter of chaste parents? I have friends, for instance, who are honest, scrupulous, trustworthy and conscientious to the last degree; to their great distress, their only daughter steals anything she can lay her hands on and lies as often as she tells the truth. How has this happened?

Occasionally, this may be because of genuine mental illness, which can strike anybody, regardless of how lovingly and skilfully she has been brought up. But it may be because the parents have not fed their children's most basic needs and followed the principles laid down in Part I of this book. If, in his early years, a child has felt insignificant, insecure or worthless, he may signal his distress by rebelling against the values his parents demonstrate.

Don't despair. Parenting is a long haul. Go back to first principles. Build up her security and self-worth all over again; keep teaching him how significant he is by rewarding his good behaviour. Persevere. At the moment, this twelve-year-old daughter of my desolate friends is a hair-raising little kleptomaniac. I very much doubt that she will still be pinching things in six or seven years' time; in a decade she will probably be a hardworking, honest and absolutely delightful citizen.

A child is like wine. You do all the right things: and then you wait. It is years before you know how good the result is going to be.

Manners

'I can't stand manners. They're just a waste of time.'
Bink

'Nonsense: manners are what stop us being foul to each other.
You fat-headed cretinous moron.'
Alexander

Morality is a matter of doing what is right; manners, of doing what is kind.

Manners are not absolute, in the way that morality is. If adultery is wrong, it is always wrong, regardless of what the society around us thinks of it. But when it comes to manners, behaviour that we might think shockingly rude can be acceptable elsewhere and vice versa. A couple of years ago we went to Pakistan for Shaun's brother's wedding. On our last evening there, we and the groom were invited to dinner by the bride's adoptive father, a clergyman and the most loving, kind and gentle family man you could hope to meet. Nevertheless, he was the only member of his family who entertained us: his wife and daughters, including the new bride, cooked and waited on us but did not sit at the table or eat with us. In London a man who presided over such a division of labour would be considered a cad of the first water. In Lahore it denoted no lack of respect or affection.

The outer form that manners take is shaped by the social environment and varies with time and place: it is continually changing. The inner consideration for others that powers those different manners does not: it is always constant. Fifty years ago an elderly gentleman would immediately have vacated his seat in a crowded tube train if a young lady entered. Nowadays it is the other way around, so a teenager with her wits about her would jump up for a senior citizen instead. The opposite behaviour springs from the same impulse: respect for more vulnerable members of society. In other words, it stems from thoughtfulness and kindness.

As with morals, the first way to give our children manners is to demonstrate them. It's extraordinary how bad we can be at this. Men who are courteous to a fault towards other people's wives and children can become oafs and boors in front of their own. I have a friend who is charm itself when he is out at a party or staying in someone else's house. He would be appalled, and very surprised, to be described as bad mannered. But visit him at home and watch him carefully. Or rather, watch his teenage children. Their mother cooks the dinner, brings it to the table, serves it, clears it away, and washes up. On her own. There is a wildly hopeful rota in the kitchen telling the children when they are supposed to be on duty to help. Their father can't understand why they never take any notice of it. I can. I overheard a family friend once ask the children to help their mother, to which one of them replied, 'Why? Daddy never does.'

But manners can be taught as well as caught, explained as well as demonstrated. Moral values run so deep that living them is far more important than talking about them. (It is, of course, a good idea to talk about our moral ideology as well as living it out, but discussion will only ever be the icing on the cake.) Manners, however, need to be reinforced by instruction as well as example. It's all very well being a brilliant letter-writer yourself, but if you don't also tell your children how and when to put pen to paper they may not pick it up.

Thank-you letters

The single change in modern manners that seems to distress the older generation most is the neglect of the thank-you letter. When I wrote a weekly question-and-answer column, this dilemma came up over and over again. Poor old Granny would scrape together her hard-saved widow's mites, research into the current must-have item, queue all night for the latest Harry Potter, wrap it up in jolly holly Christmas paper, make it into a parcel with old-fashioned brown paper and string well in advance, nearly bust what remained of her bank balance on the postage, send it off to Tristram, imagine his delight on Christmas morning … and then what? Nothing. Absolutely nothing. By February she still has no idea whether it even arrived, let alone whether he already had three copies and has now moved on to an ear-busting CD from Darkness. The same happened at his birthday, and the Christmas before that, and the one before that. Tristram has probably never heard of a postage stamp and doesn't realize there is human communication beyond the text message and the email, but Granny hasn't got either of these and she is close to tears. And I don't blame her.

I understand where Tristram is coming from, really I do. Modern parenting is like trying to juggle hot sausage rolls while pogo-ing the wrong way around a moving carousel, simultaneously listening to *Arithmetic for People Who've Forgotten it All* over the headphones and knitting the breakfast. The idea of adding letter-writing to the list of essential chores when you already owe your children three days of help with their homework and two weeks' laundry and five weekend treats and you haven't changed the bedsheets since spring, seems madness. My in-tray sometimes has letters going back years (I do get around to answering them all eventually, but usually only by writing off several weeks of my life and refusing to go on holiday until I can see the bottom). And sometimes, I admit, the older generation can be a little unforgiving. When ours were little, we went to the birthday celebration of a distant older relative. Not only did I spend hours arranging and then rehearsing 'Happy Birthday' for a string quartet whose combined age amounted to less than twenty-one, but when we got home I managed to organize each of them into writing a thank-you note. I was expecting to be nominated for Mother of the Year, but all I got was a raised eyebrow that it had taken three weeks for our thank-you letters to arrive. I ask you. I have no sympathy for this kind of churlishness. Nevertheless, bear a thought for tearful Granny.

So on Christmas Day no one, *but no one*, must open a present without your being there with pencil and paper to write down what it is and whom it is from. Yes, everyone does have to slow down a bit, which has the great side effect of making the whole thing slightly less manically, materialistically, graspingly ghastly. Then write off one day between Christmas and the New Year when the whole family sits around the table together and writes. Put it in the diary. It can be done. I say this in faith, you understand: one day we will succeed at this wonderful plan.

Other situations in which thank-you letters are absolutely *de rigueur* are nights spent under someone else's roof and the receipt of any presents, for any occasion, that were not handed over personally and opened in front of the donor with a verbal thank-you. They are also much appreciated for parties, dinners, all other presents, and indeed any effort that someone else has made on our behalf. And *replies to invitations*. For goodness' sake. How can anyone plan a party if no one replies? (Not that I expect replies to invitations any more. I omit the RSVP and take a wild guess. The friend who very kindly cooks for our parties would have torn out his hair by now if he had any.)

If all else fails, at least teach them to lift up a telephone. As I keep telling myself, she is just as busy as I am, and has cooked it, bought it, organized it or wrapped it somehow. I now give myself an ultimatum after dinners. If I haven't written a thank-you note by the end of the next day, I will telephone. I will. Really. I won't find time and a pen next week if I haven't found them today.

Table manners

Here is another common cause for complaint. No doubt this is largely because families don't eat together any more, so the poor things think that they are supposed to eat out of a trough like a pig or off a telly tray like a zombie. The very event of sitting up at a table with your children will teach them that plates are for putting food on, implements are for lifting the food to the mouth with, and human beings are for talking to. This should give you confidence to move on to the finer points.

One of these being that conversation is an art, requiring skill and practice. And that it is primarily to do with being interested in other people. I was deeply ashamed when our new *au pair* came with us to my parents' holiday home to help out. Within half an hour my mother had discovered something that had eluded me for the entire week she'd already spent with us, which was that she had recently failed an English exam and would love to have some conversational help before sitting it again. My mother had taken the trouble; I had not.

Although paying attention to someone else does not come automatically, as with most manners the basics can be devised through a few easy rules. You can write your own, such as: (i) Make sure that more of the conversation is about the other person than yourself. (ii) See how many things you can find out about him. (iii) If you get stuck, try asking what she does, where he went on holiday or what her favourite hobby is. Plenty of adults of my acquaintance could do with a bit of help like this.

Children pick the principles up quickly, rise to this kind of challenge and, if they are regularly reminded how to do it, will soon become charming and attentive members of the human race. One summer holiday some years ago, my mother organized a modest lunch party and invited a distinguished academic and his wife, who also have a holiday house on the coast nearby. Planning the seating imaginatively, as she always does, she put Alex, then about nine, next to the professor of theology, thinking that they were likely to find something in common. For the whole of the first course neither of them said anything. Just as we were clearing the plates, however, Alex – who had clearly been racking his brains all the while for a topic that might interest both his neighbour and himself – turned to him and asked, with no preliminaries at all, 'Do you think robots could be capable of independent thought?' The two of them were lost in animated conversation for the rest of the meal.

A dining table is an excellent place to teach children to attend to others' needs before their own. If you went to a snooty enough girls' boarding school (I didn't), you will have been trained to starve rather than ask for food for yourself. 'Would *you* like some butter, Laeticia?' is what the gels from St Trinian's say to one another when they want to butter their own toast, when the rest of us would yell down the table, 'Chuck us the spread, mate.' I know someone who thinks this is the most hypocritical thing she ever heard of: why not just say what you mean? It may not be coincidence that even her best friend thinks her children have the table manners of piranhas celebrating the end of an over-strict diet.

Any guidelines will seem contrived, because they are. But once a child is taught to act as though he is thinking of others, he will start to think of them for real. However artificial it may seem, going through the motions of attending to our neighbours before ourselves eventually teaches us to start thinking of them spontaneously. It is a mistake to believe that kindness must always start with a *feeling* of kindness. A kind *act* is quite adequate, and usually prompts the right feelings sooner or later. We know that we should, in theory, be ever watchful that those on either side of us have all they need to eat. But if you are as forgetful as I am (and many children are), it's easier to remember to ask them whether they want the gravy every time we want it ourselves. Again, I sometimes wish half the adults I eat with could be taught this simple rule. By being taught to behave as though they are considerate, children will become considerate, as surely as night follows day.

Clothes

Surely children can wear what they like? If what we wear is entirely superficial and doesn't harm anyone else, doesn't this mean it couldn't matter less and should come under 'Freedom of choice', discussed earlier?

Yes, usually, but not always.

We were going to a wedding, and on the way called at the house of a delightful, somewhat loopy university don and his extremely socially correct wife. They were going through a spot of Lord Emsworth regarding his wardrobe. He was clinging on to his tatty old corduroys and sports jacket with the leather patches on the elbows. His wife was trying to squeeze him into his morning suit. It was tempting to see his lack of vanity as delightfully eccentric and smirk at his wife's bossy nagging; surely no one would have taken offence at his ghastly garb. But she was right and he was wrong. As she pointed out, the bride's family had gone to considerable trouble and expense, and it was a very special day for them. The least their guests could do was put on their glad rags and make it a colourful celebration. (It's not as if he didn't have a morning suit, which would have been a very different matter.)

When we are someone else's guests, we should dress appropriately for the occasion. Every year my father takes his grandchildren to the pantomime, just as he was taken as a child. I can't remember what we usually wear, but last Christmas someone wanted to wear jeans, so I insisted on a telephone call to my parents to check this was all right. It was, of course, but it was still right to ask: my father organizes the outing months in advance, is unburdened of a small fortune for the tickets, runs up and down the aisle buying us all ices in the interval and has to endure our shouting 'Behind you!' incessantly for the entire evening. His guests can jolly well take his feelings into consideration when deciding what to wear.

If others have invited us out we should dress with them in mind. It is courteous to take trouble over our clothes, as an acknowledgement of the trouble they have taken over our food or entertainment.

The second reason why clothes matter is because they can affect our behaviour. Some years ago, just as Serena and Bink were getting to the age when they might show an interest in frocks, my mother found some moth-eaten old dinner jackets in the attic. The millennium was coming up, so we decided to dress for dinner on New Year's Eve. And we discovered an extraordinary thing. As soon as we put Benjamin in a dinner jacket, dress shirt and black tie, his manners became as formal as his outer garb. He started handing drinks round. He pulled chairs away from the dining table – not to cause us all to fall on the floor with a bump, ha ha, as he might have done the night before, but to enable the women to sit down … yes, even his own sisters. He stood up at the end of the meal and proposed a toast to the cook. It was really rather frightening.

This is why some businesses abandoned Dress Down Friday after brief experimention: they found that when their employees wore casual clothes, they displayed a more casual approach to their work. By contrast, the other Saturday Alex wanted to get lots of homework done, so he got up early and put on a suit, tie and cufflinks. I know Alex is a law unto himself, but he did get more done that day than he has in many a weekend.

Funnily enough, it seems that the clothing principle applies more to boys than to girls. A few years ago I visited a school where the boys were allowed to wear what they liked, and they were all in jogging trousers, trainers and hooded sweatshirts, slouching about in corners with their shoulders hunched. Whereas the school our daughters went to had no uniform either, but they were very workmanlike about it, wearing sensible clothes that reflected their sensible behaviour; they were also spared the bother of working out how to wear a bottle-green gabardine skirt of the regulation length in such a way as to stand out from five hundred other people in bottle-green gabardine skirts of the regulation length, which was what we had to do at school. But then girls are more individualistic and take pride in their appearance anyway, whereas boys respond to uniform and like to conform. And I'm not sexist at all.

The third reason why clothes can matter is that they affect how others treat us. As any man who has ever tried hitchhiking knows, if you wear a suit, you are far more likely to be offered a lift. Some years ago I had a problem with a hospital procedure and rang Shaun to ask him to come in, and the first thing he did was to change into a suit and tie so he would be taken seriously. This obviously harks back to the class memories of an earlier generation, when the people who were considered more important dressed in a certain way, but that is neither here nor there. The relevance for our children is that they deserve access to this information.

Just as they should know that some language or behaviour is not appropriate in certain situations, in front of certain people, so they should be aware of the language of garments. Most of the time children should wear what they like. But when they are invited out by someone else or turning up for an important interview, we owe it to them to let them know that there is a code of courtesy in their clothing that their contemporaries may not be aware of.

Chivalry

Alex has a ploy when he has a seat in a crowded tube train and a woman enters. By the standards of today, he believes it can be just as rude to stand up and offer her his place as to stay put while she stands. Or, perhaps more to the point, she is as likely to slap him around the face as smile graciously and sit down. So instead of saying, 'Would you like to sit down?' he gets up and hovers somewhere. The shortcoming of this technique is that a fat pinstriped stockbroker will then sit in his seat instead. And I think this subterfuge a shame, because the joy of having a door opened for you is not that you don't have to open it yourself – after all, an automatic door never brought a smile to the face of a girl – but that someone considers you worth opening it for.

I have tried to bring my sons up to be shamelessly chivalrous. In their case it wasn't difficult, because one is quite chivalrous anyway and the other loves spending money, so if I tell him he ought to treat a woman rather than expect her to go Dutch he welcomes it as yet another opportunity to relieve me of my cumbersome cash. And I firmly believe that any sensible woman would rather have a humble cup of tea bought for her, than to have to chip in anything towards a slap-up five-course meal.

Yes, I know many of the reasons are outdated and women earn as much as men, but I still find that a man who stands when I enter the room is invariable far better looking than one who doesn't. And the original reason is still there, in Genesis 3: men are stronger than women, and have the power to dominate.

Bringing them up to care for their sisters makes men feel strong and women feel cherished. It is hopelessly, outrageously, archaically old-fashioned.

And it works.

Respect

It wouldn't go amiss to teach our children one or two other things, for instance, how to use titles. I don't mean aristocratic titles: the fact that Lady Diana Spencer, Princess of Wales, was never, and never could have become, Princess Diana (ouch: it's like a nail across a blackboard just writing it). Yes, it might be handy if one's children should know this, though almost all the British media *still* get it wrong, even now. But if you don't know how to use a title, just don't use it, unless you want to look like a complete bumpkin. Better to call an earl simply Tom and be thought a *Guardian* reader. (In fact, this is quite a good solution anyway, as it is pleasantly friendly and egalitarian. Provided his name is Tom, of course. Otherwise you really do look stupid.) But all this comes under etiquette, which we shall come to in a moment.

I was actually referring to commoners' titles, which are still in the realm of manners, being, as they are, a token of respect. Children should use them. (So should a lot of adults, actually; including anyone working on a geriatric ward. It's humiliating enough, I imagine, to be given a bed bath at the best of times, without being called 'Ducky' or 'Love'.)

The simplest rule is always to address someone older than you using her title and surname, Mrs Jones, until she tells you to call her Suzie. Churches are very sloppy in this regard, with tiny tots using everybody's Christian name like the great big happy family it is, and very jolly it is too. But anywhere else beware, as it can irritate. Teach your children to err on the side of formality. Excessive reserve never annoys: excessive familiarity does. And if they grow up to become insurance salesmen or financial investors it will lose them a lot of business. Would you buy life assurance from a man who calls you John? I never do.

I think it's still meltingly charming when boys call adult men Sir, and quite a good wheeze the first time you meet your girlfriend's father, but I never quite had the nerve to teach my sons to do so: they could so easily come across as smarmy.

Talking of which, men should of course walk on the traffic side of the pavement when accompanying women, which is fun to teach your son when he is five and you are thirty-five. 'Why, Mummy?' 'Because you're so big and strong,' you say, bending down to his level, 'that you can protect me when ...' Whoosh: another ten-ton articulated lorry tears past, spraying him head to toe with mud.

Etiquette

'Etiquette, then. I can't stand etiquette.'
Bink

Etiquette is entirely culture-specific. What is right for the Masai is wrong for the Innuit, and what is acceptable in a rugby club changing room might be eccentric at a Buckingham Palace garden party. There is, of course, a great deal of overlap with manners: a good etiquette book will contain considerable information about what is kind and considerate. But there is inevitably an element of etiquette that is simply there because it's there.

It's pretty arbitrary, relatively pointless, and its main purpose was probably originally to define your pedigree, which nobody cares about nowadays anyway and if they do they can mug up their Nancy Mitford. You know, if you say 'sofa' and 'napkin' you come from the now extremely unfashionable middle classes. If you say 'settee' and 'serviette', your granny was probably a parlourmaid and you are doubtless excessively proud of her. If you say 'looking glass', goodness knows where you come from (certainly nowhere I've been) and you're probably eighty-fourth in line for the throne. But none of this holds much water now: good grief, I heard an Etonian mother say 'uni' the other day – and she was talking of Oxford – so nothing can be trusted any more.

But rules of etiquette are less harmful than shooting up heroin, more fun than bridge, and my mother taught me various things I've found invaluable since; so don't feel embarrassed about telling your children how to address an envelope to a Duchess, what to do with a marrow spoon or how to wear spats. Random table etiquette includes all sorts of fascinating details, such as tipping the soup dish away from you to scoop up the last bit (unless you are at sea, Bink tells me); not using butter at dinner, according to Shaun (I've no idea why); nor of course having soup spoons or fish knives, because they were invented so recently (the latter under George III, I seem to remember, not that I was there) that it suggests your silver is horribly modern. The definition of a gentleman is supposed to be that he uses the butter knife when breakfasting alone, and of a Cordon Bleu cook that she decorates the butter with parsley in similar circumstances ... though a Cordon Bleu cook told me you should *never* have parsley at breakfast. I knew that; of course I did. And did you know that 87 per cent of men, if left alone with a tea cosy in a room unobserved for five minutes, will put it on their heads? How did they work that out? Hidden cameras? Suddenly one understands why bishops wear those daft things: they've been left alone with tea cosies for too long.

Enough. Buy an etiquette book and have fun.

• • • • • • • • • • • Action Page • • • • • • • • • •

It's easy to be polite to the rich and powerful: even the heathen are well-mannered towards those they think will invite them back to dinner. The real test of courtesy is whether it is given to the vulnerable and insignificant. Real manners are extended even towards little children.

When you are with a child try to do the following:

1. Get down to his level to talk to him. (If he is your own child, you probably lift him up to yours, but this is a bit of a presumption if he is not related to you.)

2. Listen without interrupting.

3. Let her take as long as she wants over her food.

4. Refrain from personal or intrusive remarks.

5. Respect his views, opinions and interests.

Treat her, in other words, as you like to be treated yourself. If in doubt, ask yourself, 'Would I behave like that towards an adult?'

joy

'We may look dysfunctional on the surface,
but deep down we're as undysfunctional as it gets.'
Benjamin

We all want the best for our children.

What can we give them? Something that will last, perhaps even outlast us. Dedicated parents set up trust funds, help their children buy their first house, support them as students … we do all we can. If I could, I would give them perfect health, take them skiing every year, buy them beautiful clothes, make every day a happy one, buy the summer seaside house I fell in love with as a child, organize all their washing for them, empty Alex's cat's litter tray to save him a few minutes each day, enable Ben to have a glittering career at whatever this week's enthusiasm is, buy Serena a herd of Saddleback pigs or Gloucester Old Spots, learn Bink's Greek for her and Rosie? What wouldn't we get Rosie? We would all give Rosie the earth and all that's in it.

What wouldn't I do? If I had world enough, and time …

But even if I had, most of these gifts would melt away with the morning dew. Investments fail or get used up. Treasures rust and the moths eat them. (Yes I'm puzzled too, as to what kind of treasure is subject to both rust and hungry moths, but I'm sure I've remembered it right.) I can't do most of these things for them, and perhaps it's just as well. They wouldn't last.

So what can I give them?

Money?

Speaking for myself, whatever money I have I will spend first and foremost on the best possible education I can get for my children, because that will last longer than anything else my money can buy. I know there will be sharp intakes of breath, and what-about-our-public-duty, and how-can-we-abandon-the-others-in-the-state-sector, and all that kind of rot. Many of our state schools are excellent, and if your children are at one of these, lucky old you. Most of us can't afford anything else anyway and make the best of what we can, and good for us. A few of us believe that the social benefits our children get from a wider circle of friends at a state school are more important than whatever other benefits might accrue from a private education, and I sympathize and partly agree.

But if there is anyone reading this who genuinely sends his children to one school rather than another for the advantage of other people's children, then you deserve all you get. May your children rise up and ask you *why*. Yes, we have a duty to society, but this is expressed first and foremost in our duty to our children, to whom we owe a greater duty anyway. So I'm not going to sacrifice mine to propping up a school or a system that could be better than it is. I think they will be more use to society if I get them the best education I can afford, whether that is in the form of unlimited books, extracurricular music lessons, a particular school trip, or the full fees at Millfield. And I will get them as much as my resources will stretch to, because, unlike their fashionable trainers, their education will still be with them right up until the Alzheimer's sets in.

Money is a great help in bringing up children, and I don't want to underestimate it. It is currently the fashion to denigrate all the hard work that parents put in, and always have put in, to give financial support to their children. Time was, when a man would set off for work in the morning to provide for his wife and little ones, and be admired and respected for it. Now he is constantly told that he is neglecting the nappy-changing and slacking on the housework. All right, fair enough, he almost certainly *is* slacking on the housework, but give the guy a break: he's probably exhausted. And his wife, if she goes out to work, most definitely isn't slacking on anything, since she (as all the research tells us) puts in a whole load more hours running the home after she gets back from the office; and yet she is given an even harder time, being told she is disadvantaging her children by not teaching them home-baking skills and giving them a round-the-clock model of someone who is supported by someone else's income. The parent who can be at home with her children when they are small is extremely fortunate, sometimes very self-sacrificing, and undoubtedly able to spend more time with them. But the parent who goes out to work is bringing up her children by providing for them from the boardroom or factory floor, just as much as is the mother, or father, who is lucky enough to be at home.

When Serena and I had the break of a lifetime in Australia that I've already mentioned – which we were only able to do, incidentally, because I was writing about it – I took the opportunity (since I was supposed to be writing about 'bonding' with her, whatever that is) to ask her whether I spent too much time working. I was, of course, expecting the agonized reply which the media have led us all to expect, that she misses her mummy when I'm at my desk and would be quite happy to live off bread and water if only she could have me read to her at bedtime. So it was rather a shock to hear her say I should work much harder, to provide her with a university education, a farm for all her pedigree cows, and who knows what else.

Make no mistake, money comes in handy for the child-rearing business. But it is severely limited in what it can do. Not just because, for many of us, it is severely limited in our pockets, but also because most of the things our children want don't have much to do with money. The three essentials, security, self-worth and significance, were outlined in Part I. In this Part II we have looked at some of the other important things we can give our children, such as siblings, intellectual rigour, table manners, and so on. We will go on, in Part III, to consider what is arguably the most crucial aspect of all.

But there is something else. As well as discipline, moral values, maturity, all the responsible, grown-up things we impart to our offspring, we want to give them a *happy* childhood. Something they look back on with a spontaneous smile. Sepia-tinted memories to bore their grandchildren with. A shrug and a laugh to confuse the shrink when she asks, 'Tell me about your traumatic early years'.

Fun. Delight. Gladness. That elusive welling up of energy that C.S. Lewis called Joy.

The good news is that it costs nothing. And it multiplies our own satisfaction more than we could ever have imagined.

Humour

> 'Explaining a punchline to Bink is like trying to tell a joke to Hitler.'
> **Serena**

> 'Actually, Hitler had a very good sense of humor.'
> **Benjamine**

What do you remember about your childhood?

I remember my father, one breakfast time, taking a heavy bulldog clip and gently attaching it to the long hairs on Lucky's feathery retriever tail. He was a happy dog who loved to please, and would wag his tail at every opportunity. Wag, clunk. *That's funny, I thought I heard something; let me turn round and have a look. Odd: nothing there. Wag, clunk. There it goes again. Let's turn the other way and see if we can catch it. Nope. They're all laughing: I'd better join in and wag my tail, clunk, clunk. I wish I could spot whatever clunk that clunk is, but it doesn't clunk seem to matter much because they're all holding their sides and rolling on the clunk wag clunk floor* ...

In later years my father thought that Lucky, who had once been described as golden, was looking somewhat elderly and white about the whiskers, so he took the Marmite from the table and spread it on his chops to give him a little more colour. Try it. Wiping your paws over your face and then licking them like Cornettos is a great crowd-pleaser.

There is nothing like a shared sense of humour to keep a family together through hard times and liven it up in good ones. In-jokes. The anecdote you all know by heart. The punch line you don't even have to give because you are all so familiar with it. Alex and I have somehow built up a complicated, and to anyone else completely incomprehensible, gag that started with the Jasper Carrott sketch about the two goldfish and their notorious attention span or lack of it, going round the bowl commenting on the castle that they can't remember is there; it then continued on a tortuous route through his circular explanation to me as to why musicians on transposed instruments can't jolly well read their notes in C major like everyone else; and it ended up with my inability to remember what Structuralism is for more than four seconds after it's explained to me. Now the joke goes round and round like the goldfish. If ever either of us is confused about anything, one only has to say to the other, 'Nice Structuralism. What Structuralism?' in the manner of a muddled goldfish, and we both hoot and slap our thighs in a way that must be extremely alarming to any onlooker.

This can be very handy. When our daughter was in hospital, we were once or twice invited to meetings as a whole family. There must have been some purpose to these unspeakably awful sessions, though as far as I am concerned, looking back, they were all part of a catalogue of errors that formed the nadir of our family life to date. But there were moments that I still remember with an irrepressible bubbling up of anarchic mirth, which almost make the experience worthwhile. On one occasion the psychiatrist had placed her chair injudiciously, and it was possible for Bink to see the rest of us, and for us to see her, without the consultant being able to look at her face. At some extremely sensitive moment when we were all searching our hearts for emotional scar tissue that might date back to when we were being potty trained or some equally weighty issue, Bink chose to go boss-eyed and stick her tongue up her nose.

As if this were not enough, Alex – with perfect sincerity – happened to tell the doctor that he 'thinks like a fork'. Anyone in her right mind would have turned to him in astonishment, told him he was off his trolley, and probably called for a straitjacket and the nurses to cart him away ... or at least asked him what on earth he meant. It was on the tip of my tongue to say that I think like a spoon, and Bink probably thinks like a kitchen drawer full of sharp knives, corkscrews, an apple corer, a twist of string and a broken garlic crusher, when the psychiatrist nodded solemnly and said to Alex in all seriousness, 'I know what you mean.' I'm sorry, but it finished the rest of us off. When you've lived with Alex for a while, you realize that nobody could possibly know what he means most of the time. In fact, what he meant was that he thinks like a fork of lightning, going off in unpredictable directions and striking innocent passers-by at random. And if you learn that kind of thing in shrink-school I'm the Queen of Sheba. Nothing could have been a better reminder that we knew more about our family than the professional who was trying to pronounce on it.

I remembered this recently when a distraught mother, whom I didn't even know, rang me out of the blue for advice. Her daughter was going through a bit of teenagerishness, and unfortunately, because she had gone off to a friend's house for a day or two without telling her parents where she was, social services had got hold of the story, decided she was 'at risk', and booked the whole family into compulsory sessions with a clinical nurse who knew nothing about them and was determined to persuade the girl that she was suicidal and the problem almost certainly sprang from her Christian family background. I told the mother that one of the best weapons in the fight against interfering busybodies trying to wreck their family would be their corporate sense of humour. And so it turned out. For the next appointment the therapist had not prepared the furniture adequately – the girl herself had caught him unawares by turning down the first half of the session on her own with him – and there was one chair too many. The mother waited for everyone to be seated, then took the chair nearest the therapist. At which he stood up, moved the furniture around, and sat down again with an empty chair between them. So she stood up, and took the empty chair. So he got up again and rearranged it all. So she got up and replaced her chair ... and by the time they'd spent the first few minutes playing musical chairs he was extremely jumpy and the family was feeling much more of a (barely straight-faced) team.

When our son contemplated jumping off the school roof at the age of ten we naturally talked extensively afterwards, and some of our conversations were of a profoundly serious nature. (During one of them I explained, with extreme political incorrectness, that suicide is wrong, just as killing anyone is wrong; and when he looked at me with round eyes and said, 'Is it?' I could tell at once that he would never contemplate it again – nor has he.) At one point, however, Shaun said, 'Listen mate: you've got a first-rate brain in there, but it's not much use to anyone spread out like jam on the school tarmac.' He laughed and laughed, and wrinkled up his face and laughed some more. For months, even years afterwards I would wake in the small hours and shake till the dawn or struggle not to cry suddenly in public at the thought of that brave little boy, alone and afraid, not knowing how to face the future. But now, though the tears have all gone, the laughter at that comment still remains and presumably always will.

'The best way to drive out the devil … is to jeer and flout him, for he cannot bear scorn.'[1]

Holidays, projects and expeditions

When we first moved to our current parish, fourteen years ago, there were very few children attending the church, so I decided to run a summer holiday club for three- to ten-year-olds. We offered plenty of activities including music, art, puppet-making, swimming and much else besides. Naturally I needed plenty of leaders, and someone put me in touch with a whole family that was willing to come and help: mother, father, two daughters in their early twenties, a teenage boy and a girl of eight. They were multi-talented. The father taught the nine- and ten-year-olds, the mother looked after the tinies, while the girls ran music groups and produced much of the artwork for the week. The teenager played the drums for us, though he studied in the mornings – as did the youngest (taught by her sisters) – so he only joined in with the afternoon's activities.

They were from New Zealand, and had taken a year out to travel around the world together. I was bowled over. From that moment I conceived a dream that we would one day do the same. After seven years in one parish Shaun would be entitled to a sabbatical, so he put money into a scheme to save for this, while I collected ideas, planned to rent out the house to help pay for it, and plotted where we would go. In the meantime we were further inspired by friends of ours who went on a six-month sabbatical around North America, taking their three children out of school and teaching them themselves.

Alas, the summer we set aside to do this (from late May to early September) was the year when one of our children finally left the school that had been so disastrous for him and had nowhere else to go to, so we had to abandon all other plans in order to organize his future. We postponed the idea and downsized it, but the next summer that we allocated was the one when another of our children became ill. In the end Shaun was told he had to take his sabbatical anyway, and spent a few weeks reading instead. Now it is too late: Serena has embarked on six years of study, and Shaun will have to wait till he has earned another sabbatical. But it remains a great idea, and I recommend it to anyone who can succeed in doing it.

Though we will now never have what I dreamt of, we have had other times instead that have been wonderful in their own way. And I've learnt that you just have to use what you have, and do what you can do. Some have plenty of money to have terrific, if brief, holidays snorkelling in the Caribbean; others can take time off work to pursue a once-in-a-lifetime ambition, sailing round the British Isles; still others can embark on a project together, renovating a house.

When our children were younger we couldn't afford to spend any money on holidays. Luckily we had several friends who were extremely generous in lending us their houses: a cottage in the New Forest; another on a remote beach in Cornwall; a little house on Loch Ness. Some of our most magical and memorable times have been spent in the loveliest house in the north-east of Scotland which we have gone back to again and again. I still have a photograph of the six of us, grinning insanely at a camera set on autopilot, a borrowed picnic basket at our feet, on the banks of a salmon river that the children said they would never forget as long as they lived and which no doubt they've forgotten already. It didn't cost us a bean. Which is just as well, because we didn't have a bean. But we did have a very hospitable friend with a fabulous holiday house.

As they got older and I earned more of a living with my pen, I was able to organize trips that I paid for by writing about them: first a modest week on a longboat, then a slightly more ambitious expedition in an

8. Joy

Irish horse-drawn caravan, and so on. Then a few years ago I took Shaun riding across the steppes of Mongolia for an article I was writing. When Ben saw all our exciting camping equipment he wanted to come too, but I told him it was out of the question: too expensive, and the riding would be too gruelling. But when we were out there we met a family of four who went on all such holidays together, trekking in Nepal, discovering pyramids in Egypt, galloping across Mongolia. They weren't rich; they simply saved hard all year and splashed out on really exciting expeditions. So I thought, if they can do it, we can. A few months later I met someone who runs horseback safaris in the Okavango Delta,[2] I got a commission to write about such a holiday, she gave us a very generous discount in exchange for the publicity, we scraped together the rest of the money somehow, and the next summer we all went together, for a fortnight. It was the most spectacular time we've ever had.

Our daughter was already ill and wasn't really fit to come, but she bravely did anyway. She didn't ride, but she joined in everything else. And after our light aircraft touched down in Maun and we all piled into the amphibious Land Rover for the last two hours to our destination, I kept thinking: We did it! We're here, all of us together, on the trip of a lifetime. And so it turned out. Even now we will mention some trivial aspect of the fortnight – the food we ate one night, or a camp joke, or the way the staff would pile hot coals under our dining chairs late in the evening as the cold drew in and call it 'central heating', or the humorous English of one of the guides (like Bottom, he genuinely said one day, 'You see, the lion hear the smell'), or the magnificent lion we saw on the last morning when Alex had forgotten to put his spectacles on and nearly missed it, or the time we thought an elephant was going to charge us ... and at such moments we will all be back there together, sharing it again. The memories stretch far into the years ahead.

I sometimes wonder whether the value of such trips is in inverse proportion to the ease with which the parents can organize them. For those lucky millionaires who can afford two or three such holidays a year, their children will probably take them for granted and barely register that they need to treasure them. But if they know you have saved up for five or ten years and you may never be able to do it again, the chances are it will be more dearly remembered.

There are, of course, plenty of other things a family can do together. We know one family that built their own house. It was superb: so good, in fact, that as soon as it was finished they sold it and built another. The second time they were even better at it, and did everything themselves except the electricity and the plumbing. And the only things that ever went wrong with it were the electricity and the plumbing. Coincidentally, the two brothers in that family could perform one of the most extraordinary feats I've ever heard. Both could whistle and hum at the same time; not just in the droning kind of way that I can for a second or two if I practise all week, but actually whistle one tune and hum another. So between them, they could perform endless rounds, or complicated four-part harmony, just the two of them. I've heard it. On several occasions. And still don't really believe it.

Music is a great activity for members of the family to engage in together. Harmonizing with others is so much more fun than playing music alone, and chamber music so much more rewarding in some ways than being in a large choir or orchestra, that the gratification amply repays the effort. When I was on my gap year I stayed for a while in France with a family. One of the sons played the violin and one of the daughters the recorder, while I borrowed the harp of another daughter who was away. The three of us used to get together in the evenings and massacre Bach's Double Violin Concerto (violin, recorder and harp continuo). If his grave looks churned up you know whose fault it is. But I've loved that piece of music ever since, perhaps more than any other.

When my parents celebrated their diamond wedding four years ago, we managed to put on a concert with every single descendant taking part in one way or another, from the youngest who tried to read out A.A. Milne's 'Vespers' until he was overwhelmed with shyness and the rest of us had to take over, to the eldest who simply gave a toast because the last instrument he played was the mouth organ and that was a very long time ago. And somehow or other we managed to rehearse Pachelbel's 'Canon' and Vaughan Williams' 'Greensleeves' and the Beatles' 'When I'm Sixty-four' and various other duets and trios that will never be quite the same again. Such a feat costs next to nothing. And in case you're feeling daunted it doesn't need any particular talent either: we had violin Grade I in there, and my brother hasn't played the trumpet since he was at school and had to practise his half dozen notes for weeks beforehand. All it really takes is the ability to organize everyone.

Another couple I know took six months off work after they got married, and sailed from Thailand to the Mediterranean with the groom's parents. I know a grandfather who took up riding so he could accompany his children, and then their children, out hunting: he found that the activity that is supposed to be so socially divisive combined young and old, rich and poor, male and female in a glorious egalitarian exploit. Some play tennis foursomes. I have tried to learn to ski, now that my children love it. The pain is indescribable and the humiliation worse, but it has taught them great patience and care for the elderly as they sit at the bottom of the slope they got down in seconds while I sidestep for half an hour sobbing with fear; and when we get into a forest, quiet with the dripping of snow on bough and a lone bird somewhere, and go gently on down, one or other of them leading the way, for a whole leisurely afternoon and the occasional cool beer stop, before the long ski home to our chalet and the waiting cheese fondue, deliciously exhausted and hungry, I have to admit that there is nothing like the exhilaration of learning someone else's passion and joining in with an activity that your loved ones love to do.

It is never too late, and never too difficult, to find activities to do or adventures to go on together. Other families' interests will inevitably strike you as too expensive, or too specialized, or too unspeakable to engage in. Rack your brains. The love of my father's life is swimming in the North Sea at seven o'clock in the morning. You see: it takes all sorts. And the truth is that every summer somebody swims with him, though we take the agony in turns a bit. And once you get out there, with the seagulls soaring silently in the empty sky or screaming from the cliffs, the water slapping on the returning fishing smacks, the rough waves sparkling with early sunshine and the cold taking your breath away, you can see why he is addicted to it and why he still seems so young and how a few weeks of ice-cold water in the summer keep him going through the winter.

Sometimes we might want to try something once or twice, then reject it. Sometimes something is fun the first time, but you don't want to do it again. But do *something*. If you simply take your children to Rock, dump them at the nearest nightclub, then go home and play Scrabble until the time comes to collect them again, your life will be the duller.

Family traditions

Children love routine. (They love breaking it too. Obviously they can't do this if they don't have it in the first place.) Continuity is a great thing, if you can provide it.

Shaun's family always went to Ireland, to stay with his grandparents, for a month every summer. He spent the other eleven months looking forward to going back again. When he told me how much he had loved returning to the same place every year as a child, I said, that's odd, because we always went to Norfolk and I couldn't stand it. But the strange thing is that we're still going, and now that I see it through a child's eyes again, I love it. My mother stands in the same place in the back garden where my grandmother used to stand, unable to walk down to the beach now, just as her mother-in-law was then, waving to the rest of us swimming in the sea just as my grandmother did. She sits in the same chair presiding over the dinner table, and we still make summer pudding because that's what my grandmother used to make forty years ago. And we still have Norfolk beef, roast on the bone. There is something very potent about this. All the happy memories merge into one another, and if you have a year that is not so good and it rains all the time it becomes absorbed by the other years and you still end up with nostalgia. Whereas if we went to Majorca one year and Skegness another and happened to have a bad year in Majorca, we'd write it off as a wasted holiday and not go there again.

Christmas is another great time for continuity. When I was a child, a family we knew always used to organize a hockey match every Boxing Day. I don't know why it was hockey, or how it started, or where they got all the hockey sticks from, or what you had to do to be invited, or indeed – the biggest puzzle of all – why we all longed to be asked to play and relished it so much though we hated school hockey more than anything else on the timetable.

We're still playing hockey every year, in a different city with different people wrecking a different piece of common land with different hockey sticks, but still on Boxing Day, without fail. And part of the tradition is that every year Shaun, who hates all the mud being tramped around the house even more than he hates being whacked on the shins and letting a goal through, says feebly, 'Shall we give the hockey a miss this year?' and is drowned out by boos and hisses and a general thumbs down all round.

Somehow it has also come about that my cousins come every Boxing Day and stay for the whole day and into the evening, which has now grown into a substantial party, almost more important than Christmas. Which also has its traditions: the same menu every year, with the same stuffings, the same recipes, the same silver charms in a pudding made out of the same ingredients, and if ever we try to ring the changes, there is uproar. Though of course things do get changed. The year before last, by mistake, instead of having twenty people round the Christmas dinner table there were just the six of us. It was the day we told the others that the following year we would be joined by Rosie. And it was so lovely eating a hot Christmas dinner for the first time, and actually getting to sit down and relish it rather than serve another half dozen second helpings before we'd even started, and not having to spend the whole evening washing up, and even having time to give each other a present or two – and, best of all, having the amazing secret of Rosie just between the six of us, for several whole hours … until Serena rang her boyfriend – that we have started a new tradition of small, quiet Christmases.

I do recommend vast gatherings and lots of people at Christmas though, especially if you are fed up with the commercialism of it all. It turns the day into a festival about people, not presents. If you start with a rule that you don't open presents until the evening (a trick I picked up from my best friend at school, who said it's easy once you're used to it), go to church in the morning, have friends round for drinks, then Christmas dinner for more people than you can see at the table, with a game of sardines between courses to get your appetite up again, then invite neighbours in for charades in the evening with real old-fashioned candles on the Christmas tree and the fire brigade on call, it's amazing how far into the

Ten Days of Christmas you find you have gone without remembering to open any presents at all. There is always a stocking every year for everyone who wakes up in our house, but there is also an understanding that there is no compulsion on anyone to get presents for anyone else.

And thus tradition is trimmed, and tailor-made, and worn – the tradition that all tradition is voluntary, and never has to be kept unless people want to, but if they do want to, it will always be there for them.

Joy

Have you ever heard a comedian telling jokes about 'the missis' – how fat she is, or how much she nags, or some such moan – and wanted to rise up out of the audience and punch him on the nose? Perhaps it's just me. I want to shake him by the lapels and say, 'You married her, you stupid git; presumably because you were in love with her. What's your problem? Of course she nags if that's the kind of thing you're saying about her.' Okay, okay, I know they're only jokes. I'm not a feminist-fundamentalist really.

It's the same with children. Sometimes I hear the way grown-ups talk about them, and I almost want to say, 'Of course they behave like that if we say those kinds of things about them.'

Sometimes we need to remind ourselves why we had children. It's true that we were doing a great service to society by bringing them into the world, but that's not why we did it. We had them because we *wanted* them. And at some stage after their squashed-up, hideous little faces saw the light of day, we felt an uncontrollable surge of love for them. For many of us this happened at the extraordinary moment when they first appeared; for others, it wasn't until we'd got over the postnatal depression or pain from the Caesarean or had the first good night's sleep a long time later. But it happens to us all. As they lay in their cots asleep (funny how it's always when they're asleep), we wanted to scoop them up and smother them with kisses. When something threatened their safety we would have ridden wild horses across the sea to protect them. We discovered that we adored them in a selfless, self-sacrificing way that we couldn't even have imagined when we were footloose and fancy-free.

They are the same people. Yes, even when they are covered in acne and trying their first fags. When they are throwing their toys on the floor and screaming fit to be sick. When they are crying all evening with colic. When they bunk off school and steal things from our handbags and then look us in the eye and say they didn't.

We had them because we wanted them.

We had them because we knew they would give us pleasure. We had them because we had an overwhelming instinct to have them, because they impart an exquisiteness of joy that nothing else gives. We need to remind ourselves of this, and reclaim the delight. If I had to level one criticism at modern parents today – not that I would, because there are quite enough criticisms levelled at us already, but if I *had* to – I would say we have forgotten to *enjoy* our children.

If all the parenting books that told us how to feed them and discipline them and make them sleep and wake them up again, how to feel guilty if we let them sleep in our beds or guilty if we don't let them sleep in our beds, or guilty if we get up in the night for them or guilty when we smack them when they're naughty, or guilty because we give them crisps in their lunchboxes … if they gave parents one or two ideas for what we could do with our children to remind us how happy we are to have them around and how glad we are they were born, perhaps some of the other things might fall into place – or at least fall off the agenda of things to worry about.

So let's put a little more energy into thinking of ways to enjoy them, and spend a little less time agitating about what we might or might not be doing wrong. Eat with them. Talk to them. Watch telly with them. Throw a party for them. *Laugh* with them, for goodness' sake …

We will be giving them something that will last them a lifetime. We will be giving them happy memories.

There's only one gift that will last longer than this, longer than a lifetime, and that is the subject of Part III.

• • • • • • • • • • • • Action Page • • • • • • • • • • • •

'Stage a competition for who can burp the entire alphabet.'
Serena

'A game that would be great for our family — though I'm not sure it would suit anyone else's — is the Questions Game. You ask a question and the next person has to respond with another, with no hesitation, statements or rhetoric. You know: "Do you like elephants?" "What kind of elephants?" "Does it matter what kind?" "Well, African or Indian?" "Which do you prefer?" And so on. Or of course, there's always Burp Tennis.'
Benjamin

'Or Reverse Tennis Elbow. Everybody knows the word association game. With this version, you have to say a word that has no provable connection at all with the previous word. So if someone says "telephone", you mustn't say "orange", obviously.'
Alexander

'Ooh, ooh, the best game of all is the one with the trump cards that I'm not going to tell you about because I'm going to patent it.'
Bink

part III:
The Life
and Soul

'Nobody's perfect.
It's just that some of us come pretty close.'
Benjamin

Our children are fed, clothed, housed and educated. We trust they are reasonably secure, we believe they are learning to value themselves, we hope they respect those around them. They may not be perfectly happy, healthy, wealthy and wise, but they make us laugh, give us profound satisfaction and make it worth coming home after a long day at work. Indeed, they make it worth leaving the house to put in the long day at work in the first place. They are all we wished for, and more. And we aim to give them all they could ask for, and more.

But is this all? If we have children who are contented, confident and self-assured, is there anything left for us to do for them? Is there more to it than this?

Well yes, there is. There is more to *life* than this. Material success, good human relationships and physical wellbeing are not everything. And it is often when we have children that we begin to seek something else, ask the bigger questions, probe deeper into why we have been given them and what our ultimate duty towards them is and which direction we want them to end up facing in. A baby does indeed arrive trailing clouds of glory. It is as if the gift of a new human being is so extraordinary, so miraculous, that it puts the seed of wonder in our minds. By prompting us to discover the most important gift we can give them, they sometimes have the effect of enabling us to find it for ourselves.

In our parish church the largest area of growth is amongst young parents. For years they have been perfectly satisfied with their comfortable existences. They have made friends, made money, made love, made a success of their lives. Now they have children. And they want more.

Happily, there is more.

It is not so much the last piece of the jigsaw; more the picture on the box. It enables us to take what sometimes seemed a tricky, incomprehensible collection of apparently random pieces and suddenly see how they fit together.

My emphasis in this book has been on the simplicity of childrearing, on the idea that it is not a highly complicated technical skill, but an instinctive act of love. And so it is. But I have not yet told the whole tale. Love is indeed the key to the story, the beginning, middle and end, the alpha and omega and all the rest of the alphabet in between, and it is when we engage in the act of love that is raising our children that we may start to consider the source of the love, Love himself.

I have said that I consider childrearing to be an intuitive process, that in my experience we all have the wherewithal to do it naturally, and that by and large we are making a much better fist of it than we are usually led to believe. If we only have the confidence to listen to the parental impulse within us all, I believe we will not go far wrong. But sometimes we struggle to hear our instincts. The world is so noisy, the madding crowd so clamorous, that we can become confused and find it hard to pick out the voice of nature. She is there all right, telling us how to love our charges. But so is the thunder of materialism, extolling the advantages of wealth; so is the shrill sound of feminism, insisting we should be our own persons; so is the drumbeat of the masculine ego, telling us to look macho; so is the hollow rattle of post-existential individualism, confusing our notions of fulfilment. There is an alternative, authoritative voice in the storm, but it is a still small one.

Earlier on I suggested that we sometimes need a compass, just to help us follow our noses. Well, there is a compass, and in my experience it is infallible. Whenever I am not quite sure if I am going in the right direction, I pull it out of my bag, in the shape of a tatty little book printed on thin India paper with a scruffy leather binding, and it helps me get back on track. Sometimes, I admit, I have problems going the right way, but that's not the fault of the compass. I get impatient, for instance, and lose my temper. If I take the trouble to look at the compass (though I don't need to any more, over this particular issue, I've made the same mistake so often), it tells me the value of self-control, so I scramble back onto the path, say sorry and try again . . . and whoops, within a week or a day or five minutes, I've fallen off the path into the ditch of impatience again. But at least I know that I'm not supposed to be down here.

Sometimes when the sun goes in and it gets rather dark we can lose our sense of direction altogether, and the compass becomes even more important. When one of ours was ill, everybody seemed to be twirling us around in every direction to try to confuse us. 'Put your foot down!' 'Be firm!' 'Children need boundaries!' a number of people shouted at us. Even, 'Why don't you throw her out?' from one helpful friend (who subsequently, and most graciously, apologized). But we looked at the little compass, and it said no: love is patient and kind, and endures all things. And sure enough, what she needed in order to get well (or rather, to get over the mess the professionals had made of her treatment) was patience and kindness by the bucketful.

Perhaps your marriage is going through strain. You're overworked and tired, and don't feel in love any more, and keep having pointless arguments, and perhaps one of you has even fallen for someone else. There is no shortage of confusing and contradictory advice from friends, and magazines, and shrinks, and the culture all around us. But what does the compass say? Take delight in the wife of your youth. Do not let the sun go down upon your wrath.

Everything I have said in this book is based on my reading of the compass. And at the end of the day I'd much rather give you the compass than give you my reading of it. You may read it slightly differently. You may say the compass suggests to you that children should have strict bedtimes, or unlimited television, or a parent who stays at home. Though we follow the same compass we may take slightly different routes, certainly over unimportant details such as these. But if we read it regularly we will all end up going in roughly the same direction, trying to give security and self-worth and significance to our children.

And we will also give them something much more important. The compass doesn't just tell us which direction to go in to have the most fulfilling journey, though it does do this. It also gives us a destination to reach. Happiness, health and success are all very well, and make the going far more comfortable and the landscape much more attractive as we trudge along our way. But they are not the end of the journey.

Take the long view. If there is such a thing as eternity (and the evidence convinces me that there is), it will surely contribute more to our children's happiness in the end than a dozen good years at the right school or a few more decades in the right job. The physical and emotional aspects of childrearing are important, of course they are. But if there is more to life than the immediate here and now, then their spiritual health is even more vital to their wellbeing than their physical and emotional fitness.

Now of course you may come to the conclusion that this is all there is, there is no more, that death is the end, and that all we can hope for, for our children, is a journey as enjoyable as possible to nowhere. Fair enough.

But we surely owe it to our children to explore the possibility, even more than we owe it to them to ensure that they have shoes to wear or a good education or can talk openly about their feelings. And we should do so with all the dedication, open-mindedness, commitment and intelligence we can muster.

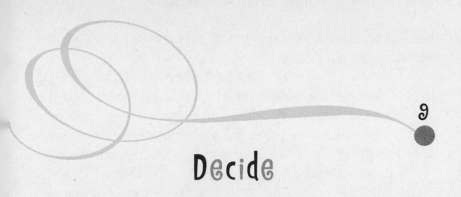

Decide

'Young children tend to believe what their parents tell them —
and so they should. But there are limits. You'll never
persuade a four-year-old that brussels sprouts taste better
than rhubarb crumble and custard, for instance.'
Alexander

As a clergyman, Shaun hears one comment more often than any other
from parents, with regard to the spiritual welfare of their offspring,
which is that they want their children to 'decide for themselves'.

This springs from a noble impulse. A truly liberal upbringing for our
children means giving them the opportunity and ability to be themselves.
We want them to find the sport that they most enjoy, the musical instrument that comes most naturally to them, the academic subjects at which
they shine, and eventually the vocation to which they are called. We
wouldn't dream (in the West anyway) of choosing our son's marriage partner. Why should we choose his religion?

Why?

As we have seen, there are things we can, and should, let children decide
for themselves. What to eat for tea, which pyjamas to wear, what colour
to dye their hair and what to give Granny for Christmas, for instance,

because the consequences dependent on these choices will not be either serious or long-term.

But there are some things we don't let them decide. Take the MMR jab. We investigate it thoroughly, weigh up the arguments on either side, and take the decision for them. Responsible and intelligent people come down on both sides of the debate. But no parents who are either responsible or intelligent expect their children to make up their own minds.

We do a similar thing over their early education. There are principled parents who believe passionately that the state system is the best, and don't send their children to private schools even though they could afford it. There are other, equally principled, parents who can't afford it at all, and yet scrimp and save and bankrupt themselves to give their children advantages they wish they had had. Both sides, I hope, respect each other. There are even those who decide to teach their children themselves. But there is not a parent in the country whom any of us would respect, who opts out of education altogether; who says to his child, 'Whether or not you go to school is your own personal, individual decision.' We even, as a society, penalize those who do. If it were not illegal, though, it would still be highly irresponsible.

Whether or not we want to have a relationship with the God who made us is surely the most serious decision, with the most long-term consequences, that anybody can ever make. We don't expect them to decide whether or not to take medicine when they are ill: if we believe it will do them good we make jolly sure they swallow it. (We may be wrong; but no one could accuse us of being negligent.) We don't let them determine whether or not to be educated: we ensure that they turn up at school on a Monday morning whether they like it or not. (Again, we might be resented for doing this; but we could hardly be criticized.) Surely their attitude towards God, if he exists, is more important than their education or health.

And yet time and again one hears parents say, in a well-meaning sort of way, 'I want my children to have the choice.' 'We want them to decide for themselves.' 'We thought we'd take them to Sunday school and let them make up their minds later.'

If God doesn't exist, it is surely irresponsible to subject them to a fairy tale. And if he does exist and will call us to answer to him one day, it is far more irresponsible to present him as an optional extra.

They will choose what we have chosen

Let's consider for a moment what happens when we let our children 'decide for themselves'.

Soon after Molly or James is born, after we have registered for all the really competitive schools in the area (let's get our priorities right, after all), we ring the vicar and arrange the christening (which is not in fact letting them decide for themselves, but don't let's split hairs). We choose godparents who are fun, generous and likely to remember birthdays, we organize a sumptuous lunch, order in the champagne, put on our best hats, and get the creature dunked.

We then (in contravention of the solemn vows we have just taken, incidentally) forget all about it until he or she is of an age for Sunday school. At which point we ring the vicar again, find out the time of Sunday school, bundle Molly and James into the car, drop them off at ten-thirty, pick up the Sunday papers on the way home, make a pot of coffee and look forward to an hour's peace and quiet. And it doesn't matter how good the Sunday school is, how well taught, how committed those who run it, how interesting or helpful or convincing – or even true – the content, the still small voice of God will not deign to drown out the deafeningly loud alternative clamour emanating from the parents: that religion is something you grow out of. That it's for the kiddies. That reading the papers is the activity of choice. That, as soon as you are old enough, you elect to stay at home instead of going to church, because church is somewhere you dump young children who have no choice, in order to set free the adults who do have a choice and use that choice to opt out. And that on the one weekend in the month when there isn't a Sunday school but a service that the guitar-strumming friendly curate calls 'family worship' we take advantage of this and all go out for the day, leaving family worship to the over-sixty-fives because otherwise Mummy and Daddy might have to go too.

Even if the vicar has strategically dropped Sunday school – because he believes that Christianity is something we grow into not out of, and church is a family that should do things together as families do – so that Mummy (and it usually is good old Mummy) is selfless enough to accompany the children to church while they are young, they may still get this message. Children are not stupid. They will notice if you don't believe in Christianity on the other days of the week. It is very kind and dedicated of you. It is also a great deal better than nothing, and an excellent way of learning more about the Christian faith and helping you decide what you do believe. But if, deep down, you think it's nothing but a collection of pretty stories for children that you yourself have grown out of, your children are likely to grow up and think the same one day. If you don't believe Jesus is worth following for his own sake but only for the sake of your children, the chances are that your children will soon agree with you. And why shouldn't they?

They will copy us. It is what children do.

There is no such thing as religious neutrality

There is no such thing as English spoken without an accent. It seems to me that I haven't got an accent, because I speak what my drama school used to call Received Pronunciation; it's the Geordie or New Yorker who has irregular vowel sounds. But to the Geordie or the New Yorker I'm the one who speaks funny: he doesn't think I talk without an accent at all. I think it's normal because I've lived with it all my life, so I labour under the misconception that I speak a perfectly neutral form of English. But as Professor Higgins said, it is impossible for any Englishman to open his mouth, without alienating himself from other Englishmen.

It's the same with our religious assumptions. We think we haven't got any. Having lived with Western relativism all our lives, we don't notice it and think we enjoy a perfectly neutral philosophical position. But anyone coming from a fresh perspective can spot our assumptions a mile off.

We believe that we can give our children a genuine choice of religion. We lay out all the creeds on offer like supermarket brands of soap, and don't see that this is imposing our assumptions on our children just as much as if we brought them up as Orthodox Jews or Sunni Muslims.

When we let our children 'decide for themselves' we are teaching them something very clearly. By implying that it is all right for them to choose and that we are happy for them to do so, we are telling them that one choice is as good as another and there isn't a great deal between them. They will receive the unambiguous message that a religion is like a breakfast cereal, and it doesn't matter much which one you go for: some taste a bit better than others or do you a bit more good, but as long as you eat something you'll get through the day.

They know that we wouldn't dream of giving them a choice between swimming with armbands under proper supervision and swimming alone with no buoyancy aids. They know that we wouldn't let them choose between wearing seatbelts in the car and crawling around all over the back seat. So by giving them a choice about religion we are teaching them, most eloquently, that religion is not particularly important – certainly not a matter of life and death.

They also know no one would let them choose the date of the Battle of Hastings, or that water should be made up of HO_2 rather than H_2O. Somewhere in our attic we have a chart of the kings and queens of England, with all the royal dates and family trees. Once, in a fit of enthusiasm, I pinned it up somewhere, in the hope that I would know it by the time the children came to learn it at school. It never once occurred to me to put up various alternative charts so they could choose which reality they preferred. If I had, I would have been teaching them an unmistakable lesson about the reliability of historians: that they're all a bunch of cranks and we might as well make it up ourselves. But this is exactly what we do with religion. If I give them a choice, I am telling them that no one religion can be exclusively true.

Ergo, any religion that makes this claim must, one way or another, be telling porkies.

This is the assumption that we don't notice in the developed West. Why do we frown on any proselytizing religion? Because it is inconceivable to us that one religion might be right and another wrong. But this is what some of the religions themselves teach and believe. If we disagree with this, then we shouldn't introduce our children to the three monotheistic religions for a start; certainly not in their orthodox forms.

In addition, some religions would say that they can't be tasted on a trial basis. We like to think we can give our children a smattering of this, that and the other: a friend's bar mitzvah, a Hindu wedding, church at Christmas and lashings of materialism, so they can see which one appeals to them the most. All very balanced and politically correct, like *Thought for the Day* for a lifetime: Islam this week and Sikhism the next.

This may be fine as a curriculum for RE, and right and proper as a strategy for balanced religious broadcasting, but as an approach to the meaning of life it is superficial in the extreme. Like thinking you know what it's like to be married because you've taken half a dozen girls out to dinner. No, in order to experience marriage, you have to take the risk and commit yourself to one, to the exclusion of all the rest. Being a guest at Hanukkah or Purim might give you some idea as to why Judaism has survived so long against all the odds, but it would not introduce you to the Jewish God. To do this you would need to turn your back on other gods, convert to Judaism and enter the covenant. Clearly you cannot do this while trying out half a dozen other religions as well.

Christianity is the same. It is an all-or-nothing type of faith. You can find out a great deal about the Christian gospel before you make up your mind. But you will never understand it unless you realize that you can't experience Christianity without committing your life to it to the exclusion of all others.

Something is either true or it isn't

All religions make claims. Some of these are purely subjective. If you meditate cross-legged for twenty minutes before breakfast you will find your day more serene. Prayer calms you down. Going to church will help your marriage. Religious schools get better results. And so forth. These kind of 'truths' are not really truths at all. They are trends. As such, they can be 'true' for some people but not for others. It is easy to see that prayer might calm some people, but not everyone. Many children will respond well to the structure and teaching of religious schools, but not all. So, like a diet, you find the one that suits you. It doesn't much matter whether it is calorie-controlled or non-carbohydrate, as long as you can keep it up and lose weight on it. If this were all religion was, it would simply be a matter of personal choice. Find the one that appeals to you, and stick with it. Your children might as well make up their own minds indeed.

But this is not all it is. Some religions make objective claims. 'The only God is Allah and Mohammed is his prophet', for instance. Or, 'Yahweh brought the Israelites out of Egypt'. Or, 'Jesus Christ was born in Bethlehem in Judea'. Well, either he was or he wasn't. It is only in the ivory-towered never-never land of academic theologians that a statement like this can be both true and not true at the same time; true on a mythical level but not true on the historic level or some such daffy talk. To the rest of us, a table is either there or it isn't. Jesus was either born in Bethlehem or he wasn't. He either rose again as he said he would, or his bones rotted away and he turned to dust like everyone else.

And, just as we owe it to our children to research the MMR jab and weigh up whether the risk of bowel disease and autism is real or imagined, acceptable or unacceptable, and make a decision on behalf of those who are too young to decide for themselves, so we owe it to those same children to weigh up whether the claims made by Christianity are credible or not, backed up by evidence or not, worth committing to or not. One day we will know the truth about MMR; in the meantime we must make the most responsible decision we can. One day we will know the truth about God. Today, we have to bring up our children in the light of the best decision we can make.

The one thing we should not do, however, is leave them to make up their own minds. Either Jesus was who he said he was, or he was a dangerous lunatic. If the former, we should bow down and worship him ourselves. If the latter, what on earth are we doing introducing our children to his teaching?

How?

When our son was eleven we ran completely out of ideas. He was off the top of the scale on some IQ tests, but he failed almost every exam he sat. He could work out things that were way beyond us, but he couldn't work out how to get down in time for breakfast. We had found a school where we knew he would be blissfully happy, but we couldn't see any way of persuading them to take him.

One afternoon I was sitting in a television studio waiting for the cameras to roll, and I found I was next to a top psychologist. I poured out my troubles, and he told me it sounded as thought my son's brain was 'miswired'. He told me where I could find the best consultant who would be able to tell me (on payment of a suitable fee) whether this was indeed the case.

'And then what?' I said.

'Oh, there's nothing you can do about it,' he said. 'But at least you would know.' I decided to keep my cash.

It was a friend who told me about David Mulhall.[1] To be honest, his method sounded stark raving bonkers. She told me that he tells you how to rub paintbrushes all over your child's body, and by this method cures all sorts of ills, from dyslexia and dyspraxia to attention deficit hyperactivity disorder. You'd have to be desperate.

We were.

When I spoke to him on the telephone, he had told me that he couldn't treat innate conditions like Asperger's syndrome, and by an extraordinary coincidence the day our son was due to meet him was the day he finally received his diagnosis of Asperger's. But David's first session was free so we had nothing to lose, and it was too late for him to give the appointment to someone else, so he had nothing to lose either. And as soon as they met he dismissed the Asperger's theory. 'I think his brain's miswired,' he said. 'And I can rewire it for him.'

How do you decide whether something is worth trying? You look at the evidence, weigh up the cost, talk to those who have done it. But in the end you'll only know for certain by giving it a go.

Look at the evidence

David explained his theory to us. It was plausible enough. It is based on an analysis of various given reflexes and what they do. It wasn't by any means the only possible explanation of what causes developmental problems, but it was intellectually tenable. I didn't go into it in great depth, but I made sure I understood enough to know what David says he is doing and why.

Christianity isn't the only possible explanation of why the world is as it is. But it is an explanation that holds water, that is intellectually respectable, that makes sense. Some people need to go into it in great depth, and if you are one such I recommend that you do so: look at the sources for the New Testament and how many early manuscripts there are and how well attested they are, and even go and look at them if this means you will be able to assess them better. You cannot know too much about it.

Some people don't need to do as much as this. They just need to understand the basics and see whether they make sense. I didn't have time to study David's philosophy at length: I just knew there was nothing else to try and that what he said made some sense. I could see he wasn't a charlatan and was convinced enough to take it further.

The best place to find out about Christianity is in the Gospels. You can tell quite quickly that the people who wrote them weren't frauds, and it doesn't take long to know whether the accounts warrant further investigation.

Talk to people who have tried it

David must have expected me to be sceptical. He gave me the telephone number of a family whose son had just finished treatment. He told me the parents had volunteered to talk to anyone who wanted to know more.

I rang and spoke to the father. He couldn't speak highly enough of David's work. His son had always been bright, but incapable of performing at school; he struggled with homework, failed school tests, and couldn't achieve anything. Now he was top of his class in one of the most academic schools in London. Mother and father were so pleased that several members of the family were now having treatment. And I also had the recommendation of the mother who had suggested David in the first place, who hadn't seen quite such clear results but was impressed enough to put her second son through it as well.

Most of us know people who have committed their lives to Jesus Christ. I don't mean those of us who simply put 'Church of England' down on the form because we're not sure what else to put, and describe ourselves as Christians because we know we're not Buddhists or Jains. I mean those who say they have a personal relationship with him. Ask them whether they think it's worth it and would recommend giving it a try and what difference it has made to their lives?

Weigh up the cost

David's treatment was costly. Not just the fee every six weeks or so when we had to see him. We also had to embark on doing his treatment for ten minutes every morning and evening, without fail, for as long as it would take. It should have been about nine months, but in our son's case it took nearly three and a half years.

So we stood to lose quite a lot of money, even more time, and have the embarrassment of telling Matron that it really was important, however late he was running for breakfast, and his treatment absolutely couldn't be skipped. And I tell you, when it was late at night or Christmas Day, or we were camping in a cramped tent or taking an overnight flight somewhere, I hated David's treatment more than I can say.

But what did we have to gain? The worst it could be was useless; it wasn't going to do any positive harm. And if it worked … oh, if it worked, it was worth all the time and money we could spend on it.

Christianity is costly. If you really decide to go for it, it will take your whole life, all your time and money and commitment and everything else. But the worst it can be is mistaken.

And if it's true … well, the benefits, as they say, are out of this world.

In the end, all we could do was try it. We would only know for sure by giving it a go. Our son was convinced it changed his life, and for years said David's analysis was the only one that made any sense.

Now our daughter is having treatment from David too, for her Obsessive Compulsive Disorder. The longer we try it the more convinced we are. But we'll only know quite how effective it is at some distant date in the future.

The same is true of our Christian faith.

Action Page

1. Read a Gospel

Mark is short and accessible, and would only take a couple of hours. Or you could try my favourite, Luke; and after reading volume one, the Gospels, move on to volume two, the Acts of the Apostles, also by Luke. Ask yourself whether the writing, the people, the events, but most of all the central character himself, are credible. If so, what are the implications?

2. Try visiting a church that teaches the Bible

Remember that Jesus came for sinners, and his churches reflect this. If the first one you visit isn't friendly and the teaching doesn't make sense, don't give up; try another.

3. Talk to a Christian friend

Again, some Christians are still young in the faith or muddled about what they believe. This doesn't matter, but it will help you to find one who is articulate, committed and clear.

Ask him what he believes and why; what difference it has made to him; and whether he would recommend his Master.

4. Read a Christian book

Such as *Mere Christianity* by C.S. Lewis (HarperCollins), *Basic Christianity* by John Stott (InterVarsity), *The Case for Christ* by Lee Strobel (Zondervan), or *A Fresh Start* by John Chapman (Good Book Company).

5. Try it

Implement

10

> 'Richard Dawkins says he can't respect any scientist
> who believes the Bible. But what makes science different from
> witchcraft or alchemy is that it's sensible about admitting what it
> does and doesn't know. So I can't respect any scientist who doesn't
> understand the limitations of science; the Bible takes you places
> where science just doesn't go.'
>
> **Alexander**

If Christianity is true, what then?

If you have come to the conclusion that it isn't, or you are not sure, or you still need time to think about it, then this chapter is not really for you. Read it by all means if you wish, for the time when you have an essential message that is vital for you to pass on to your children. For now, though, you presumably feel you have enough to do loving them and enjoying them and giving them a good time.

But for those of us who come to the conclusion that the teaching, claims and promises of Jesus of Nazareth are well documented, reliably evidenced, credible, coherent, reasonable – to the best of our knowledge, true – we discover a new ambition for our children that eclipses all else. If Jesus Christ is the Son of God, nothing is as important as to know him. Once we believe in the chance of eternal life, the only thing that ultimately matters for our children is that they should have the benefit of it too.

So bringing them up in the Christian faith becomes the issue. What else compares, if it is true? If Jesus' promises still hold true, our ultimate duty must be to pass them on to our children in such a way that they can understand, believe, respond to and claim them for themselves.

How can we do this?

Believe it

'You can tell the Bible's true because it says how awful life can be.'
Benjamin

It sounds obvious, but the first way to pass on a belief is to believe it. It is easy to pay lip service to a creed without really taking it to heart. To be honest, we all do this to some extent.

Jesus tells us not to worry about laying up treasure on earth; we should make our investments in heaven, where stockmarket fluctuations can't reach them. But how many of us could put our hands on our hearts and say we are never anxious about our children's future job prospects? Consider the birds of the air and the lilies of the field; even Solomon in all his glory was not arrayed as one of these. But are we *really* more concerned for little Lucy to love Jesus than that she should have clothes to wear – or even that she should have friends at school and pass her exams?

I am not suggesting, of course, that we should show no interest in our children's material wellbeing, and should care nothing for their worldly happiness and success. To do this would be to indicate that we cared nothing for the children themselves. If we love them we will naturally share all their concerns, great and small. Nor am I implying some simplistic formula, that we never let them miss church to cope with an essay crisis, or that we insist on sending them to a Christian school rather than one with inspirational teaching or good results.

However, if we really believe the gospel, we will have our eyes on a different future. We will have alternative priorities. We will want our children to do well; of course we will. But what we'll really care about will be their eternal futures. And they will spot this, as sure as eggs is eggs.

We never succeed in fooling our children. It is possible to swindle a boss, deceive a neighbour, dupe a best friend and sometimes even to cheat on a marriage partner. But I've never yet come across anyone who succeeded in fooling his children. They see through us every time.

So they are not likely to pick up any belief from us unless we *believe* it through and through.

If we do, we will want to talk about it. Tell them why we hold it to be true. Explain what difference it makes to us. Pray with them. Read the Bible to them. Encourage them to call on God when they hit bad times, and thank him when they have good ones.

I know lovely Christian people whose children have never even thought of following Jesus Christ themselves. But then they never heard him talked about when they were little. Their fathers didn't kneel at their bedsides saying their prayers with them; their mothers didn't open their Bibles and read them a story. So it never really dawned on them that Jesus and his teaching mattered to their parents at all.

Live it

The wise man builds on foundations of rock. What makes him wise? He hears my words, Jesus said, and puts them into practice. The wind blows, the rain falls, the hard times come and his house stands firm. The fool builds on soft soil and his house cracks.

The New Testament teaches clearly that true Christian faith results in a true Christian life. If we believe, we will put that belief into practice. Which is just as well, because our children won't embrace our faith unless they see us living it as well. You don't have to go far in literature or real life to find people who say something along the lines of, 'My father was a very religious man, but he was such a brute to my mother that I never want to have anything to do with religion again.'

I realize that this is not, strictly speaking, logical. Jesus came for the whores and the swindlers and the domestic brutes of this world, not for the good people. The church is for sinners: that's the point of it. So it ought to be possible for us to see through a rotten Christian to the glorious character of Christ; to recognize that there can be a bad advertisement for a product without the product being bad; to realize that our parents were lousy Christians but that doesn't mean Christianity is lousy. It ought to be possible – in theory.

In practice, however, Christians are ambassadors for their faith, even to fellow adults. And as far as children are concerned, we stand in the place of God to them. If their earthly father is forgiving, affirming, loving and kind, they are likely to be enthusiastic about the idea of a heavenly Father. If he is a drunken, miserable, violent bully, they won't warm to the notion of an omnipotent, omniscient version of this. If we want our children to grow up as Christians, we have to behave like Christ towards them. Which is the best way to love our children anyway.

I think of the families that I admire most, the ones that are intimate, kind, funny and affirming and stand by each other through thick and thin. In each case the rock supporting the family is the rock of Jesus himself. It is certainly true of the home I grew up in. Of course there are wonderfully happy, loving, humorous, liberal-minded families that have no faith whatsoever. And yes, sadly, there are families that are broken and struggling despite their strong and well founded beliefs. Nevertheless, it is true that Jesus' teaching, properly followed, will naturally result in the parenting principles laid out at the beginning of this book. Take an obvious example: Christianity encourages the permanence of marriage; and a stable, secure marriage is one of the greatest assets we can give our children.

This is why the teaching of Jesus is the picture on the front of the jigsaw box. It is possible to put the jigsaw together without it. It's possible to stay married, to love our children unconditionally, to forgive all their failures, to admire them regardless of their success in the eyes of the world, to discipline them without disapproving of them, to listen to them and respect their views ... and so on and so forth. These are all the individual pieces of the jigsaw, and there are people who sort them and fit them together and create a beautiful, composite whole without any apparent help from God.

In fact, however, we all have help from God, whether we acknowledge it or not, because he is the one who put the parenting instinct within us. He gave each of us the eyes to see where the corners of our children's lives go, and the mind to work out how the edges of the brothers and sisters fit together, and the patience to do the endless hours of homework and cooking and driving around that make up the boring sky. It is natural for us to be able to put the jigsaw together, and God gave each of us the nature to do it.

But he also gave us a picture on the box, and we don't get any bonus points for doing it the hard way. If someone else has put it together already, why not take advantage of this and have the completed picture at the outset, so we know what it's supposed to look like?

'Husbands, love your wives,' Saint Paul says. What is the most important thing a man can do for his children? Love their mother, of course.

How many times should we forgive our children, if they are cheeky, disrespectful, dishonest, thieving, lazy, and goodness knows what else besides? Seventy times seven, Jesus says.

He also teaches me that, if the bank has cancelled a debt I owe worth fifty thousand pounds, it's a bit ungracious to insist on the fiver back from the friend who can't repay it. And if I know that God has forgiven me everything despite all the years I've neglected him, it's much easier to go on loving my children when they're being rude and ignoring me.

The patience, endurance and commitment that are the stuff of child-rearing are all the qualities that God first showed towards us.

Obey Jesus' teaching, and it will help you bring your children up. It will also enable you to pass your faith on to them.

Put the children first

'There is one good qualification for being a parent: your love must be stronger than any negative emotion (anger or rage, disgust or contempt) your child may ever be able to inspire in you (and if anyone can, your child will be able to).'

Bink

So far, so much common sense. If we want to share the gospel with others, of course we have to believe it and live it. But when it comes to children, there is another condition that also seems to be crucial. And it is perhaps particularly relevant to those readers who are already active, committed Christians, and have long known everything I have said so far about believing the gospel and living it.

Before we were even married, when we considered the possibility of children, our ultimate concern was how to bring them up as Christians. In the light of eternity nothing else is truly important. So we looked around at those Christian friends of ours who were a generation older and who had teenage children themselves, to see how they had got on.

Most of them, I'm happy to say, had children who had embraced their faith. The popular myth that children grow up and automatically reject their parents' values is self-evidently untrue. If God cares for us, he will care about our children, hear our prayers on their behalf and care about their futures even more than we do ourselves.

But there were exceptions. We did have a few friends who were deeply committed Christians, who lived the gospel, believed it, talked about it, demonstrated its love every day in the way they lived – and who, incidentally, were wonderful, kind, generous people – who, to their great distress, had seen one or more of their children turn away from Christianity. And when we asked ourselves whether it was possible to see any reason why, a pattern seemed to emerge.

It appeared that those parents whose children rejected their faith had mostly done something that seems very noble and worthy, but is possibly mistaken. To put it rather simplistically, they seemed to have put God before their children.

I realize this must sound puzzling. Doesn't God ask to be first in our lives? Isn't that what he wants? Won't he honour us if we make him a priority?

Yes, God does want us to love him above everything, and I suppose everyone, else. But how do we do this? 'When I was thirsty, did you give me a drink? When I was in prison, did you visit me? When I was cold, did you shelter and clothe me? When I was a stranger, did you welcome me in? When you do this for the least of my brothers and sisters, you do it for me.'[1] God expects us to love him by loving one another. And that sometimes means loving others in his place.

A wife should love her husband as if he were Jesus himself.[2] A husband is to love his wife even more than this, again as if he were Jesus himself.[3] Parents stand *in loco Dei* to our children, and that means loving them as he has loved us. If we do less than this, how can they understand the extraordinary love of God?

The truth is that when parents put God before their children, this isn't actually what they are doing. What they're really doing is putting his *work* first, rather than God himself. If a tramp comes to our vicarage door and I abandon my children's supper in order to give him a sandwich, I may fool myself that I'm putting God before my children. But I'm not. I'm putting a stranger at the door before them. (I know: I've done it.)

If Alex is busy trying to explain to Shaun about negative energy or space being turned inside out or how to travel in time or even how to read electronic mail, and Shaun tears himself away from this fascinating subject to listen to a parishioner talking about her problems of faith, he's not giving God priority in his life; he is simply attending to someone else instead of to his son. So what we're telling our children is not that God is more important than they are (which of course is true) but that other people are.

And children can't understand this. Or rather, they understand it all too well. They see with the clear sharpness of vision that their bright young eyes give them, that they are not as important to us as the bishop, or the Bible study group, or the other people at the church prayer meeting. They know that our leftover love isn't enough. And they reason that, if God's love is leftover love too, that won't be enough either.

It is said that an Irishwoman once wrote to the preacher C.H. Spurgeon, 'Dear Mr Spurgeon, please advise me. I feel called by God to be a preacher. But the trouble is I have ten children.'

'Dear Madam,' he returned, 'I am delighted God has called you to preach, and overjoyed that he has given you a congregation.'

A clergyman's wife said to me recently, 'Oh, if only I didn't have little children, just think how much more Christian work I could do.' I have thought. And however hard I think, I can't think of any Christian work she could do that could be half as important (or a tenth as enjoyable) as the work she's been given already. It is a comment that sends a chill through the bones. I have a horrible feeling that, if she goes on thinking it, her children will reject her faith.

Of course, this is not inevitable. God is gracious and overrules our short-comings, and children can make their own decisions and overcome them. I knew a vicar who never used to leave his study to greet his children when they came home from school. He would sit unmoved, in splendid isolation, a few yards away from the kitchen where they had to get their own tea, for a conscientious hour and a half until he reckoned that his working day had finished at five o'clock. Nevertheless, they have all grown up into committed Christian adults.

But if 'Daddy can't do my prayers tonight because he's got to chair a meeting of the church council', or 'Daddy can't come to my sports day because he's away on a preaching conference', or 'Daddy [and it is more often Daddy] can't ever spend Saturday with me because that's the day he writes his sermon', what is such a child going to conclude about God? That God comes between me and my Daddy, and takes him away from me. Who would want such a deity?

Does this mean we can never attend to others (or even to our work) in case our children should resent it? No: that would be neither practical nor possible. Last year I was contributing to a conference on 'The Surgeon and the Family', discussing the pressures that can come between a medical man and his children. Someone told an account of a friend who was driving home from hospital to be at his daughter's twenty-first birthday party when his mobile telephone rang. One of his patients had gone into a critical condition; he knew her better than anyone else; could he turn round and go back to the operating theatre and attend to her? He did, and he saved her life. When he finally got home the party was over. His wife said it was the last straw, and initiated divorce proceedings.

What, I was asked, should the man have done? Well, of course he must save his patient's life, if that's what it comes down to. The wrong decision wasn't the one he made that night, which anyone can understand and forgive, even the disappointed twenty-one-year-old and her exasperated mother. The problem was not in the choice he made then, but in all the wrong choices he had made throughout the preceding quarter-century, so that when his wife said it was the last straw that was exactly what she meant. Goodness knows how many birthday parties he must have missed to have driven her to such a point; there can't always have been a life hanging in the balance, however good a surgeon he was.

Christian work is not the only work that comes between us and our children. But when it does, the effects are more disastrous. That surgeon's children will probably never go into medicine. That's all right; there are plenty of other worthwhile jobs. But the clergyman who makes the same mistake drives his children away not just from his job, but from Christianity itself. And that is serious.

Members of the cloth, being professional Christians as it were, provide an archetypal example; and clergy families in particular should be ruthless on behalf of their children. Is the vicarage needed for a worthy meeting? It's not a church building; it's the children's home, and they should be consulted before anyone else is allowed to use it. Does the parish want the vicar to be available on a Saturday? They can want away; it is the only day the children have at home. Do members of the congregation always telephone during the children's bathtime? Take the wretched thing off the hook; they will find another time to ring, but you will not find another time when you can read your children a bedtime story.

To the seeker at the door, the enquirer on the end of the line, the couple needing marriage guidance, the family whose baby is being baptized, you are not the only answer. He will knock on another door, she will try another clergyman, they will call again, or get advice from someone else, or find somebody else who can explain Christianity to them. But your children will never find another father, another mother. They are the only people in the world to whom you are indispensable. Make them your priority, as you are theirs.

Before we were even engaged we were blessed with extraordinary good fortune. It was the long summer vacation, and I spent two months travelling to, and staying with, a missionary doctor and his family in Nepal.

There I found our answer. He and his wife provided the best model we could possibly have been given.

Dr Graham Scott-Brown was in charge of the Shining Hospital in Pokhara, oversaw Green Pastures Leprosy Hospital, was Director of the Nepal International Fellowship and responsible for liaising with the government. He was also, perhaps more to the point, saving lives on most days of the week. With such responsibility, one might have expected him to be attending meetings every night, working all weekend, and leaving the house before the family was up, as many men with far less important jobs are doing. But Graham also had three children. Every morning he had breakfast with them and read them a Bible story. Every afternoon he was home by teatime. Before supper I sometimes heard him playing the guitar with them and singing. Eventually I asked him whether he was out on many nights of the week. 'One and a half,' he said. He and Margaret, his wife, went to the Sunday service every week, which was in the evening. And they took it in turns to attend the weekly prayer meeting. That was all.

Their example impressed me so much that it shaped our family life. Thanks to Graham and Margaret, I was never in any doubt that our children were infinitely more important than anyone else, parishioner or pauper. Sometimes people talk to me about a broadcast I have done or article I have written, and by the way they speak I know they consider such work influential. How we delude ourselves! I might have the ear of a few million people for two minutes and forty-five seconds on a Wednesday morning when I am broadcasting *Thought for the Day*. I know people appreciate it because they often write and tell me. But not a single listener is likely to change his life as a result of two and three-quarter minutes while he is dressing his toddler and searching for the marmalade before dashing out of the house. That's not to say it isn't worthwhile; after all, I've got to pay for my children's breakfast somehow, and if you hand me a microphone and half a chance I can't think of anything better to do with the time than try and tell the gospel before you shut me up again. But I don't expect anyone to take much notice.

Shaun, on the other hand, preaches to a hundred or so every Sunday for half an hour. Most of these people will also see something of the way he lives. Consequently, many of them may change a little and one or two will change a lot. His work as a preacher is certainly more influential than the work I do as a writer. But if he were not there, his congregation would find another vicar, or listen to someone else.

But there are five people who witness the way we live our lives, and believe our beliefs, and put Jesus' teaching into practice or more often fail to, for twenty-four hours a day, seven days a week, fifty-two weeks a year, for fifty years or more.

That is real influence.

· · · · · · · · · · · Action Page · · · · · · · · · · ·

1. Pray

   a. With your spouse.

   b. As soon as your baby is born.

   c. When you put your children to bed.

   d. When you are stuck in a traffic jam with them and worried about being late.

   e. When you are waiting for exam results.

   f. When you get good news.

   g. Every day.

   h. Whenever.

2. Read them the Bible

   a. At breakfast, or

   b. When they go to bed, or

   c. As a special treat, or

   d. On holiday, or

   e. Whenever they ask, or

   f. Whenever.

3. Talk to them about your faith, what it means to you, why you believe, and what difference it makes

   a. Whenever.

   b. Live it, believe it, and put your children first.

Celebrate

'If we contribute to your book, do we get some of the royalties?'
Serena

'How much will you pay me for writing in your book?'
Benjamin

'No man but a blockhead ever wrote, except for money.'
Samuel Johnson

Every family is a cause for celebration. Hang on: did I say *every* family? Well, you show me one that isn't. Occasionally you read of exceptions in the newspapers, but I've yet to come across one first hand – and, what with my work and Shaun's, we meet a pretty wide variety of people. Admittedly, I once met a boy on a television show who got his girlfriend pregnant when she was eleven and he was twelve; when I asked him whether his parents minded, he replied that his sister was bringing him up and she didn't care what he did. Presumably if someone had taken more interest in him he wouldn't have needed to turn to sex for love. But isn't it a tribute to families in general, his family in particular, and his sister especially, that she bothered to take him in under her roof? What did she stand to gain by it? Why should she put up with the inconvenience and expense? Somehow his absent parents had managed to instill in his sister enough sense of the value of sibling love that she was prepared for the burden of his upbringing without directly benefiting anything from it at all. Even his story is a reason for rejoicing.

I know, I know: it's not hard to find people who say that their fathers did them down and their mothers undermined them, that their parents are full of imperfections and have left them with permanent problems. Indeed, I'd only have to walk a few yards into my children's bedrooms to stumble over several of them. But I hope they would also say that we have given them life and love, sustenance and education, and the wherewithal to overcome most of our lamentable lapses.

Living in a vicarage, we see people at their worst as well as their best. Our doorbell is rung by those who are facing the most gruelling traumas and coping with life's toughest tragedies. And yet all the parents I've ever met love their children. They feed and clothe and shelter them. They put sticking plasters on their knees and kiss their hurts better and even put up with their multi-pierced, half-shaved boyfriends. And every family I've ever seen is a place of joy and affirmation. Yes, it's a place of mistakes too; of words that would have been better unspoken, hurts that take time to heal, and deeds we wish we hadn't done. After all, families are only run by amateurs. But for this particular job, amateurs are the best people to do it.

I realize many professionals out there think we're making a mess of it. But the trouble with professionals is that they only see the bits that don't work. Suppose you were to ring up your plumber, and ask him to describe your house. What would he say? 'Yours is the one with the shower that leaks, and the dishwasher that broke down last May.' He wouldn't say the bath is watertight, the basins are all fine, the washing machine has never faltered and even the dishwasher has worked beautifully all but once. He certainly wouldn't know that the roof keeps the rain out, the garden is lovely, the Sunday lunch is to die for and the family members all listen to each other. Why would he? He was called in to fix a very specific thing that went wrong. That's all he knows about you. Even when it comes to the plumbing he is not interested in how well it works most of the time. And as regards the cooking or the conversation, he hasn't got a clue. No reason why he should have.

Similarly, if you were to ask your GP what his impression of your family is, he would probably give you a list of your ailments. (When I was a child we knew our GP socially, so he could have described us when we were fit and healthy too, but this is seldom the case now.) Even if you were to enquire solely about his area of expertise, your physical health, he would be unlikely to give an accurately optimistic appraisal of the overall situation. And he would know next to nothing about the emotional or spiritual welfare of the household.

Most plumbers and GPs have the wit to realize that theirs is not the full picture. They know that their knowledge is specialist. They do not assume that most people's houses are permanently flooded, or that your children are usually in bed with appendicitis. They certainly wouldn't argue for legislation that made this assumption. 'We've got to do away with water pipes because they're always bursting.' Or, 'We shouldn't allow children to go to school, because when they do they get nits.'

But do childcare 'professionals' have a similarly broad perspective? I was recently on a television programme with a woman from a children's charity who wanted smacking banned. I painted a thumbnail sketch of normal, loving, reasonable discipline that included the controlled use of disincentives, including smacking; I asked her what was wrong with it. She looked at me as if she had never heard of such a thing.

'If everyone did it that way,' she said, 'there wouldn't be a problem. But you should see what I see.'

I have no doubt she has witnessed dreadful, distressing cases of violence towards children. I am equally sure that legislation would not make the slightest difference to this – such abuse is already illegal, after all. But I also know what she and others like her seem to have forgotten. That people who perpetrate these shocking instances constitute a tiny minority. And that even within that minority there are hardly any adults who are biologically or maritally related to the children they mistreat: they are usually foster parents or care workers or the mothers' temporary boyfriends. Healthy, married parents who abuse their own offspring are rarer than mare's eggs. There aren't many who hurt their legally recognized stepchildren either. But those who work with these exceptional cases seem to forget that they are exceptional, and want to pass laws dictating to the vast majority of ordinary, competent parents how they should bring up their children.

This widespread pessimism about the family is not confined to legislation, to the macro level, if you like. It has an impact on individuals, on the micro level, too. The sister of a very good friend of mine went for counselling on the advice of her doctor: she was feeling desperate, discouraged and dispirited because one of her children was mentally ill. Later, when she had had time to reflect on the counselling sessions, she realized that if she had believed half of what she was told by her therapist she would have killed herself. Despite her protestations to the contrary, he repeatedly told her that her marriage was unhappy and always had been, her children had almost insurmountable problems and her family life was dysfunctional. Presumably her only hope was the magical cure for all her ills that he would deliver one day in the future.

That day never came. After nearly a year she began to ask herself why she was seeing someone who insisted on perpetuating such a dismal view of her life and her family. Notwithstanding the therapist's dire warnings that she had only just started therapy, she bid him goodbye. Instead, she decided to listen to friends and family who affirmed her in what she was doing, who knew what it was like to care for a sick child, and who could see that she was coping. And who would occasionally bring round a chicken casserole. In other words, fellow amateurs.

They, like she – like you and me – know that childrearing isn't always easy, and sometimes needs considerable amounts of stamina; but they also knew that the difficulty is not *knowing* what to do, but just plain *doing* it. And let's be blunt: by and large it is only parents themselves who care enough to go on doing this for their children. I know there are exceptional teachers around, who give the best years of their lives to the children in their care and are still remembered by them five decades on; I know there are still doctors who come out in the middle of the night, and move heaven and earth to get the right treatment for a sick child. But by and large it is the parents, the amateurs, who make the world go round. And since the politicians and policy-makers are not going to congratulate us, perhaps we should congratulate ourselves more often.

I said at the beginning of this book that no family runs completely smoothly, and ours is no exception. We have endured failure, rejection, illness, discouragement, misdiagnosis, disability, depression and heart-ache. And I'm sorry to say, because of the society we now live in, we have some-times suffered some of these things at the hands of professionals, who have occasionally made our job of parenting far harder. But there was also the teacher who gave our son a computer at the age of eight; the hospital doctor who crossed London several times because our daughter didn't want to visit another hospital; the housemaster who uttered not a word of rebuke after anxiously searching for our son all evening after he forgot to say he was going out for tea; the school chaplain who visited our daughter in hospital; the busy professor who gave our son a whole afternoon just because I emailed him in desparation out of the blue; the NHS midwife who came out twice, in mufti, for most of the night, in her own time, because she had delivered our first baby and wanted to deliver her siblings.

And yet despite all these wonderful examples of professional love shown to our children (and yours), it is primarily we, their parents, who have given them the support to get where they are now. Where are they now? Well, I won't bore you or I would sound like a doting mother. You wouldn't be particularly interested in what my children have achieved or overcome or become. Suffice it to say that when I look at them, my heart swells with pride. (Or bursts with annoyance. One or the other. But more often the former, actually.) As does yours when you look at your children. As it should. Because from the moment they were born they have been learning and growing and living and loving, and mastering life's problems, and you are the ones who have enabled them to do so.

A friend of ours, who has experienced the same illness as one of our children and understands it well, was most encouraged and even astonished to see her progress. He asked me what had prompted the improvement. I reflected on his question for some time. In the end there was only one answer I could honestly give, however smug it sounded. Apart from her own effort and determination, there was one thing, above and beyond all else, that had provided the healing. 'Old-fashioned love,' I said. (Which, presumably – going right back to the beginning – had encouraged her effort and determination in the first place.) I can say this without arrogance because it is no more, and no less, than you are giving your children.

How do I know? Because, by virtue of being a parent, you have a fail-safe mechanism. Parenting is foolproof. You cannot fail. What children need, above all, are people who don't give up on them. You, their parents, are those people. You don't give up on them because you can't. They will always be your children, and you will always love them, if you allow yourself to follow your instincts.

What most of us need to know is not the discouraging stuff that professional counsellors throw at us, the minute, nit-picking little ways in which we (or our parents) may not have measured up to some artificial standard of clinical-therapeutic-functioning. Nor should we listen to journalists and media commentators, telling us parenting is in crisis and nobody knows how to do it any more. Nor do we need to know what many baby books tell us, that if we don't throw off the duvet and jump out of bed in the middle of the night at the slightest whimper from the nursery we will traumatize them for life. Or, according to fashion, that if we *do* throw off the duvet at the slightest whimper we will ..., et cetera.

What we need to know is no less than the truth: that we have succeeded, and will continue to do so. Of course our children are not perfect human beings. No one is. But they're pretty good, nonetheless, aren't they?

When our eldest was fourteen she asked if she could have a cast party after a play that her girls' school was putting on in conjunction with the boys' school. We took our lives in our hands – apparently – and agreed. I say apparently, because every other parent thought we should be certified. Sixty teenagers in the house? Were we lunatics, or what? Well, we drew up endless rules about no pot, no sex, no condoms, no going upstairs, no spirits, no smoking in the house, no excluding her younger siblings ... and perhaps it's just as well we did. But in the event, after the first hour during which they tried the loud-music-and-snogging-in-the-garden thing, they gave up and behaved better than most adults at parties. By the time

I went to bed sometime before midnight, two were playing an exquisite duet for violin and piano, others were sitting around a game of chess, and most were simply talking. If we believed the media, by that time of night they should have been committing serial murder.

So let's celebrate our success. Agonize less. Congratulate our children more. Enjoy them. Admire them. Credit ourselves with their good qualities. And tolerate their less attractive ones, as they tolerate ours.

A girl I know is currently causing her parents despair. Talk to them, and you will hear that she is doing no homework, smoking dope, and shoplifting. But recently I was lucky enough to spend an afternoon in her company, and realized what she is really like. She has a sense of humour, a love of children, and an ambition to be a hairdresser. What she needs is a little encouragement and a little more confidence. What her parents need is to know that she does them credit: she is a kind girl, who admires them and wants to succeed. And, given half a chance, she will.

As will my children, and yours, given half a chance. As will they all.

'I think having children is so irresponsible, that anyone who does it should spend the rest of his life making up for it . . .'
Bink

•••••••••••• Action Page ••••••••••••

1. Prepare

   a. Buy a bottle of champers – or lemonade.

   b. Put it in the fridge.

2. Wait

How long for? Well, that's a tricky one. How long till you see the full success you've made of bringing up your children? A lifetime. How early on in that lifetime should you celebrate? The minute they're born. Or as soon as mother and baby have had a bath, anyway. Unless they both like drinking in the bath, in which case there's no need to wait at all.

    On the other hand, how long does it take to chill a bottle? A couple of hours. Unless you've got one of those chill-sleeve thingies, in which case about five minutes. So I should compromise, and go for the five minutes.

3. Celebrate

   a. Open the bottle.

   b. Share it with the children.

   c. Put another bottle in the fridge for tomorrow.

That's it. That's all you need to know, to bring up children successfully. The rest is instinct. As the current jargon goes:

4. Enjoy

Celebrate

'What, Shaun? The Internet? You press
on the little button that says "Internet" . . .'
Alexander

'Internet.'
Rosalie

'That's right, Rosie. Clever girl. The Squinker just said Internet.
She pointed at the computer, and said Internet.'
Alexander

'Yeah, right.'
Bink

'Oh, I'm sure she did, if you say she did.'
Benjamin

'Yes dear.'
Serena

'Never mind, Boo-boo; I heard you. Now, up on my knee,
there we go: this is how we use it . . .'
Alexander

About the Author

Anne Atkins has written several novels, *The Lost Child*, *On Our Own*, and *A Fine and Private Place*, acclaimed for their sensitivity to a child's viewpoint on an adult world. She is well known for her controversial broadcasts, particularly 'Thought for the Day' on Radio 4's flagship 'Today' programme – and her commonsense advice as agony aunt for the *Daily Telegraph*, ITV's Sunday, and as parenting advisor for femail.co.us. She has five children, who are amazed at her temerity in writing a book about parenting but think they are good advertisement for it anyway.

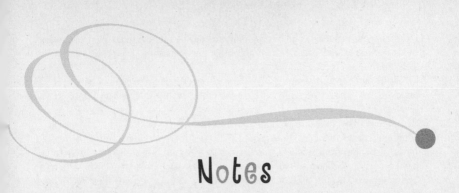

Notes

Introduction

1. At the Liberal Democrat autumn conference, 2003, a motion was proposed by Paul Burstow that there should no longer be any defence in the law for parents who smack their children. It is now part of Liberal Democrat policy that physical punishment of children by parents be redefined as child abuse and classified as a criminal offence.
2. Frank Furedi, *Paranoid Parenting*, The Penguin Press, 2001, page x.

Chapter 1. Security

1. *Othello*, Act I, scene 3, lines 214ff.
2. Serena has insisted on a disclaimer to the effect that she doesn't put any of our missing items in her room. Everyone else dumps them there: brothers, poltergeists, retriever-rabbits – they go round the house collecting things and hiding them in her bedroom.
3. J. McDowell and D. Day, *How to Be a Hero to your Kids*, Word Publishing, 1991, page 126, quoted by Rob Parsons in *The Sixty Minute Father*, Hodder & Stoughton, 1995, page 105.
4. See, for instance, *Divorce and Separation – The Outcomes for Children* by Bryan Rodgers and Jan Pryor (The Joseph Rowntree Foundation, 1998), including the summary on pages 4–5 and further references on pages 58–68. See also *Experiments in Living: The Fatherless Family* by Rebecca O'Neill (Civitas, 2002) for extensive and detailed research, which can be downloaded from www.civitas.org.uk/pdf/Experiments.pdf.
5. For instance, in England and Wales during 2000, babies born to single mothers (i.e. registered only in the mother's name) were *seven times* more likely to die of cot death than those born to married couples; those born to separated couples (registered in both names but at different addresses) were three times more at risk. See *Mortality Statistics: Childhood, Infant and Perinatal. Review of the Register General on Deaths in England and Wales, 2000*, Series DH3 33. Office for National Statistics (2002).
6. M. Hetherington, *For Better or Worse: Divorce Reconsidered*, W.W. Norton, 2002. Also, J. Elliot and M. Richards, 'Parental divorce and the life chances of children', *Family Law*, 1991, pages 481–84; J. Wasworth et al., 'The influence of family type on children's behaviour and development at five years', *Journal of Child Psychology and Psychiatry* 26, pages 245–54. See also H. Joshi et al., 'Diverse Family Living Situations and Child

Development: A multilevel analysis comparing longitudinal evidence from Britain and the United States', *International Journal of Law Policy and the Family,* Volume 13, 1999, pages 292–314.

7. C. Harper and S. McLanaham, 'Father Absence and Youth Incarceration', San Francisco, 1998, paper presented at the annual meeting of the American Sociological Association.

8. O. Lundbert, 'The impact of childhood living conditions on illness and mortality in adulthood', *Social Science and Medicine* 36, 1993, pages 1047–52. After controlling for poverty, children from single-parent families were found to be 70% more likely to have circulatory problems, 56% more likely to show signs of mental illness, 27% more likely to report chronic aches and pains and 26% more likely to rate their health as poor. They were 30% more likely to die over a 16-year study period.

9. Robert Whelan, *Broken Homes and Battered Children,* Family Education Trust, 1994, page 29. For this risk , see also P. Cawson, *Child Maltreatment in the Family,* NSPCC, 2002.

10. Lady Longford. Possibly. Or perhaps Lady Churchill first. All right, it's confession time. My first book was meticulously footnoted, cross-referenced, triple-checked, what have you. In those days this involved laborious weeks in the library, which one could hardly expect the pampered reader to put in. Besides, I barely had one embryonic child when I started writing it (though I distinctly remember giving birth to our third child the day before I finally sent off the finished manuscript). Now I have five. I haven't got time for all this. You want to know who said it, you look it up. Which you can probably do more easily than I anyway, because you understand the Internet. Except that you haven't time either, because you have children too. Which means you can't be doing with endless flippings backward and forward to all these footnotes, losing your place, putting the book down to empty the potty and then coming back having forgotten where you are. So can we reach an agreement on this? From now on, no more footnotes. It'll save you time, reading them; me time, investigating them; even save some benighted reviewer time, because if he wants to pan my book he can just say I haven't researched it properly. Win, win, win …

11. Yes, I know I said no more footnotes. Consistency is one of the most important characteristics of good parenting: we must always mean what we say, never go back on our word, and carry out threats and promises alike with scrupulous regularity, as I go to great lengths to point out in the chapter on discipline. Anyway, as I was saying, this misquote is from *To Lucasta, Going to the Wars* by Richard Lovelace and the original is of course 'honour' not 'Mummy'. Right, positively no more footnotes now. For the moment anyway.'

Chapter 3. Significance

1. Look, I managed a whole, chapter, alright? Fine, I admit it: I'm hopeless. I can't even stick with any resolution for more than five minutes. But this note about smacking is important. Since I wrote this chapter, events have moved fast, and it now looks likely that the government may change the current law. Some particularly Christian pressure groups have voiced great concern at the damage which resulting undue state interference may do to ordinary families. Essential reading – certainly for anyone involved in legislation – should be Sweden's smacking ban: more harm than good

by Dr Robert E. Larzelere, Associate Professor of Psychology at the University of Nebraska Medical Center. Dr Larzelere highlights some alarming trends, for instance that since the ban in Sweden, family assaults against children have increased by nearly 500%, and child-on-child violence by even more. On the other side, Dr Joan Durrant of the University of Manibota has privately challenged some of these findings, but as far as I am aware, her comments are not yet in the public domain.

Chapter 4. Relationships

1. There is, alas, considerable and mounting evidence that psychotherapy is at best useless and at worst harmful. See, for instance, 'Looking for a counsellor? You need your head examined' by Dr Raj Persand (*The Daily Telegraph*, 12 March 2003); also, 'Therapy is bad for your (mental) health' by Dr Garth Wood (*The Daily Telegraph*, 28 October 1997). Less well researched or authoritative, but still of interest, is 'Stiff upper lip beats stress counselling' by Sarah Baxter and Lois Rogers (*Sunday Times*, 2 March 2003).

Chapter 5. Freedom

1. *Unfinished Journey*, Yehudi Menuhin, Methuen 1996, page 35. I was doing so well: only one footnote per chapter. But I feel a spate of them coming on, so I thought I might as well let you look up this anecdote, in case you have time on your hands …
2. *The Daily Telegraph*, 6th April 2004. 'Children under two "should not watch any TV"', David Derbyshire. Dr Dimitri Christakis, of Seattle Regional Medical Centre, says: 'The newborn brain develops very rapidly during the first two to three years of life. It's really being wired. We know from studies of newborn rats that if you expose them to different levels of visual stimuli the architecture of the brain looks very different.' For good measure see also *The Sunday Telegraph*, 1st February 2004, 'Daytime TV harms children, say presenters'.
3. Safety being measured according to deaths per 100 billion passenger kilometres: in Great Britain in 2001, the rate of fatalities for rail travel was 0.1 as against 3 for those travelling by car. See www.dft.gov.uk.
4. For instance, by a staggering 44% in the year 2001/2002. See *Crime in England and Wales*, 2001/2002 Supplementary Volume 1, 'Homicides and Gun Crime' and Home Office Statistics, 22 January 2004, www.homeoffice.gov.uk.
5. As a general rule, each 1 mph reduction in the speed limit reduces accidents by 5%. More specific, introducing traffic calming schemes in residential areas to reduce the speed limit from 30 to 20 mph leads to an overall reduction in injuries of 60%, including injuries to children down 67% of which injuries to child cyclists down 48% and injuries to child pedestrians down 70%. See *Review of Traffic Calming Schemes*, Report 215 by Webster and Mackie, Transport Research Laboratory, 1996. See also *New Directions in Speed Management*, 2000.
6. This was called (rather quaintly) the Society for the Support of Home Confinements and was run by Margaret Whyte at 17 Laburnum Ave., Durham. It has now sunk without a trace. Try www.homebirth.org.uk instead.

7. For instance, a study in the Netherlands in 1986 documented only 2.2 deaths per 1,000 for babies born at home, compared with 13.9 for those born in hospital. See *Homebirth in the UK* by the Brighton Homebirth Support Group at www.midwiferytoday.com/articles/homebirthuk.asp. See also *The Safety of Home Birth* by James Hughes at chetday.com/homebirthresearch.htm.

8. Homicides of 5- to 15-year-old children per million of the population are usually around 3 or 4 a year. But homicides of 16- to 30-year old males – the group most at risk, incidentally – are generally between 30 and 40. See *Crime in England and Wales* in note 4.

9. Over half of child homicides are committed by a parent, whereas stranger danger amounts to no more than about a sixth.

10. Fewer than 10 children a year in England and Wales are murdered by people they don't know, apart from last year when there was a blip and 17 children under 16 years old were killed. Even this unusually high figure, however, is still less than a tenth of the number killed by cars in that year.

Chapter 8. Joy

1. Martin Luther, quoted by C.S. Lewis in the *Screwtape Letters*, along with Thomas More: 'The devil … the prowde spirite … cannot endure to be mocked.'

2. PJ and Barney Bestelink, www.okavangohorse.com.

Chapter 9. Decide

1. For more information, see www.davidmulhall.co.uk or telephone 0(044)20 7223 4321.

Chapter 10. Implement

1. Matthew 25:34–45.
2. Ephesians 5:22.
3. Ephesians 5:25.